# Core Economics for Managers

Joshua Gans

**Core Economics for Managers**
**1st Edition**
**Joshua Gans**

Project editor: Tony Davidson
Editor: Greg Alford
Publishing manager: Michael Tully
Indexer: Julie King
Text design: Chris Ryan
Cover design: Olga Lavecchia
Original cover concept: Patrick Jennings
Production controller: Jodie Van Teylingen
Typeset in Times New Roman PS and Gill Sans by Linotype


Any URLs contained in this publication were checked for currency during the production process. Note, however, that the publisher cannot vouch for the ongoing currency of URLs.

For product information and technology assistance,
**in Australia call 1300 790 853;**
**in New Zealand call 0800 449 725**


For permission to use material from this text or product, please email **aust.permissions@cengage.com**

**National Library of Australia Cataloguing-in-Publication Data**
Gans, Joshua.
Core economics for managers.

    Includes index.
    For tertiary students.
    ISBN 978 0 17 012475 1.
    1. Managerial economics - Textbooks. 2. Economics - Textbooks. I. Title.

338.5


**Cengage Learning Australia**
Level 7, 80 Dorcas Street
South Melbourne, Victoria Australia 3205

**Cengage Learning New Zealand**
Unit 4B Rosedale Office Park
331 Rosedale Road, Albany, North Shore 0632, NZ

For learning solutions, visit **cengage.com.au**

Printed in Australia by Ligare Pty Ltd.
2 3 4 5 6 7 8 13 12 11 10 09

# Core Economics for Managers

Joshua Gans

CENGAGE
Learning™

Australia • Brazil • Japan • Korea • Mexico • Singapore • Spain • United Kingdom • United States

# About The Author

Joshua Gans is Professor of Management (Information Economics) at the Melbourne Business School, University of Melbourne. He studied economics at the University of Queensland and Stanford University. He currently teaches introductory economics and incentive theory to MBA students.

Professor Gans's research ranges over many fields of economics including economic growth, game theory, regulation and the economics of technological change and innovation. His work has been published in academic journals including the *American Economic Review, Journal of Economic Perspectives, Journal of Political Economy* and the *Rand Journal of Economics*. Currently, he is a co-editor of the *International Journal of Industrial Organisation* and the *Journal of Economics and Management Strategy*. He has also undertaken consulting activities (through his consulting firm, CoRE Research), advising governments and private firms on the impact of microeconomic reform and competition policy in Australia. In 2007, he was awarded the Economic Society of Australia's Young Economist Award for the Australian economist under 40 who has made the most significant contribution to economic knowledge.

Professor Gans lives in Melbourne with his partner, Natalie Lippey, and children, Belanna, Ariel and Annika.

# Contents

# To the instructor

This book was written with four related aims in mind:

1. To fill a perceived gap in the market for strictly economics texts that focus on those aspects of pricing, competition and incentives that economics deals with best; i.e., the core competencies of economics.

2. To utilise a negotiations framework, alongside traditional posted pricing theories, to teach issues in price formation to MBA students.

3. To provide an integrated framework to deal with price formation, competition, contracting, ownership and incentives.

4. To complement existing case materials rather than include detailed discussions of them. The focus of the book will be theoretical with simple examples (usually numerical) to illustrate basic principles.

Let me outline each of these in turn.

## 1. Focus on core competencies of economics

This book is based upon two subjects taught at the Melbourne Business School. The first is entitled Managerial Economics. It is a compulsory introduction to economics and, in particular, pricing and competitive strategies. The second course is entitled Incentives and Contracts. It is an elective subject that covers issues in writing contracts and providing incentives in those contracts. In my mind, these two subjects cover the key economic principles that are valuable for business.

For economics subjects taught at the Melbourne Business School, we required a text that was business-oriented but kept to those issues that economics could deal with best. That is, we did not want to stray into issues of corporate strategy (e.g., ideas like Porter's Five Forces) or issues of human resource management (e.g., personnel or promotion policies within firms). These are dealt with in separate subjects. As such, I believe there is a need for a text that complements the subjects that achieve this perspective and focus; i.e., a text that focuses on the core competencies of economics as a discipline.

## 2. Price formation through negotiations and posted pricing

Traditional neoclassical economic textbooks have a very limited view of price formation. Essentially, all markets are seen as mass markets where all of a firm's customers are charged a single, linear price. There is some discussion of price discrimination but, in many respects, this view of price formation misses key aspects within the experience of many MBA students. For those students, when negotiating supply agreements and the like, the mass market model of price formation can seem distant and unrealistic.

In contrast, this book uses a negotiations framework to model price formation. Adam Brandenburger and Barry Nalebuff's popular management book, *Co-opetition*, uses an intuitive negotiations framework based on the concept of added value. While their discussions are descriptive, a textbook based on the concept of added value can be more precise and quantitative. Added value is a concept readily reducible to numerical and graphical analysis – already common in economics texts. This allows one to bring in a more realistic view of price formation and cases based on added value. As such, it is my belief that the added value approach enriches the applicability of economics to business thinking and reinforces economic principles in a business-like environment.

## 3.  Integrated framework

One key advantage of building an economics text on a negotiations framework is that it makes accessible the discussions and analyses of issues in contracting. Recent economic research on contracting and ownership is based on a negotiations model of price formation. This is particularly useful when discussing the consequences of contractual incompleteness, imperfect commitment and opportunism that plague many contracting situations. It also provides a context from which to discuss the Coase theorem and results regarding firm boundaries: in particular, when vertical integration will be an efficient business structure. Finally, it allows a more detailed discussion of how contracts mould incentives in a business relationship. As such, this text unifies the tools required for analyses of price formation and issues of internal organisation that are spanned by many recent MBA-oriented economics texts.

## 4.  Style of the book

The object of the book is to provide clear discussion of economic theory and principles and illustrate them by way of simple stylised examples. Hence, while there might be references to real-world situations, there is no rich discussion of particular cases. It is left to individual lecturers to add the cases they see as most appropriate.

The intention is that the book be a reference for students to come back to again and again to receive a clearer understanding of principles discussed in class.

This book would best be utilised in conjunction with a book such as Brandenburger and Nalebuff's. That book provides very interesting discussions of real-world cases and could be used to motivate a student to examine economic principles in more depth and face the complexity of the environments they will have to deal with upon graduation.

Joshua Gans
May 2005

# Acknowledgements

This book arose as a result of continuous development in the economics curriculum at Melbourne Business School. In many respects, the changes to that curriculum were an eight-year collaborative effort among instructors and so I would first like to acknowledge Vivek Chaudhri, Jenny George, Bruce Grundy, Michael Ryall and Philip Williams for their critical roles in that endeavour. I also want to thank Stephen King with whom I co-wrote a textbook (Gans, King & Mankiw, 2005); he provided significant contributions to Chapters 1 and 9 of this book. Thanks also to Niko Matouschek and numerous students for useful comments but, in particular, Richard Hayes and Robert Arculus who should be commended for their very thorough reading of earlier drafts of this text.

The most thanks, however, goes to my colleague Catherine de Fontenay who showed the way to integrate decision theory with cooperative game theory that now is the cornerstone of the first part of this book. She also demonstrated that MBA students can enjoy learning quantitative methods when they can see their immediate useful applicability.

Some of the key new concepts introduced in this book were inspired by a developing academic literature. The notion of added value, upon which Chapters 4 and 5 are based, was initially developed by Adam Brandenburger and Gus Stuart (1996) and popularised by Brandenburger and Barry Nalebuff (1997). Glenn MacDonald and Michael Ryall (2004) provided a formal definition of competitive advantage that is utilised in Chapters 6 and 7. Brandenburger and Stuart (2004) provided an analytical means of dealing with bi-form games that is the foundation for Chapter 7. Finally, I make use of Oz Shy's notion of an undercut-proof equilibria to model price competition with differentiated goods in Chapter 9.

Finally, it goes without saying that my own interest in managerial education, and education generally, continues to be inspired by my partner, Natalie, and our three wonderful children, Belanna, Ariel and Annika. I owe everything to them.

## References

Brandenburger, A. & Stuart, H. (1996), 'Value-Based Business Strategy', *Journal of Economics and Management Strategy*, Vol.5, pp.5–24.

Brandenburger, A. & Stuart, H. (2004), 'Biform Games', *mimeo.*, Columbia.

Gans, J., King, S. & Mankiw, N.G. (2005) *Principles of Microeconomics* (3rd Asia-Pacific edition), Thomson: Melbourne.

MacDonald, G. & Ryall, M. (2004), 'How do value creation and competition determine whether a firm appropriates value', *Management Science*, Vol.50, pp.1319–33.

Nalebuff, B. & Brandenburger, A. (1997), *Co-opetition*, Harper Collins: London.

Shy, O. (2001), *The Economics of Network Industries*, Cambridge University Press: Cambridge.

# 1 Introduction – why should managers study economics?

Economics analyses your business's place in the world. Who does your business interact with? How does it interact with these different parties? When is it desirable to cooperate and when does your business need to compete? How can your business best place itself to profit from these everyday interactions?

By studying economics, managers can better appreciate the forces that act on their business. These forces include both constraints and opportunities. Some parties, most notably competitors, constrain your business's activities and limit the amount of profit that your business can earn. Other parties enhance your business's ability to earn profits. For example, without customers a business creates no value and makes no profit.

A key role for a manager is to steer your business through the sea of constraints and opportunities that it faces. In the absence of effective management a business is like a rudderless ship, pushed this way and that by forces of the marketplace that are beyond its control. The role of economics is to provide both a rudder and a map. Economics provides a map for your business by explaining and analysing the forces that act on your firm. Economics helps you to determine your competitive environment and to understand the constraints and opportunities that face your business. Economics provides a rudder and helps you to guide your business by providing a variety of concepts, ideas and decision-making procedures that assist in reshaping the market environment.

A course in managerial economics, however, does not provide you with a simple formulaic approach to business. There is no one correct way to handle business situations, and so economics provides you with a variety of ways to analyse the market circumstances that face your business. In this sense, economics provides you with a 'tool kit'. A plumber, carpenter or other tradesperson brings a set of appropriate tools with them. When faced by a particular problem, they are equipped to deal with that problem – they reach into their tool kit for the right tool to use to deal with the job. And if the tradesperson cannot deal with the problem then he or she knows where to seek appropriate help. In the same way, the tools of economics can be applied to a wide variety of market interactions that face your business. Part of the skill of economics is determining which tool is appropriate for a particular situation. And, like the tradesperson, part of the skill of managerial economics is learning when your business needs extra assistance and where to seek that assistance.

The tool kit of economics involves a variety of different ideas and concepts. If you have a background in undergraduate economics, then you will be familiar with the concept of perfect competition and how it can be used to provide insight into a wide range of government policies such as taxation, restrictions on international trade, wage and price controls, and other market interventions. Perfect competition is a device well suited to government policy analysis, but it has limited use for a manager. This is because the perfectly competitive model in economics takes a very wide-ranging view of trade and the market. While this is appropriate when considering broad government policy, it does not help you manage your firm on a day-to-day basis.

Economics, particularly over the past 30 years, has developed a variety of new tools that can aid managers. Game theory, the mathematical analysis of strategic situations, has been used by economists to consider alternative business strategies, including their strengths and weaknesses. Models of imperfect competition allow managers to formalise their interactions with other businesses in the marketplace and to characterise the key factors that guide effective business decision-making. Bargaining theory allows managers to consider the likely outcomes of day-to-day interactions and to formulate processes to ensure the best possible results for their businesses. A course on managerial economics will focus on these recent advances in economic theory and practice as these tools will be most valuable to managers in guiding their businesses.

While these tools focus on the 'local' forces that buffet businesses, firms also face 'global' forces in the marketplace. Inflation, exchange rate fluctuations, interest rate changes, government taxation policy and a range of other global forces interact to create the broader business environment. Unlike local forces of the marketplace, a manager will often have limited (if any) ability to influence or control these global forces. While businesses may complain about particular government policies or even lobby to change these policies through business associations, individual managers must often take the broader business environment as given. This does not, however, mean that managers can take this broader environment for granted. Successful firms are those that are led by managers who can manipulate the local business environment to best suit their firm, and who can predict longer-term changes in the broader business environment and prepare their firm for any changes to this environment. Thus, a key part of economics for managers involves the broader investigation of government policy and how this impacts on individual businesses.

Roughly speaking, the tools that deal with the local business environment are called microeconomics, while understanding the economy-wide business environment is part of macroeconomics. A manager needs to be up to date with both the tools of microeconomics and macroeconomics if they are to successfully chart a course for their business.

## Understanding your business's place in the world

Before you can guide your business and shape its future direction you must first determine the place that your business occupies in the world. In particular, where is your business located *in the marketplace*? As a manager you may not like where your business is located. You might want to shift your business and change its market position. But before you can do this you need to understand where your business is currently located and what opportunities and constraints are currently placed on it.

The marketplace is not a physical location. Of course, your business has an address or a 'place of business', but this physical location is often of less importance than your firm's market location. Market location is given not by physical space but by the interactions and relationships between your business and other participants in the process of buying and selling products that is the 'bread and butter' of your business.

For example, suppose that you operate a small retail business selling sports equipment. Clearly your physical location is important. It will determine the degree of 'passing trade' for your store and may be the difference between success and failure. However, your market location is at least as important. Your market location is given by the complex web of interactions that allow your business to thrive and prosper. It involves your suppliers, such as the wholesalers of sports equipment, the landlord who owns your premises and your employees who supply you with labour. It also involves your customers, whether they are individuals who are after a single item, a sporting team that wants to make a bulk purchase, or a corporate client who requires ongoing highly personalised service. Your business interacts with these suppliers and customers and the success of your business depends on how well you deal with them.

The web of market interactions goes much further than just your customers and suppliers. It also involves other market players who may either create opportunities for your business or who constrain your business through competition. For example, suppose that a branch of a large retail sporting goods chain opens just a few shops away from you. The new store is clearly going to be a competitor. The prices charged by the new store will limit your pricing. If you price too high then your customers will simply go to the new store and buy there instead. The new store may also change the way that you deal with your customers. If the new store offers a higher level of service then you may need to increase your service levels to maintain your sales.

Alternatively, suppose that a new sporting team in a national competition commences operations in the same city as your store. You may not supply the team or its players but this does not mean that the new team is irrelevant for your business. If the team is successful then their fans will want to buy merchandise and other products that relate to the team and the sport. It is likely that your sales will rise with the success of the new local team. Rather than being a competitor, the new team complements your business.

The complex web of interactions that define your business's location in the marketplace are summarised by Brandenburger and Nalebuff as the 'value net' (see Figure 1.1). The other participants in the marketplace, who we will call 'players', can be customers or suppliers, and they can also be competitors or complementors. Customers are those individuals or businesses who buy your product. Suppliers are those firms or people from whom your business buys goods or services. Customers and suppliers are easily recognised by considering the flow of goods, services and financial obligations. You provide your customers with goods or services in exchange for payment. Your suppliers provide you with goods or services in exchange for you paying them. Put simply, to identify your customers and your suppliers, just 'follow the money'.

**Figure 1.1** The value net

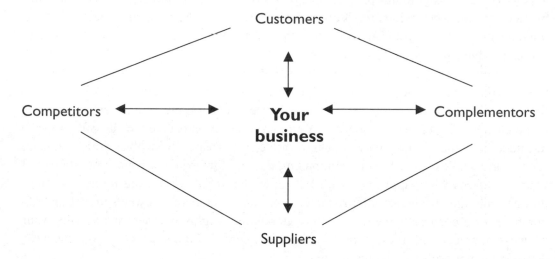

Complementors and competitors can be harder to identify. Complementors increase the value to another party of dealing with your business. Competitors reduce the value to another party of dealing with your business. Thus, complementors and competitors affect your business by altering your interactions with customers and suppliers. The rival store in the example above was a competitor because your customers value your products less if they already have the products supplied by your rival. To see this, suppose that a customer wishes to buy a tennis racquet. If they buy a racquet at the new store then that customer is unlikely to come into your store and buy another racquet. The customer only requires one tennis racquet and if they buy from your rival then their potential purchase is lost to you.

The new sporting club in our example above is a complementor because individuals who become supporters of the new club will value your products more than if the new club did not exist. The new club raises the value of your goods and services to some potential customers.

Identifying the other players in your market and their roles is of critical importance to managing your business. This is obvious for customers and suppliers. Without satisfied customers your business will lose sales over time and head towards bankruptcy. Without reliable suppliers, you will be unable to properly serve your customers. However, the importance of both competitors and complementors is often overlooked. Competitors constrain your business and a manager needs to identify relevant competitors and understand how to best deal with these competitors. Economics provides guidance by highlighting the different dimensions of competitive conduct that businesses can exploit, as well as showing the range of competitive alternatives that your firm can embrace – from harsh one-on-one competition through to collusion and cooperation.

Complementors help your business. They expand the opportunities that face your business so that in general it is desirable to assist complementors. Thus a key element of success for your business can involve encouraging complementors. To continue with the sporting example, your store might choose to sponsor the new team. This is directly beneficial to your business in the sense that such sponsorship functions as advertising. It is also indirectly beneficial for your business. To the degree that your sponsorship helps the new team become successful, your sponsorship aids a complementor and this will feed back into increased sales for your store.

While the value net provides a simple framework to help you determine your business's location in the marketplace, it must be used with care. In particular, some players may fill multiple roles. If the new sporting team establishes its own club outlet store selling merchandise, then it will be both a complementor and a competitor. It benefits your business to the degree that the club's success raises demand for your sporting goods, but it also competes with you for retail customers through its own store. Similarly, a rival sporting store may be both a competitor and a complementor. It competes with you for customers, but by forming a 'mass' of sporting stores it can also encourage more customers to come to your store's physical location to buy sporting goods. Similarly, by providing an additional outlet for suppliers, the rival store may make it easier and cheaper for your business to buy stock. When players fill multiple roles in the marketplace these roles need to be carefully identified and your interactions with these players need to trade off these multiple roles. For example, starting a price war to wipe out your retail rival may lead to your business having fewer competitors. But it might also mean that you have access to fewer suppliers and that sporting goods customers simply 'go elsewhere' to shop.

## Economic decision-making

Economic decision-making aims to guide managers in making the best possible choices for their businesses. A key element of this decision-making is the concept of economic profit.

Economic profit is different to accounting profit. In particular, economic profit considers costs not in simple expenditure terms but in terms of foregone opportunities. To capture this idea, economists use the term 'opportunity cost'.

The opportunity cost of an action is the best alternative that you give up when you undertake that action. This need not be a direct monetary cost but it is a real resource cost to your firm. It measures the best alternative that you gave up when you made a particular decision and provides the appropriate benchmark for evaluating your actions as a manager. Economic profit measures the gain to your firm by your decision relative to the next best opportunity that was blocked off by your decision.

To give a simple example, suppose that your business employs Sunita, an IT professional who maintains the computer systems. Sunita is a regular employee and receives a fixed monthly salary, so that from the perspective of your business Sunita's salary is a fixed cost. It does not matter how busy Sunita is at any time, your firm pays her the same salary each month.

Suppose that one department of your business has purchased a new computer system and wants you to deploy Sunita to the department for a month to set up their system. The head of this department argues that this will be cheaper than getting in an outside firm to set up the new computer system. After all (argues the department head) your business pays the same amount to Sunita each month whether she is setting up the new system or maintaining the computer systems for other departments in your firm. So (the argument goes) this means that there is no cost in deploying her to set up the new computer system.

Right? No, absolutely wrong! If Sunita is busy setting up the new computer system in one department then her other duties will be neglected. There is an opportunity cost associated with deploying Sunita to set up the new computer system. The size of this opportunity cost is the potential damage that your business faces by neglecting the maintenance on its other computer systems for a month. If the other computer systems around the firm are relatively stable and reliable, so that usually Sunita spends much of her time doing low value work that could easily be ignored for a month, then the opportunity cost is small. However, if having the other computer systems neglected for a month substantially increases the probability of a major system breakdown and potential loss of business, then the opportunity cost of deploying Sunita for a month might be huge.

Should Sunita be redeployed or should an outside firm be brought in for a month? Suppose that the cost of having an outside firm set up the new system is $10 000. If the opportunity cost of having Sunita redeployed for a month is more than $10 000 then it is more profitable for you to bring in the outside firm. While this costs your business $10 000, this is less than the potential cost of neglecting your other computer systems for one month.

While the concept of opportunity costs might seem relatively straightforward, it is amazing how many businesses just do not get it. To give one example, in the early 1990s a major Australian real estate business had a computer system that only allowed a maximum of 50 terminals to be in use at any one time. The system had over 100 terminals but worked on a first-come-first-served basis. So as long as you were 'logged in' to a terminal then you could keep using that terminal for as long as you liked, even if there was a queue of people waiting to use the computer system. You had to 'log out' before someone else could 'log in'. Further, individual departments within the firm faced no internal charge for using the computer terminals but everyone knew that on Wednesdays, when the main board meeting was on, that the terminals would quickly become congested as there was a last-minute rush to finish reports and papers to present to the board. As a result, the firm developed a Wednesday morning ritual. Employees would race each other into the office on Wednesday morning in order to log in to the computer. Successful employees would then leave the office and get breakfast, have a coffee or work out at the gym for one or two hours before beginning work for the day. Of course, those 'late' employees who missed out on accessing the computer were left to fume, unable to complete their work no matter how important it was to the firm.

The problem for the firm was clear. The business faced a potentially huge opportunity cost of computer terminal access once the system became congested. But no individual employee or department faced that opportunity cost. A simple solution would be to instigate an internal charge so that departments had an incentive to moderate their computer use – and allow employees more sleep on Wednesdays. In fact, luckily for the business, technological progress solved the problem for them and the business ended up replacing its computer system during the 1990s with an up-to-date network.

From an economic perspective, the best way to evaluate alternatives is to consider the relevant opportunity costs. Of course, in many situations, it is difficult to determine the exact value of these costs. The costs may not be reflected simply in dollars, but may involve factors such as employee health and workforce morale. For example, how do you measure the cost of having employees race each other to work on Wednesday mornings?

When faced by opportunity costs that are difficult to measure it is tempting to simply give up. But the fact that a decision is difficult, or that it is hard to gather the necessary information, is no excuse for inaction. Simply put, you will be paid as a manager to make the hard decisions, and saying that they are 'too hard' is no excuse. Economics can help by providing a framework to assist you in making the right decisions for your business, and by pointing out the type of information that you will need to gather in order to make better decisions.

## Creating value and bargaining

Businesses such as General Motors, IBM or Time-Warner earn money for their shareholders by receiving payments from their customers that exceed the payments to their suppliers. Their ability to do this depends critically on there being some 'money on the table'. That is, customers will not pay a firm more for a product than the value of the benefits they derive from that product and suppliers will not accept payments that do not cover their own costs. So ultimately, for there to be something left for the business, customers' benefits must exceed suppliers' costs.

By bringing customers and suppliers together, businesses can create value, and by doing this they can appropriate some of this value for themselves as profit. For this reason, a key part of economic analysis for managers involves identifying the source of value and understanding how this value is divided between various market players.

To understand the concept of value, consider a simple example. Suppose that Raymond has a second-hand Corvette for sale. Robert is interested in buying the car. How do we work out the potential value (if any) created by this sale?

First we need to consider Robert's willingness-to-pay for the Corvette. This is simply defined as the highest price that Robert would be willing to pay Raymond for the car rather than 'walking away' from the deal. For example, this maximum price might be $25 000. In other words, Robert is willing to pay up to $25 000 for the Corvette but would prefer to walk away rather than pay any more. Of course, Robert would prefer to pay less than $25 000 for the car. However, when calculating a buyer's willingness-to-pay we need to consider the highest price that the buyer would be willing to accept.

Second, we need to consider the opportunity cost to Raymond of selling the car. This is given by the next best alternative that Raymond gives up when he sells the Corvette to Robert. For example, Raymond might have already talked to a car dealer who offered to pay $16 000. Alternatively, Raymond might value using the car himself at the equivalent of $16 000. In other words he would rather keep the car himself rather than sell it for anything less than $16 000. In either case, the opportunity cost to Raymond of selling the car to Robert is $16 000. This is the value of the *best* alternative that he gives up by the sale. Clearly, Raymond will not sell the car to Robert for anything less than $16 000.

In this situation, the value that can be created when Robert buys the car from Raymond is $9000. This is the difference between Robert's willingness-to-pay ($25 000) and Raymond's opportunity cost ($16 000). As there is positive value then there is 'money on the table' and both Raymond and Robert can gain from the trade. Notice, however, that the size of the value created by the trade does not depend on the price that is agreed by Raymond and Robert. While the difference between willingness-to-pay and opportunity cost gives us the value created, the price tells us how the value is divided between Robert and Raymond.

To see this, suppose that Robert and Raymond agree to a price of $20 000 for the Corvette. Then, Robert has gained $5000 as his share of the value created. This is just the difference between Robert's willingness-to-pay ($25 000) and the amount he actually pays ($20 000). Raymond gains $4000 of the value created – the difference between the price he receives and his opportunity cost ($16 000).

This simple example provides two important economic lessons for business. First, profits are derived from creating value. It does not matter how good you think your product is, if no-one is willing to pay more for your product than the cost of producing it then no value is created and your business will not make a profit. Business is about creating value.

Second, pricing matters because it divides the value created between different market players. As a result it is important for a manager to understand the forces that shape prices in the marketplace and how to influence and alter prices in a way that is advantageous for his or her business.

Initially this second statement might appear odd. After all, don't businesses set their prices? How can prices be shaped by the marketplace? Some thought, however, quickly shows how the marketplace constrains firms when setting prices. If a business tried to set a price significantly above its competitors' prices then that business is likely to lose most of its customers to its competitors. Of course the business can set a high price – but if it makes few sales then such a price will not be profitable!

The marketplace constrains pricing from the perspective of both sellers and buyers. To see this, consider again the example of Raymond selling a second-hand Corvette. As before, suppose that Robert is willing to pay up to $25 000 for the car. In addition, however, Deborah is interested in buying the car. Her willingness-to-pay is not as high as Robert's and she is only willing to pay up to $24 000 for the Corvette.

Initially, it might appear that Deborah is irrelevant. After all, the maximum value is created if Raymond sells the Corvette to Robert. Such a sale creates $9000 in value whereas selling the car to Deborah only creates $8000. So if Raymond sold the car to Deborah then this would mean 'wasting' a potential $1000 in value. So long as bargaining between the three players leads to an outcome that maximises the total value created then Raymond will sell the car to Robert.

Deborah matters, however, because she changes the bargaining power in the negotiations between Robert and Raymond. Even though Deborah is unlikely to be the eventual purchaser of the car, because she is a *potential* purchaser she will affect the price paid by Robert. In particular, we can now predict with some confidence that Robert will pay more than $20 000 for the Corvette. The reason for this is clear. If Robert was about to buy the car for $20 000 then it would be in Deborah's interest to offer Raymond a higher price and to try to outbid Robert. After all, Deborah's willingness-to-pay is $24 000 so she is willing to pay up to $24 000 for the Corvette. If Robert was about to buy the car for $20 000 then she would be willing to offer say $20 500 to try to outbid Robert. And Raymond would prefer to sell the car for $20 500 than $20 000.

Of course, the same holds true for any price below $24 000. If Robert is about to buy the car for less than $24 000 then it would pay Deborah to try to outbid Robert by offering Raymond a higher price. As a result, even though Deborah is unlikely to buy the Corvette, because she is a potential purchaser the price that Robert pays is likely to be bid up above $24 000. Only if Robert pays more than $24 000 will he be able to 'shake off' Deborah and buy the car.

Even though Deborah is unlikely to actually buy the Corvette from Raymond, her presence as a potential buyer creates competition for the car. This allows Raymond to charge Robert a higher price for the car. Competition from Deborah as a potential buyer makes other buyers worse off but makes the seller better off.

This example captures a general rule for the division of value. The more competition there is on one side of a transaction, the lower the bargaining power for the parties on that side of the transaction. By increasing buyer competition, Deborah makes Robert, another potential buyer, worse off but makes Raymond, the seller, better off.

The types of interaction between different parties to a trade have been extensively analysed in the economics and management literature. Economics provides a variety of tools to help managers understand their position in the marketplace and how to modify that position to improve their business's bargaining position.

## Understanding the market

If you are a connoisseur of popular management books, then much of the discussion in this chapter might surprise you. After all, according to many of these popular books, business is like a form of warfare. In contrast, economics tells us that much of business is about cooperation and value creation. Businesses profit when they create value with their customers and their suppliers. These profits can be enhanced if businesses coordinate with complementors. Rather than business being about conflict, economics shows us how cooperation can help business.

At the same time, we have seen that competition can limit the value that is received by market players. Whether you are a buyer or a seller, an increase in competition on your side of the market tends to lower the value that is available to you and to increase the value that is seized by other market participants. While cooperation is important to maximise the value created in the marketplace, competition can shift the distribution of this value.

From the perspective of market players, competition on your own side of a market transaction is undesirable but competition on the other side of a transaction is beneficial. But how can a manager use market competition to his or her business's best advantage?

From an economic perspective, competition is like a game. Given the behaviour of other players in the market, it benefits any particular business to compete hard. Such behaviour increases sales and undermines competitors. So competing hard is unilaterally desirable for a business. But when all businesses compete hard, this simply disperses profits and makes consumers better off. The businesses in any market would all be better off if they could avoid competition and cooperate instead.

Such games reflect the dilemma faced by competing firms. When engaged in competition in the marketplace, each business individually has a strong incentive to compete, steal its rivals' customers and raise its own profits. However, if all competing businesses do this, they all end up losing, by setting lower prices and having lower profits. If businesses could coordinate then they would be able to avoid competition and raise their total profits.

Explicit collusion between firms to avoid competition is illegal in most developed countries. For example, in Australia collusion is deemed illegal under section 45 of the *Trade Practices Act*. This does not mean that managers are helpless when faced by the 'competition dilemma'. Rather, it means that managers must carefully think about the strategies that their businesses adopt to deal with competition. Should the business compete hard to try and 'wipe out' its rivals in order to be able to raise prices back up in the future? Or should a business try to signal to its rivals that a strong price war is mutually destructive and that they should both set higher prices? Can a business adopt strategies that limit exposure to a price war, for example by locking in customers? Long-term customer contracts, customer loyalty schemes and incompatibility of standards can all be used to limit customers' ability to switch suppliers and to moderate competition. But each of these strategies also involves a cost for the relevant business. Does the benefit outweigh the cost?

Economics can help managers to answer these questions by providing powerful tools of analysis for competition and related strategic situations. There is no simple solution to these problems and the correct strategy will depend on the particular market circumstances that face a business. Economics, however, can help a manager to navigate through the sea of alternative strategies in order to choose the best path for his or her business.

## Summary

In this chapter, we have presented a brief overview of the type of tools and analytical skills that economics provides to managers. This book will explore all of these tools and economic issues in much more detail.

Economics is an invaluable tool for managers. By helping managers to better understand where a business is located in the marketplace and how businesses interact with other market players, economics can change the focus of managers. At its heart, business is about creating value. Understanding the process of value creation and the division of value is a key element in understanding business. While competition is sometimes an unavoidable necessity in the marketplace, managers can moderate and alter the nature of competition. Economics assists managers to understand the competitive options and alternatives that face their businesses, both locally, in their marketplace, and globally, within the wider economic environment.

# Part I

# Decision-making

As mentioned earlier, by bringing customers and suppliers together, businesses can create value, and can ensure that they appropriate some of this value for themselves as profit. For this reason, the first important set of tools of economic analysis is concerned with identifying value and its sources so as to understand the role of a business in value creation.

Value is not often a readily quantifiable concept. It cannot simply be reduced to monetary terms. A natural question to ask is how profit, which is a distinctly monetary measure, can arise from value, which has elements that are often not monetary? The answer lies in the way in which money, something people and businesses prefer to have more than less of, can assist in guiding the decisions of rational individuals.

The benefits a person derives from consuming an ice cream cannot be readily quantified; however, that same person can be asked to name the highest price that they would be *willing to pay* for an ice cream. This would give a monetary equivalent for the benefit that that person places on ice cream. Moreover, it can be related back to the payment that an ice-cream supplier would need to receive in order to cover supply costs.

By stepping into the shoes of key decision-makers, you can potentially determine the monetary equivalents of different actions. This exercise allows you to analyse whether there is an opportunity to create value. In this topic, you will learn how to put yourself in the place of decision-makers to establish the existence of value-creating opportunities for business.

From an analytical perspective, there are two key dimensions upon which decisions might be distinguished: (1) the degree of uncertainty associated with outcomes, and (2) the interdependence of those outcomes with the actions chosen by others. The figure below shows how certain types of decisions can be classified according to these two dimensions. Your decision regarding what to have for lunch today does not involve much uncertainty as you are aware of the range of options and your experience tells you how you might enjoy any particular one. In contrast, if you undertake extreme sports there is a high degree of uncertainty as to whether you might be injured or not. For each of these decisions, the outcomes do not depend upon others' actions. The same is not true of your decision as to how hard to study. If your school grades on a curve then if others study harder, you will also have to study harder to achieve a higher grade. Similarly, when your firm enters a new market, there is uncertainty as to whether consumers will like your product but also whether your profits will be affected by the reactions of established firms in that market.

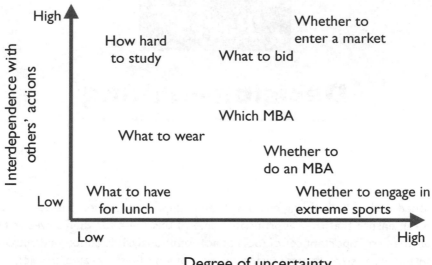

We begin our study of decision-making with the simple case of *non-strategic* decisions. These are decisions where outcomes do not depend on the actions of others. A decision is *strategic* if it requires you to take into account how others will react to your decision. For instance, if your firm raises the price of its product, it has to consider how your competitors may react. Strategic decisions are the focus of Chapter 4. In a *non-strategic* environment, on the other hand, either there are no other competitors or their response can be predicted. Such decisions are simpler to analyse and so we deal with them first, in Chapter 2. Also, it is possible to use non-strategic decision-making to define what we mean by value and trade. That will be the subject of Chapter 3.

# 2 Individual decision-making

Almost every business school teaching case is posed in the form of a decision. As a student, your job is to work out what options are available to the perplexed manager in question, what the consequences of each one are likely to be and to ultimately recommend a course of action. In short, the task is to model the decision faced by the manager.

In this chapter, we introduce a tool that helps you *frame* a decision and then *solve* it to eliminate undesirable options and work out what the most desired option may be. The tool to frame a decision is called a decision tree and the method to solve it is called roll-back. We look at each of these and then use them to identify and explain some common decision-making pitfalls.

## Framing decisions

To understand how a decision problem can be represented by a decision tree, it is instructive to consider a 'business case' situation:

> TimeScape Ltd currently has a successful program for time management that is used on handheld computers. Their managing director, Catherine George, is contemplating further development of their software. This development will allow the product to be used on some high-end mobile or smart phones.
>
> There are two challenges. The first will be the technical issues of ensuring a well-functioning product on mobile phones. The second will be marketing issues associated with distributing the product to mobile phone, as opposed to handheld, users. This will involve additional investments in marketing channels. Catherine wonders whether this uncertainty will make it too risky to engage in the $200 000 expenditures necessary to develop the upgrade.

At its broadest level, Catherine's decision can be represented by a tree as depicted in Figure 2.1. As you can see, the decision tree is made up of decision nodes (the square) and branches (one for each action at a given node). At the tip of each branch is a statement as to the consequence of each action.

**Figure 2.1**

Having represented the broad decision facing Catherine as a tree, it is easy to see that more information will surely be required to sort this out. Of particular importance is the fact that following any decision to develop the upgrade, Catherine will receive information as to whether the technical issues for mobiles were sorted out or not; that is, if the project was a success on this dimension or a failure. Let's add this information to the case:

> Suppose there are two possibilities: either the project is a success and the technical issues are fully sorted out or it is a failure and the mobile product will be of lower value to customers. Catherine assesses that there is a 50 per cent probability of a successful development.

We can represent this additional information by adding a node and branches to the decision tree (Figure 2.2). In this case, the additional node does not represent a decision point but a point where uncertainty is resolved. We call these nodes *chance nodes* and they are represented by a circle. The branches from these nodes do not represent actions but alternative states of the world – in this case, success or failure – that may arise. However, the tips of the branches, like those from decision nodes, still represent the consequences flowing from that branch.

There is still an important sense in which Figure 2.2 is not a complete decision tree. This requires all of the decisions to be identified as decision nodes. However, Figure 2.2 lists the entry decision for the mobile market as a consequence rather than a decision. Figure 2.3 provides the complete tree. Note that the decision of whether to enter the mobile market is considered following the resolution of uncertainty regarding whether the project is successful or not. This is represented by a new node off the success branch with the options of entering that market or not. The consequences in terms of profits are then indicated.

**Figure 2.2**

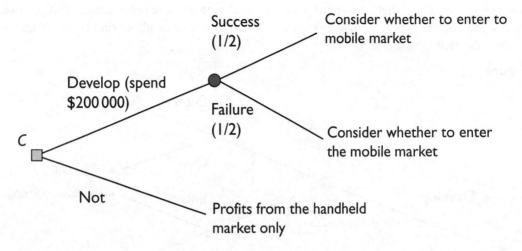

**Figure 2.3**

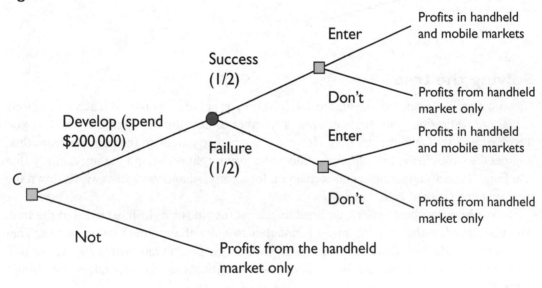

Finally, while in some situations, the *qualitative* information in Figure 2.3 is all you may have available, in others *quantitative* information may be utilised. Specifically, profit outcomes and the costs of market entry can be calculated, or at least considered. For instance, even without putting numbers to them, Figure 2.4 depicts the components of profitability. There, *h* are the profits that would arise in the handheld market. In the mobile market, the costs of entry are *c* and the potential profits (after entry) are *M* (if the project is a success) and *m* (if it is not). Given this, it is reasonable to suppose that $M > m$. Notice that this representation contains a hidden assumption that the profits you would make in the mobile market do not depend on those in the handheld market and vice versa. You would have to judge whether in reality such an assumption were reasonable. What is true, as will be shown below, is that this type of assumption does allow one to more easily analyse the decision at hand.

**Figure 2.4**

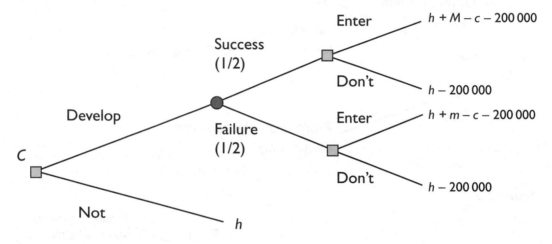

## Solving the tree

Faced with a decision tree like Figure 2.4, how do you solve it in order to reach a decision? If you are Catherine, your first decision is whether to develop the upgrade or not. If you develop, you will spend $200 000. However, in order to calculate the benefits from this, you need to anticipate any subsequent decision you might make and the uncertainty that you face. Such anticipation requires that you look forward and work backwards down the tree: this is a method called *roll-back*.

To see how roll-back works, we need to start at the tip (or right-most side) of the tree. The last decision that may be made is whether to enter the mobile market or not. That decision is made with full knowledge as to whether the project has been a success or not. If the project has been successful, Catherine would only choose to enter rather than 'don't enter' if:

$$h + M - c - 200\ 000 > h - 200\ 000$$
$$\text{or } M > c$$

This equation is saying two things. First, that the entry decision does not depend upon handheld market profits or development costs. Second, that it will be worthwhile to enter the mobile market only if the profits TimeScape expects to earn exceeds the costs of entry. Similarly, if the project has not been a success, then Catherine will only enter the mobile market if:

$$h + m - c - 200\ 000 > h - 200\ 000 \text{ or } m > c$$

Essentially, the decision to enter the mobile market will be made on its own merits given the outcome of the development project. Note, however, that if $m > c$ (entry will occur even if the project is not successful) then it is also surely the case that $M > c$ and entry will occur in any event.

In working backwards, therefore, there are three cases to consider: whether (i) $M < c$ (and hence, $m < c$, so that Catherine would only ever sell in the handheld market); (ii) $m > c$ (and hence, $M > c$ so that Catherine would always choose to enter the mobile market) or (iii) $M > c > m$ (Catherine only enters the mobile market if the project is successful). These cases determine what happens following the resolution of uncertainty regarding the success of the project.

If it is the case that (i) holds, then whether the project is successful or not is irrelevant as Catherine would not enter the mobile market anyway. For that reason, the uncertainty does not really matter: Timescape will get $h - 200\,000$ in any event. In this situation, by working backwards, we can 'clip' branches and reduce the tree to that in Figure 2.5. There it is easy to see that Catherine will choose to develop if:

$$h - 200\,000 > h$$

Clearly, this will never hold. Essentially, there is no upside to developing the software for the mobile market as entry into that market is never worthwhile. So, in case (i), by roll-back, we can see that Catherine would choose not to undertake the development project.

**Figure 2.5**

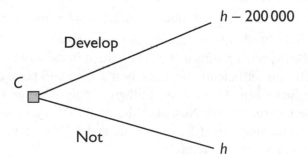

What if (ii) holds and entry into the mobile market is always profitable? In this situation, the uncertainty now matters. In order to work out what Catherine should do in this case, we must calculate the expected payoff from a decision to develop. Before doing this it is useful to reflect upon what an expected payoff is. When an action results in a payoff with certainty we say that that outcome occurs with probability equal to 1 (or with 100% certainty). In this case, that payoff is the payoff associated with that action. However, if, following an action, a payoff, say of $x$, has only a 50% chance of occurring and otherwise a payoff of $y$ will occur, then the expected payoff associated with that action is 0.5 x $x + 0.5 x $y. Alternatively, if the payoff of $x$ had a 75% chance of occurring and $y had a 25% chance of occurring the expected payoff would be 0.75 x $x + 0.25 x $y. In this sense, an expected payoff is what an agent would earn on *average* from taking this action.

Applying the notion of expected value to our case, by developing, TimeScape has a 50% chance of earning $h + M - c - 200\,000$ and a 50% chance of only earning $h + m - c - 200\,000$. Its expected payoff is, therefore:

$$0.5 \text{ x } (h + M - c - 200\,000) + 0.5 \text{ x } (h + m - c - 200\,000)$$
$$= h + 0.5 \text{ x } (M + m) - c - 200\,000$$

Taking this into account reduces the decision tree back to a tree where there is no uncertainty; as in Figure 2.6.

**Figure 2.6**

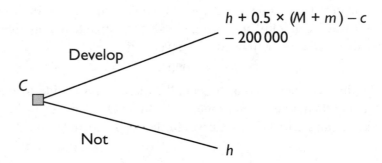

From Figure 2.6, we can easily see that Catherine will choose to develop only if:

$$h + 0.5 \text{ x } (M + m) - c - 200\,000 > h \text{ or } 0.5 \text{ x } (M + m) - c > 200\,000$$

As before, the right hand side are the development costs. The left hand side of this inequality is now the expected profits that can be earned in the mobile market. So long as those expected profits are sufficiently high, the best choice will be to develop.

Finally, in case (iii) where $M > c > m$, Catherine only chooses to enter the mobile market if the project is successful. Now it is the case that, by developing, TimeScape has a 50% chance of earning $h + M - c - 200\,000$ and a 50% chance of only earning $h - 200\,000$. Its expected payoff is, therefore:

$$0.5 \text{ x } (h + M - c - 200\,000) + 0.5 \text{ x } (h - 200\,000)$$
$$= h + 0.5 \text{ x } (M - c) - 200\,000$$

This allows us to reduce the tree to that depicted in Figure 2.7. In this case, Catherine will choose to develop only if:

$$h + 0.5 \text{ x } (M - c) - 200\,000 > h \text{ or } 0.5 \text{ x } (M - c) > 200\,000$$

This is a similar condition to that found for case (ii) although it is weaker as there is less potential for entry into the mobile market.

**Figure 2.7**

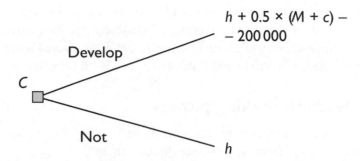

$h + 0.5 \times (M + c) -$
$- 200\,000$

Develop

$C$

Not

$h$

In summary, by using roll-back, Catherine's decision can be reduced to some simple calculations. Put simply, if $M < c$, then developing the software is not worthwhile as entry into the mobile market is not profitable. On the other hand, if $m > c$, it is worthwhile to develop if $(M + m)/2 - c > 200\,000$. In this case, entry into the mobile market is always profitable. However, if entry into the mobile market is only profitable for a successful development $(M > c > m)$, then the development decision is based solely on the expectation of that success: i.e., development should occur only if $(M - c)/2 > 200\,000$.

**Figure 2.8**

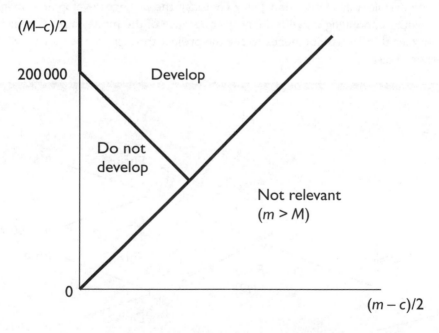

$(M–c)/2$

$200\,000$

Develop

Do not
develop

Not relevant
$(m > M)$

$0$

$(m - c)/2$

Indeed, we can graph the range of calculations that will lead Catherine to favour development over not developing. In Figure 2.8, we graph the ranges of expected profits in the mobile market with and without a successful development. Note that as $M > m$, a proportion of that graph (where $m > M$) is not relevant. When both $(M - c)/2$ and $(m$

$-c)/2$ are low, Catherine will choose not to develop. In contrast, when they are high she will develop. The downward sloping diagonal line indicates the boundary between these decisions. At any point on this line, Catherine is indifferent between developing and not. So by coming up with estimates of the various profit scenarios, using Figure 2.8, Catherine can evaluate which decision will be most attractive (based on expected payoffs).

## Common decision-making pitfalls

Decision trees are useful in that they can assist in identifying some common pitfalls in business decision-making. Here we illustrate three of these.

### 1. Sunk costs

Costs that have already been incurred and cannot be recovered are known as sunk costs. When making decisions, managers should ignore these costs; otherwise, they risk making poor decisions.

Consider the following amendment to our running case to illustrate this point:

> Suppose that TimeScape has already spent $100 000 on initial exploration of the mobile software option. Jenny Fontenay, the project development manager, favours continuing on with the project because of the money already spent. She argues that TimeScape needs to see the project through or the money will have been wasted.

**Figure 2.9**

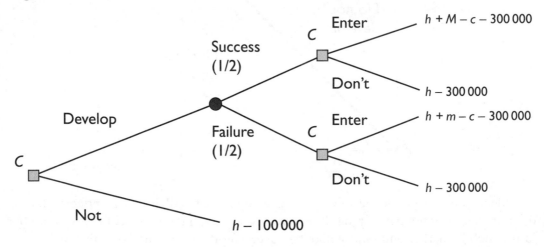

Using this new information, we can change the overall decision tree (Figure 2.9). Notice that because the $100 000 has already been spent, then we subtract it from the tip of every branch.

What this means is that if we consider any particular scenario (say, the previous case (ii), where $m > c$ and mobile entry is always profitable), the reduced tree also includes an additional $100 000 cost on each tip (see Figure 2.10 – an amendment to 2.6). Because the $100 000 is incurred regardless, the decision as to whether to develop (or continue developing or not) remains the same as before. In this case, Catherine will choose to develop only if:

$$h + 0.5 \times (M + m) - c - 300\,000 > h - 100\,000 \text{ or } 0.5 \times (M + m) - c > 200\,000$$

The $100 000 is on both sides of this inequality and cancels out.

**Figure 2.10**

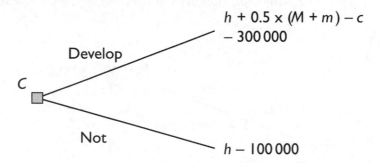

Put simply, the money spent on previous exploration of the concept is a sunk cost. Whether TimeScape continues to develop or not, the $100 000 they have already invested cannot be recovered. Using this sunk cost to justify continued development could lead to greater losses. Investment should only continue if the expected return exceeds the investment costs from this time onwards ($200 000).

This suggests a useful principle.

> *When making decisions, managers need to be forward-looking and thus should ignore sunk costs.*

## 2. Margins versus averages

When considering increasing or decreasing their production levels, firms should base their decisions on marginal cost (MC) rather than average cost (AC). MC accurately reflects the cost of producing an additional unit of output or the savings from producing one unit less. To see how mistakes can be made by not considering marginal costs, consider the following:

> A railway owner notices that their engines have the capacity to haul more carloads and is considering putting on an additional carload. At present, they operate 10 cars and receive $1000 per carload and this would not change if an 11th car was added. A look at the accounts of the company confirms that with 11 carloads, the cost per carload consists of $600 for the car itself, $300 for the allocated cost of the rail (that is, $3300 divided by 11) and $200 for physical loading and unloading. Therefore the average cost of each carload is 600 + 300 + 200 = $1100 per load.

If one were to compare this to the price per carload, one might be tempted to consider an expansion unprofitable. However, framing the decision in a tree reveals a different picture.

**Figure 2.11**

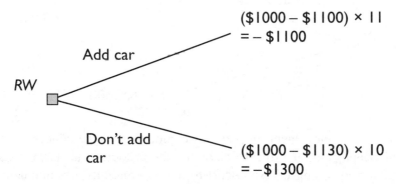

Notice that the company makes a loss regardless of whether it uses 10 or 11 cars. However, comparing those losses indicates that the company makes $200 more if it adds a car than if it does not. This happens even though on average carloads are unprofitable.

A closer examination reveals what is going on here. Adding an extra car gives $1000 in revenue. But in terms of costs, it only adds car and loading costs, i.e., MC is $800, but does not change the rail cost. The rail costs are fixed costs that would be unchanged if more cars were hauled. Hence, they are not part of the decision to add another car or not.

Average cost plays a role in some analyses, but in most cases, it is useful to follow this rule:

> *The proper cost to consider when trying to maximise profits is the firm's marginal cost.*

### 3. Economic versus accounting profit

When economists talk about a good's cost, they refer to its *opportunity cost*, a measure not only of explicit costs like labour and materials used in production, i.e., the items that are included in a firm's income statement, but also of implicit costs, such as revenues that the inputs could have generated through some other use. Consider the following example:

> For the past year, a couple have owned a trendy café in a central business district. The area of the building where the café operates is owned by the couple. In that year, the café had revenues of $334 992. One of them has calculated that *total costs* (including labour, the wholesale costs of coffee and food, equipment costs and marketing costs) are $222 578. He reports to his partner that the café is very successful, with profits of $112 414 for the year.
>
> His partner is unconvinced. She notes that they did not take into account the rent that the two could have earned on the space they used, which is as much as $8000 per month. They also did not consider the wages of $54 000 per year he gave up by choosing to manage the café. The sum of these two implicit costs, $150 000, needs to be added to the original estimate of the café's costs to get the total economic cost. With this, their economic profit is indeed a loss of $37 586. Maybe they should think about getting out of this business.

A decision tree shows that this last analysis is correct. Figure 2.12 shows the decision tree implicitly facing the couple. Because the implicit costs together are greater than the original estimate of the café's profits, in an economic sense, the café is losing money.

**Figure 2.12**

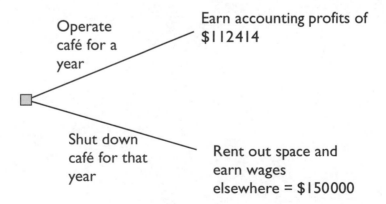

The café example suggests an important principle:

> *When making decisions, economic agents should take into account the opportunity costs of actions, not merely their explicit costs.*

The key point here is that when contemplating a decision, it is important to use only relevant costs in weighing up alternative options. If additional costs are brought in, then profitable decisions may be mistakenly held to be unprofitable and value-creating opportunities would be lost.

## Summary

This chapter has introduced the tool of decision trees as a way of showing you how to frame decision problems and then solve them using roll-back. This type of tool can be used for many decisions that do not involve a strategic element: that is, where there is only one relevant decision-maker. As we will see in Chapter 4, however, this tool can be amended to consider situations where the decisions of agents interact.

Decision trees can be usefully employed to illustrate some common pitfalls in decision-making. To be sure, you need not be aware of these pitfalls to make good use of decision trees. However, by knowing what to watch out for, you can more easily focus on such errors in reasoning when engaging in internal debates regarding what to do and how to evaluate past decisions taken.

# 3 Cooperative decision-making

Many decisions are not individual – as described in the previous chapter – but joint or cooperative. A good example of this is marriage. Two people will only decide to get married if the value they receive together is greater than the value they receive apart. In this situation, a decision node on a decision tree involves the decision of whether to cooperate or not. In addition, the outcomes on the tips of branches involve the sum of the values of all of the individuals involved when they either do or do not cooperate respectively.

In business, the main form of cooperative decision is whether to trade or exchange goods and services. Two parties decide whether they will be jointly better off by trading as opposed to not trading. To put this another way: trade will only occur of there is value created from it. If person $A$ receives a good from person $B$ that $B$ can use but $A$ cannot, there is unlikely to be surplus from such a trade. However, if instead $A$ happened to have that good, then by trading it to $B$, there is likely to be surplus created.

In this chapter, we explore a set of tools that can assist you in identifying when trade creates value (and is, therefore, likely to occur). In so doing, we will first need to explore just what value is and also how individuals can assess whether trade is worthwhile. After all, it may well be that the 'sum' of individual values is higher if trade proceeds but whether it is worthwhile for each individual to engage in trade is a different matter.

## Creating value through exchange

The value that is created by a business's activities is potentially complex and diverse. It results from that business's relationships with other players in the economy, including its customers, suppliers and other businesses who deal with those same players (i.e., competitors and complementors). Given this, it is useful to consider a stylised representation of the process of value creation in order to state a definition of value that is readily applicable to realistic situations.

A very simple way of defining value is to track a particular activity of a business. Recall that what a business does is to utilise inputs from suppliers and turn them into products that its customers desire. The flow of product from suppliers, through the business, to customers is referred to as the *value chain of production*; depicted in Figure 3.1. It shows the vertical flow of goods and services and also money between customers, your business and suppliers.

**Figure 3.1**

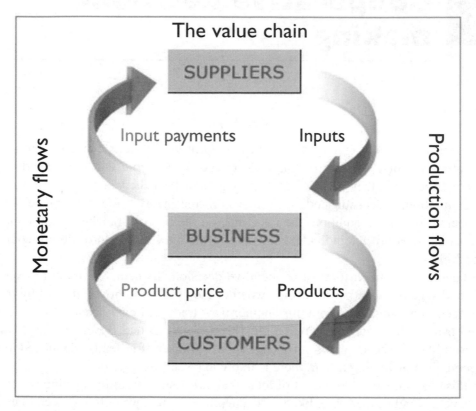

These flows will only occur if the relevant decision-makers – customers and suppliers – are willing to engage in their respective transactions. Customers must be willing to exchange money (the product price) for the business's product and suppliers must be willing to accept money (input payments) for the provision of inputs. Finally, the business will only be willing to participate in the value chain if there is a positive gap between product price and input payments (i.e., some 'money on the table'). It is only when there is such a gap that value is created.

This concept is perhaps easier to grasp if we consider a hypothetical case:

> Vases Abroad Inc. are importers of rare vases from China and elsewhere. They purchase vases speculatively and put out a quarterly catalogue to discerning buyers – some of whom are domestically located antique dealers. Each vase has a unique value to a potential customer and also a distinct acquisition cost for Vases Abroad.

Vases Abroad has acquired a Ming Dynasty era vase and a particular customer, Ming21 (a dealer), has expressed an interest in purchasing it. If they don't sell the vase to Ming21, Vases Abroad believe that the expected price they would receive from other customers would be about $50 000; although that will take some time. In the meantime, the storage costs will amount to $2000 (for security and insurance). Is it worthwhile to sell to Ming21?

If they do not sell to Ming21, Vases Abroad expects to make $48 000 (the $50 000 likely payment less the storage costs of $2000). Ming21, in turn, places some monetary value on owning the vase. Let's denote this value by $v_B$. As Vases Abroad receives no additional value if they make a sale, $v_B$ is, therefore, the joint value to both it and Ming21 from a sale.

Figure 3.2 depicts the joint decision tree for Vases Abroad and Ming21. From this tree, it is easy to see that it will be jointly desirable for Vases Abroad to trade the vase to Ming21 if $v_B$ is at least $48 000 and not otherwise. The difference in joint payoffs ($v_B$ – $48 000) is *the value created by this exchange or the gains from trade.*

**Figure 3.2**

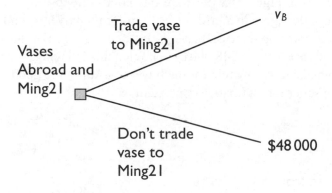

This illustrates a first general principle regarding exchange:

*Principle 1: A trade will only take place if the (potential) buyer and (potential) seller are* jointly *better off as a result of the exchange.*

In general, if a good is bought by a buyer who places a value, $v_B$, on the good, and sold by a seller who would otherwise earn $o_S$ (in the case of our example, $o_S$ = $48 000), then there is value created by an exchange only if $v_B \geq o_S$.

Sometimes it will be the case that the exchange may free the seller up to engage in other activities – allowing them to earn, say, $v_S$. It may also be the case that, if no trade takes place, the buyer would use their funds to do other things, netting them earnings of $o_B$. In this more general case, there is value created from the exchange only if:

$$\underbrace{v_B + v_S}_{\substack{\text{Joint payoff} \\ \text{from trade}}} \geq \underbrace{o_S + o_B}_{\substack{\text{Joint payoff} \\ \text{without trade}}}$$

We will see below that this more general case often arises when cooperative activities are considered by two parties who are not strictly in a buyer/seller role but are joint contributors to a productive activity.

## But what about price?

At this point, you might naturally wonder where the 'price' is in all of this. Surely the main reason that a seller trades with a buyer is the payment they receive. Thus far, we have just pointed out that for trade to occur there must be some value created. In effect, it must be the case that the joint benefits to the buyer and seller from trade exceed what they would get otherwise. However, it is also the case that for trade to occur the buyer and seller must *individually* find it worthwhile. This is where price comes into the equation.

The decision trees in Figure 3.3 illustrate this point. Suppose in our Ming vase case that the buyer and seller agree to a price of $p$. Then for the buyer to find it worthwhile to trade at that price it must be the case that $v_B - p > 0$ or $v_B > p$. For the seller to agree to trade, it must be the case that $p > \$48\,000\ (= o_S)$. What this is saying is that the price has to be low enough to make it worthwhile for the buyer to acquire the goods but high enough to compensate the seller for alternative opportunities.

**Figure 3.3**

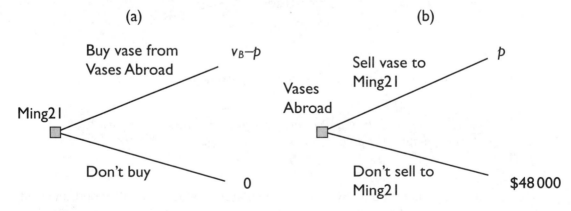

This illustrates a second principle:

> *Principle 2: A trade will only take place at a price that makes both the (potential) buyer and the (potential) seller individually better off as a result of the exchange.*

In general this means that trade will only occur if we can find at least one price, $p$, such that:

$$v_B - p \geq o_B \text{ and } p + v_S \geq o_S$$

Together these imply that:

$$v_B - o_B \geq p \geq o_S - v_S$$

Notice that:

- If $v_B - o_B \geq o_S - v_S$, this is the same as our earlier condition for the buyer and seller to be jointly better off from trade (that is, it is the same as $v_B + v_S \geq o_B + o_S$).
- If the buyer and seller are jointly better off from trade, then there is potentially a range of prices (from a high price of $v_B - o_B$ to a low price of $o_S - v_S$) at which trade will make both the buyer and seller individually better off.
- If the buyer and seller are not jointly better off from trade (that is, $v_B + v_S < o_B + o_S$), then there are no prices at which trade will make *both* the buyer and seller individually better off.

So in the case of the Ming vase, for the buyer and seller to be jointly better off from trade, it needs to be the case that $o_B \geq \$48\ 000$. However, for Ming21 to purchase the vase, $.p \leq v_B$ and for Vases Abroad to sell to Ming21, $p \geq \$48\ 000$. Thus, if $v_B > \$48\ 000$, there is a range of prices from \$48 000 to $v_B$. What price might ultimately emerge is, however, dependent on other factors; something that we explore in Part II of this book.

The concept of a highest and lowest price for which trade might occur can be useful in defining some building blocks with which to analyse transactions at an individual level. These building blocks are: (1) customer willingness-to-pay and (2) supplier willingness-to-sell.

> A customer's willingness-to-pay *is the maximum price they would pay and still choose to purchase a product.*
>
> A supplier's willingness-to-sell *is the minimum price they would accept and still choose to supply a product.*

These concepts will be explored in more detail below. For the moment consider how they relate to value created through exchange.

There will only be value created if, when price is as high as possible, this exceeds the lowest possible input payments. The highest possible price is, by definition, the customer's willingness-to-pay for a product while the lowest possible price is defined by the supplier's willingness-to-sell. Therefore, value will only be created if a customer's willingness-to-pay exceeds the supplier's opportunity costs. Thus, one can define value and the surplus from trade in these terms:

> Total surplus *is the difference between customers' willingness-to-pay for a product and the suppliers' willingness-to-sell of supplying the inputs used to produce that product.*

As an example, suppose that a customer's willingness-to-pay for an ice cream at a sports stadium was $3. An ice cream vendor at that stadium has costs of $1 if they sell an ice cream to that customer. Therefore, if an exchange or transaction were to occur, total surplus would be $2; equal to the difference between the customer's willingness-to-pay of $3 and the vendor's willingness-to-sell of $1. So long as one can determine the willingness-to-pay and willingness-to-sell associated with a particular transaction one can easily quantify that transaction's total surplus.

Business can appropriate some of the value created by bringing customers and suppliers together in completing the value chain. However, it will not usually appropriate all value created because price will often be less than a customer's willingness-to-pay and input prices may exceed suppliers' willingness-to-sell. So it is the difference between price and input price that will determine a business's profitability. The first step for business is, therefore, to ensure that it assists in creating value.

## Identifying player roles

Before looking at willingness-to-pay and willingness-to-sell more closely, it is worth digressing a moment to consider how a trade perspective can be used to identify the roles of key players – in particular, who are a business's customers and who are its suppliers. This is important because ultimately a business has to direct strategies – advertising, contracting and support – towards particular players.

Customers of a business are those players that purchase goods or services from it. They can be identified using the following:

> *A* customer *is any player who pays money to the business.*

For many businesses, identifying customers in this way is relatively simple. This is particularly true of retailing, and in those businesses it is clear who to direct marketing strategies towards. For other businesses, identifying customers is more complex. For a charity such as the Red Cross, a usual perspective is that they are in the business of helping those in need. However, according to the above test, recipients of charity are not customers because they do not pay money to it. Instead, customers would be donors who inject money into the business. Moreover, like customers in retailing, part of the task of charities is to persuade donors to part with more money; that is, to consume more gift giving.

Other businesses may have more than a single class of customers. Newspapers receive money from readers and advertisers. Moreover, these classes of customer have benefits that interact with one another. Advertisers prefer newspapers with large readerships or readerships of a matching demographic to their products. On the other hand, readers prefer newspapers with less advertising. Consequently, newspapers may face trade-offs in terms of how much they satisfy the wants of one or both customer types.

From a supplier perspective, the following is an analogous identification test to that for a customer:

> A supplier *is any player who receives money from that business.*

This definition would obviously include employees, equipment manufacturers, Internet service providers and energy utilities. But other players may be harder to classify. Shareholders are generally considered suppliers of equity financing to businesses; that is, they pay money into a business. However, they also receive money from the business in terms of dividends on return on capital. As they expect this to outweigh their initial contribution, shareholders would be classified as customers.

The same would be true of depositors in banks. They expect to earn interest payments while keeping a claim on any money deposited. But for some depositors, they keep very little money in saving accounts and use the convenience of a bank's security and electronic payment systems. For this, they are often charged account-keeping fees. Hence, they are treated like customers more than suppliers. According to our above definitions, this is appropriate as the bank is not paying them and they are receiving services from the bank.

## Willingness–to-pay

Willingness-to-pay is a concept that comes directly from looking at a customer's decision regarding whether to purchase a product or not. In particular, willingness-to-pay is the price at which a customer is indifferent between purchasing and not purchasing the product. In this sense it provides a quantifiable measure of the value a customer brings to a potential transaction. So while the benefits a person derives from consuming, say, an ice cream cannot be readily quantified that same person can be asked to name the highest price that they would be *willing to pay* for an ice cream. This would give a monetary equivalent to the benefit that that person places on ice cream. Moreover, it can be related back to the payment that an ice-cream supplier would need to receive in order to cover supply costs.

In some situations, a customer is itself a business. In this case, their willingness-to-pay for an input may be straightforward to calculate. For instance, in our case for this chapter, Ming21 is an antique dealer and so is considering purchasing the vase on the basis of the profits it may earn from selling the vase to its own customers. To see this, let's add some more detail to the case:

> Ming21 sells its products mainly by scheduled auctions. To attract discerning buyers, it must usually hold a special event – especially for high-value pieces. The marketing and staging costs associated with such an event can typically run towards $8000. However, from this Ming21 expects to find a few buyers who will bid up to around $200 000 for the vase.

Given these facts, Figure 3.4 depicts Ming21's decision tree. Notice that Ming21 (D) will choose to buy the vase if $192\,000 - p > \$0$ or $p < \$192\,000$. Thus, so long as the price of the vase is less than $192\,000$, Ming21 will purchase it. In this example, $192\,000$ represents Ming21's willingness-to-pay for the vase.

**Figure 3.4**

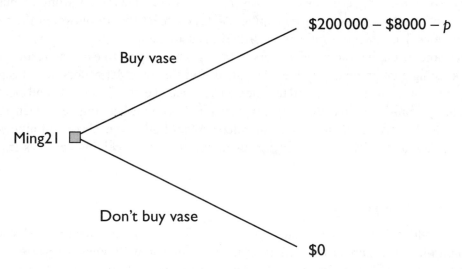

$$\$200\,000 - \$8000 - p$$

Buy vase

Ming21

Don't buy vase

$$\$0$$

In general, a customer's willingness-to-pay for a product is determined by many factors. These include the subjective benefit or utility a customer may derive from a product's consumption (such as a vacation package) or the increased profits that result from utilisation of a product (such as a more modern production technology). Consumers may be willing to pay more for a product when their incomes rise, when a complementary product becomes cheaper (such as CDs with lower priced CD players) or when they are located closer to a particular firm or that firm provides a more favourable brand image. All of these factors – often the domain of marketing subjects – are involved in forming a customer's willingness-to-pay.

Willingness-to-pay, however, is not an absolute notion. It often depends on the alternative outcome customers face if they choose not to purchase a particular product. Thus, you need to examine the overall decision customers are facing as they decide whether to buy the product or not.

For instance, suppose that Ming21 can only carry one item in each event and has identified another piece that could be sold. Ming21 expects to earn $12 000 for that piece. Now Ming21's decision tree is as in Figure 3.5. So in this situation the dealer will buy the vase if:

$$\$200\ 000 - \$8000 - p > \$12\ 000$$

$$\text{(which implies that)}\ p < \$200\ 000 - \$8000 - \$12\ 000$$

$$\text{(implying that)}\ p < \$180\ 000$$

Ming21's willingness-to-pay has fallen to $180 000 because of the alternative profitable opportunity that would have to be sacrificed if the vase were purchased.

**Figure 3.5**

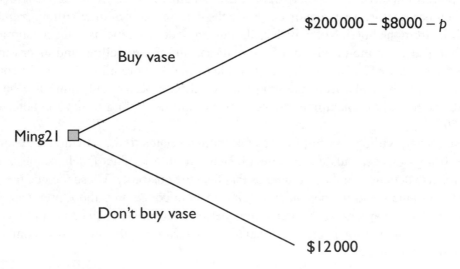

The idea that willingness-to-pay is a relative concept can be illustrated through the following example. Hotels often have honour or mini-bars. The prices of drinks in this bar are usually much higher than the price you would pay at a corner store. Why that is so has something to do with the willingness-to-pay that some hotel customers have for drinks in the hotel room. But in order to understand this we need to consider the drink-purchasing decisions of a hotel customer.

If you are in a hotel, you derive a benefit from drinking a Coke in your room. The monetary equivalent of this might be $5. One way of getting this benefit is to use the mini-bar, in which case you get $5 in value less the price you have to pay. Another option might be to go across the road to the store and buy a Coke for $1.50 and bring it back to your room. In that case, you still get the $5 value but you have to pay $1.50 as well as incurring the cost of travelling outside your room. Suppose that cost is $x$, an amount that is not specified.

Given these options, what is the customer's willingness-to-pay for a Coke from the mini-bar? More specifically, is it $5 or something less? The answer is, it depends. If $x$ were so high (perhaps because it is raining outside) that it was not worthwhile leaving the hotel room then your only option for getting a Coke would be to consume it in your room. In that event, you would be willing to pay up to $5 for the Coke from the mini-bar.

However, what if $x$ were low, say, less than $3.50? In such a situation, you would be willing to pay up to $1.50 plus $c$ for the Coke from the mini-bar. To see this suppose that $x$ was 2. If the hotel's price for Coke were $3, it would be worthwhile paying this price (it is less than $1.50 + $2 = $3.50). On the other hand, if its price were $4, you would prefer to purchase the Coke from the store. That price exceeds your willingness-to-pay of $3.50 for the hotel's Coke.

By putting ourselves in the shoes of the customer and evaluating their purchase decision from their perspective we can more easily see the determinants of their willingness-to-pay for a Coke from the hotel. Not only does the customer derive benefits from consuming the Coke but also from the proximity of the mini-bar and the travelling and inconvenience this saves the customer. Hence, the hotel is able to charge a premium for this. In contrast, if $x$ were zero, the Coke from the mini-bar would be a perfect substitute for the Coke from the store and the maximum the customer would be willing to pay the hotel would be $1.50.

In summary, willingness-to-pay is a concept that relates to the situation a customer is facing. It not only depends on the direct benefits from a product (such as consumption utility) it also depends on the alternatives that face the customer. These include the prices of related products and the customer-specific costs in consuming those products. As we will see in later chapters, such interactions between different businesses' products in a customer's decision problem play a critical role in determining the intensity of competition among those businesses.

## Willingness-to-sell

Similar to willingness-to-pay, determining willingness-to-sell involves considering the decision faced by an agent; in this case, suppliers. When suppliers choose to supply resources or inputs to a business, they are unable to supply those resources elsewhere. Therefore, suppliers essentially give up the returns they might have earned had they not supplied the business. This lost opportunity for alternative earnings is the opportunity cost incurred by suppliers. A supplier's willingness-to-sell is the minimum price they would accept and still choose to supply the resource. It is equal to their opportunity cost of supplying the resource.

To see how willingness-to-sell is determined, consider a vendor who owns and operates an ice-cream stand on weekends. The vendor needs to determine on a month-by-month basis whether or not they should continue to keep the stand open. In a typical month, the vendor can sell 1000 ice-cream cones on weekends. The cost of ice-cream materials is $0.20 per cone. Imagine that the stand itself involves no cost to the vendor. Thus, if the price per cone is $p$, the vendor expects to earn $(p - 0.20) \times 1000$ per month. Should the stand stay open so long as $p$ exceeds 0.20? If it does, the vendor will earn some money.

Figure 3.6 represents this decision. Notice that the decision tree highlights a missing variable: what does the vendor do if the stand shuts down? The vendor could work for someone else; perhaps another stand. Suppose that this employment would give $500 in wages. In this case, the vendor would be better off keeping the stand open only if $(p - 0.20) \times 1000 > 500$ or $p > 0.70$. Thus, the vendor's willingness-to-sell is $0.70 per ice cream. It is driven by the vendor's explicit cost of materials as well as their implicit cost of labour.

**Figure 3.6**

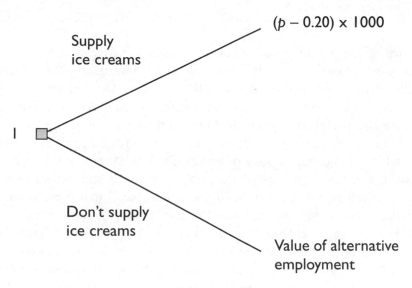

In summary, willingness-to-sell is a concept that relates to the situation a supplier is facing. It not only depends on the direct costs of producing a product but also depends on the alternatives that face the supplier. These include the potential earnings from putting resources – capital and labour – to other uses as well as earnings that could be had from selling to a different customer or group of customers. As such, willingness-to-sell is indistinguishable from the concept of opportunity cost explored in Chapter 2.

## Value creation with many agents

The above discussion considered trade between a customer and a supplier. However, many trading situations involve more than two agents. Here we consider two of the most important of these: (i) when there are many customers and sellers and (ii) when there are several providers of complementary goods.

### Many customers and sellers

In addition to being the building blocks of value, willingness-to-pay and opportunity cost are directly related to the economic concepts of demand and supply, respectively. Indeed, by definition:

> *For each unit price of a product, the* quantity demanded *for a product is the quantity of output for which customers' willingness-to-pay for a unit of output exceeds price.*
>
> *For each unit price of a product, the* quantity supplied *of a product is the quantity of output for which suppliers' willingness-to-sell for a unit of output is smaller than price.*

Notice that, given this definition, as the price falls, quantity demanded for a product will rise, as more customers are willing to pay for more units of output. On the other hand, as price falls, quantity supplied is likely to fall as suppliers face reduced returns.

Not only are the concepts of demand and supply related to the underlying sources of value, they are also useful concepts in determining what level of output would maximise the total value created. To see this, suppose that a market for a product consists of four customers, with willingnesses-to-pay of $1000, $800, $600 and $400 for a single unit of the product, and four suppliers who are able to produce one unit of output each at willingnesses-to-sell of $900, $700, $500 and $300. Recall that there is value created when the willingness-to-pay of a customer exceeds the willingness-to-sell of a supplier. So it would be tempting to think that supplier 1 could supply customer 1, supplier 2 could supply customer 2, etc. In this case, the total value created in the market would be $400 as each customer's willingness-to-pay exceeds their supplier's willingness-to-sell by $100.

This matching of customers and suppliers would not maximise the total value created. Consider an alternative matching whereby customer 1 is matched with supplier 4, customer 2 is matched with supplier 3 and the remaining two customers and suppliers do not trade at all. In this case, the total value created is $1000 (= 1000 − 300 + 800 − 500), which is higher than the situation where all four customers are supplied. Moreover, notice that, given this, if either of the other customers were supplied, value created would be lower as those customers' willingnesses-to-pay would be below the suppliers' willingnesses-to-sell. So to maximise the value created, customers 1 and 2 must be supplied by suppliers 3 and 4 and no other trades should take place.

This example illustrates a more general principle: in order to maximise the total value created, the customer with the highest willingness-to-pay should be matched with the supplier with the lowest opportunity cost, the customer with the next highest willingness-to-pay should be matched with the supplier with the next lowest opportunity cost and so on. Moreover, trades should not take place beyond the point where the willingness-to-pay of the next customer is less than the willingness-to-sell of the next supplier.

It is important that the matching exercise is used to order customers and suppliers to form demand and supply curves and find their intersection. In our example, so long as two units are sold from suppliers 3 and 4 to customers 1 and 2, the total value created is maximised. Thus, customer 1 could purchase from supplier 3 and customer 2 from supplier 4, generating the same level of value.

This situation can be depicted graphically where we rank customers from highest to lowest willingness-to-pay and suppliers from lowest to highest willingness-to-sell. This is done in Figure 3.7. The line of customers' willingnesses-to-pay is what is called the market demand curve for the product while the line of suppliers' willingnesses-to-sell is the market supply curve. Notice that the value created is maximised where the two curves intersect: that is, where demand effectively equals supply.

**Figure 3.7**

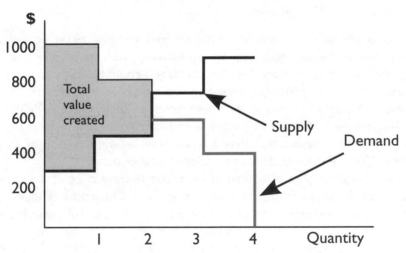

By considering willingness-to-pay and willingness-to-sell in terms of demand and supply, it becomes easier to see what quantity will the greatest value. As we will see in a later chapter, market forces, whereby prices change in response to shortages and surpluses, can ensure that demand equals supply and hence, the total value created is maximised.

## Demand, supply and new product development

Let's consider how demand and supply might assist in understanding whether or not to invest in new products to save time. According to James Gleick, the pace of modern life has accelerated.

> We are in a rush. We are making haste. A compression of time characterises the life of the century now closing. Airport gates are minor intensifiers of the lose-not-a-minute anguish of our age. There are other intensifiers – places and objects that signify impatience. Certain notorious intersections and tollbooths. Doctors' anterooms ('waiting' rooms). The DOOR CLOSE button in elevators, so often a placebo, with no function to distract for a moment those riders to whom ten seconds seems an eternity. Speed-dial buttons on telephones: do you invest minutes in programming them and reap your rewards in tenths of a second? Remote controls: their very existence, in the hands of a quick-reflexed, multitasking, channel-flipping, fast-forwarding citizenry, has caused an acceleration in the pace of films and television commercials. (Gleick, J. (2000), *Faster: The Acceleration of Just About Everything*, Vintage Books: New York.)

There are many reasons why activities have become faster. For instance, it could be that people demand more time-saving products because they now live in the rat race of modern life. Alternatively, it could be that technology has lowered the cost of producing time; that is, time-saving products are cheaper and more available. The former is a description of an increase in demand for time – people are willing to pay more – while the latter is a description of an increase in the supply of time; a given amount of time-saving can now be supplied at a lower cost. But it could also be a combination of things.

Identifying the precise source of increased timeliness could be critical if time is your business. To see this, suppose you are a producer of elevators. A decade ago, you had developed a new design for a high-speed elevator. However, at that time, you assessed there was insufficient demand. You note that today the pace of life is quicker, demonstrating that people are actually purchasing more time-saving devices and doing other things to save time. Indeed, buildings are putting in elevators of higher speeds. Should you bring out your design from the file cabinet?

It depends. Is demand or supply responsible for the increased consumption of time-saving devices? Either could be responsible. In Figure 3.8A, an increase in demand is associated with an increase in the quantity of time demanded. Similarly, in Figure 3.8B, an increase in supply is associated with an increase in the quantity of time saved. However, in the former, the last builder who purchases a quicker elevator is willing to pay more for it than in the past while, in the latter, the reverse is true: an increase in supply has led to greater elevator speed because it is more affordable.

**Figure 3.8** High-speed elevator market

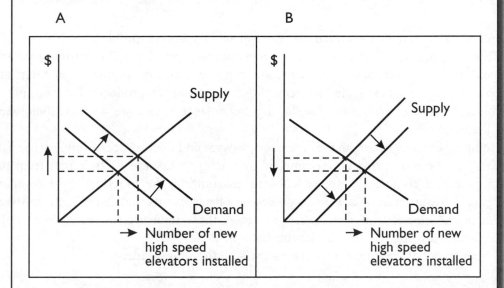

In terms of your development decision, the difference is crucial. If the changes are primarily demand-related, it may be time to bring a new product to market, as builders are willing to pay more for it than before. In contrast, if it is supply-related, there may be little reason to develop the product further as builders do not actually value the product more but there are alternative and cheaper ways of installing quicker elevators. Unless your costs have also fallen, the value of your product may have diminished.

The moral of this story is that the source of a change in consumption patterns matters in terms of how you manage your business. Observing greater consumption does not by any means signal more opportunities; it may be a signal that finding a valuable product niche is harder for your business. Disentangling the two is, therefore, a first step in any product development or investment decision.

## Cooperating with complementors

A more subtle form of value creation comes from dealing with complementors.

> *An agent is your* complementor *if customers value your product more when they have the other agent's product than when they have your product alone.*

Interdependent industries often cooperate to achieve greater profitability.

This is perhaps easiest to see with complementary products. The existence of and demand for complementary products can improve industry profitability. After all, complementary products stimulate demand for an industry's products. For example, a customer is willing to pay more for shaving cream when razors are available than when they are not.

Complementarity occurs in the computer software and microprocessor industries. The demand for the processing power supplied by microprocessors results in part from the development of complex computer software. In addition, the introduction of complex computer software necessitates microprocessor advancements that can execute software commands. As a result of their interdependence, these industries cooperate with open exchanges of information, which benefits both industries.

Another way of viewing complementarity is on the supply side.

> *A player is your* complementor *if it is more attractive for a supplier to provide resources to you when it is also supplying the other player, than when it is supplying you alone.*

If a particular supplier has a greater willingness-to-sell to you and another customer together than to each separately, then you and the other customer are complementors in supply. For instance, some customers might use a broadband Internet connection during the day while others might use it at night. If both types of customers are available, an Internet provider can provide the service to each at a lower price than it could if only one type were available.

DIGGING

DEEPER

### Specialisation and trade

In his 1776 classic, *Wealth of Nations*, Adam Smith demonstrated the importance of the value that could be created by specialisation. His famous example was of a pin factory where the labour of making a pin was divided into a number of separate tasks, each performed by a different worker. By focusing and not having to switch around, each worker could learn by repetition how to produce their task more efficiently, thereby enabling the firm to generate more pins per worker.

In the 19th century, David Ricardo built on Smith to find a subtler reason why specialisation could create value. He recognised that different inputs were able to perform functions with different productivities. For instance, some land was more suited to produce wine than wheat and some workers were better at certain tasks than others. Now if one worker's productivity at a task was greater than another then it may be obvious that they should specialise in that task. But what will happen if that worker is better at all tasks than another worker?

For Ricardo, workers should still specialise; and they should do the task for which they have a greater *comparative advantage*. To see this, suppose that two workers – Jack and Jill – were producing water. Jill could fill pails at a rate of 20 per hour or carry 12 pails down the hill in that hour. On the other hand, for Jack these rates were 12 and 4 respectively. If each had 8 hours in the day to spare, then working separately, Jill could produce 60 pails while Jack could produce only 24 pails; a total of 84 pails.

Instead, suppose that Jack and Jill were to specialise with Jill hauling and Jack filling pails. In this case, they could produce a total of 96 pails. The reason is that Jill has a comparative advantage in hauling being 3 times better than Jack as opposed to filling where she is only 1.67 times better than Jack. To put it another way, in the time Jill can fill a pail she is costing herself 3/5 of a hauled pail whereas Jack would only cost 1/3 of a hauled pail. So the opportunity cost of filling is higher for Jill than for Jack, making it better to leave the filling to Jack.

Thus, a rationale for specialisation arises whenever resources are limited (in the example above, the limited time resources of workers), so one should take into account the opportunity cost of the use of those resources and allocate productive activities so as to minimise those costs. Simply looking at technical measures of productivity alone is unlikely to generate an outcome that maximises total value created.

## Summary

Cooperative decision-making is related to individual decision-making as it requires all individuals to be satisfied with the cooperative decision being made. This chapter has focused on the value that can be realised through cooperative decision-making without considering how such cooperation can be achieved. Invariably this requires some form of compensation to be paid by those benefiting directly from the decision to those whom it costs. In the next chapter, we will examine what happens when there is no simple mechanism to agree upon compensation. However, in Part II, we turn to consider negotiations over value; specifically how these generate value maximising outcomes as well as determining a compensation or pricing agreement that allows that value to be shared among agents.

# 4 Strategic decision-making

Chapter 2 examined how individual decision-makers evaluate choices while Chapter 3 looked at how groups of decision-makers might evaluate choices if they acted cooperatively. Here we examine what happens when (i) individual choices impact on others, and (ii) individual decision-makers cannot cooperatively agree on their actions; that is, they act independently from one another. In this situation, individual decision-makers need to think strategically and forecast what actions others might take in response to their actions.

The economic tool we will apply in this chapter is that of *non-cooperative game theory*. The 'game' refers to the notion that when individuals choose actions to maximise their own payoffs they are in some sense playing a game with, and possibly against, other players. The 'non-cooperative' part refers to the fact that individuals in these situations are choosing actions independently of one another rather than agreeing to a cooperative outcome as in Chapter 3.

Non-cooperative game theory naturally builds upon the decision tree tool illustrated in Chapter 2. The only differences are (i) that there is more than one agent making a decision in a given tree, and (ii) that agents may or may not know what actions others have taken earlier in the tree. It is this latter dimension upon which we divide this chapter up. First, we deal with situations where agents can observe earlier actions taken by others (*sequential move games*) before turning to situations where those actions cannot be observed (*simultaneous move games*).

## Sequential move games

Sequential move games are ones where each agent makes moves at different times and those choosing later can observe what those before them have done. This allows later decision-makers to react to those choices. However, it also means that earlier decision-makers can benefit by 'putting themselves in the shoes' of later decision-makers to consider how their choices may differ depending upon earlier choices that are made.

Given how closely sequential move games relate to decision trees, it is useful to build our understanding of them by continuing on (in a simpler form) the hypothetical case of TimeScape considered in Chapter 2:

> Catherine at TimeScape is worried about how a rival in the mobile market, BigCell, might react to her entry. She had been operating on the assumption that TimeScape could expect to earn $400 000 in profits should she enter that market.[1] However, this was on the assumption that BigCell accommodated her entry and did not react by pursuing aggressive pricing. If this occurred, her profits would fall to $100 000.

Let's suppose that TimeScape's full entry cost into the mobile market is $300 000.[2] Notice that if Catherine expects BigCell to accommodate her entry, then entry is profitable but it will not be profitable if BigCell competes aggressively.

Catherine could assign probabilities to BigCell's choices and treat this as an individual decision under uncertainty. Alternatively, she could consider what choices BigCell might actually make if faced with them.

> Catherine considers that BigCell – which currently makes profits of $2m in the mobile market – may see those profits fall to $1.5m if TimeScape enters and BigCell does not change its pricing. If BigCell chooses to fight a price war, then BigCell's profits will fall to $1m. However, those profits would rise again to $2m should Catherine choose to exit the mobile market.

This gives us enough information to build a game tree. That tree is depicted in Figure 4.1. Notice the differences between that tree and an individual decision tree. First, both TimeScape (T) and BigCell (B) are making decisions at different points. Second, both TimeScape and BigCell receive payoffs at the end. By convention, *we always write the payoff of the first mover first and the other movers in the order they move.* In this case, the first payoff refers to TimeScape and the second to BigCell.

### Representing sequential games

Notice that, in Figure 4.1, TimeScape's entry decision comes first. Having observed this, BigCell chooses whether to accommodate that entry or fight a price war. Following from this, TimeScape gets another choice – whether to stay in the market or exit. All of these different combinations of choices give rise to five pairs of payoffs. Notice that should TimeScape choose not to enter in the first place, the game ends with each firm getting their status quo payoffs. However, once TimeScape enters those payoffs can no longer be achieved as TimeScape sinks its entry cost of $300 000. It is clear that TimeScape would like its entry to go ahead and for BigCell to accommodate it. However, BigCell would prefer entry to be deterred or, at the very least, for TimeScape to choose to exit. Neither, however, has perfect control of these outcomes.

**Figure 4.1** Game tree

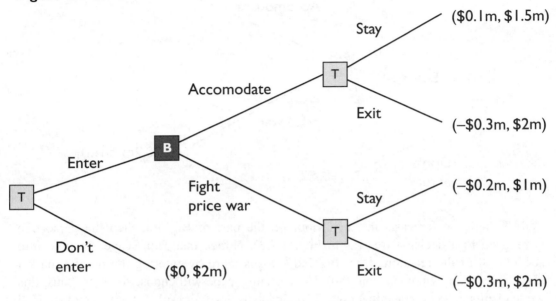

### Solving the game tree

Game trees, like decision trees, are solved by working backwards; from the tips of the branches to the root. In this case, this means considering TimeScape's decision to stay in the market or exit. This decision is made in two different circumstances. In the first, BigCell has already chosen to accommodate TimeScape. In this case, TimeScape looks at its own payoff only when making a decision and will choose to stay (earning $100 000 rather than losing $300 000). Similarly, should BigCell choose to fight a price war, TimeScape will also prefer to stay rather than exit. In each case, TimeScape makes a loss but its losses are smaller if it stays. Intuitively, TimeScape has already sunk its entry costs by that point and so these do not factor into its decision. At that point, even with a price war, TimeScape makes more by staying than exiting and so chooses to stay.

Figure 4.2 depicts the 'clipped' game tree taking into account TimeScape's 'stay versus exit' decisions. Given this, we are now in a position to analyse BigCell's choice. BigCell is effectively putting itself in TimeScape's place and has worked out that TimeScape will stay in the market no matter what. BigCell now considers whether to accommodate or fight based on its payoffs. Accommodation will earn BigCell $1.5m whilst fighting a price war will only earn it $1m. Thus, BigCell will choose to accommodate at this point.

**Figure 4.2** Reduced game tree

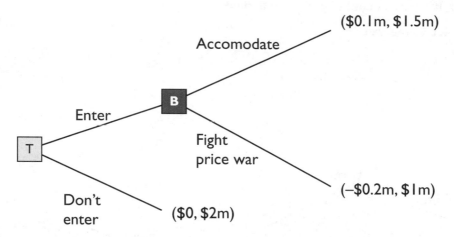

If TimeScape forecasts this behaviour on the part of BigCell, then the game tree is reduced to a decision tree (as in Figure 4.3). Notice that TimeScape – taking into account all of the reactions from BigCell – earns more by entering the mobile market ($100 000) than by not entering ($0). Hence, TimeScape will choose to enter. Thus, this game results in an outcome that gives TimeScape its desired result – it enters and BigCell accommodates that entry.

**Figure 4.3** Reduced to decision tree

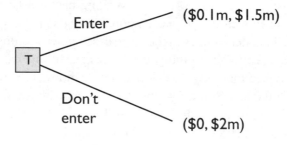

### Evaluating credible threats

Intuitively, while BigCell may have wanted TimeScape to believe it would fight a price war – in which case TimeScape would have expected to earn a loss from entry – that possibility was not credible. When put in a position to fight a price war, given that entry has already taken place and TimeScape's entry costs were already sunk, fighting a price war would only disadvantage BigCell. Hence, TimeScape – seeing through this – would realise that the possibility of a price war was remote and so chooses to enter.

The game tree allows us to illustrate what moves are likely to actually happen and what moves are unlikely. So while BigCell might appear to be threatening a price war should

TimeScape enter, this threat is not *credible*. When given a chance, BigCell would not find it profitable to carry it out.

Other threats, however, might be more credible. For instance, suppose that BigCell – instead of accommodating or fighting a price war in the mobile market – themselves entered the handheld market. This could be something useful for BigCell as it could mitigate their losses due to TimeScape's entry by allowing them to offer a mobile phone with handheld functions. It also might be something that BigCell might otherwise not have done but for competitive pressure from TimeScape. In this case, the game tree might look as in Figure 4.4. Notice that for BigCell, entering the handheld market improves its profits should TimeScape stay in the market but causes losses if TimeScape exits (i.e., is only worthwhile given the competitive pressure). For TimeScape, BigCell's entry into handhelds hurts it by costing it $100 000 in profits in that market.

**Figure 4.4** Alternative threats

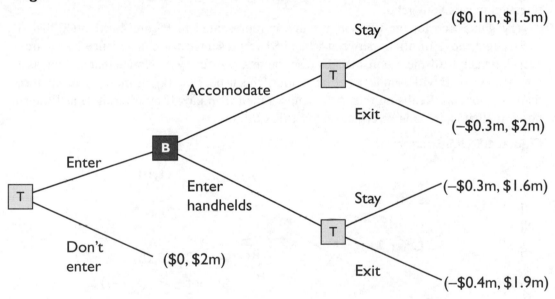

Solving this alternative game tree, we still find that TimeScape will want to stay in the mobiles market but that, given this, BigCell earns more profits from entering handhelds than from simply accommodating TimeScape's mobile entry (i.e., it earns $1.6m from entering handhelds as opposed to $1.5m from not entering). Given this, TimeScape now faces a loss of $300 000 from entry into mobiles and so chooses not to enter.

This demonstrates that the likely outcomes in a game tree are very sensitive to small changes in the payoffs and actions available to different agents. While before, BigCell could not credibly threaten to fight a price war, in this alternative game, the threat to enter handhelds was credible because TimeScape's entry into mobiles made this choice worthwhile for BigCell. Faced with a credible threat, TimeScape chose to avoid the mobile market.

## Bargaining

To provide an alternative example of a sequential move game, consider structured bargaining. This occurs when one party to a negotiation makes an offer to another. The other party can respond by accepting or rejecting that offer. In this situation, the negotiations may come to an end or, alternatively, may progress with counter-offers. The key question becomes: when will an agreement be reached and how will any surplus between parties be divided?

Perhaps the simplest bargaining game is the ultimatum game. For example, suppose that two parties – A and B – are negotiating over how to divide $1. They can only have the $1 if they come to an agreement – that is, when someone's offer is accepted by the other party. In the ultimatum game, there is a single round of offers and potential acceptances. Here, A makes an offer of a division of $1 to B (e.g., $x$ goes to A and $1 - x$ goes to B) and B chooses to accept or reject that offer. Acceptance means B gets $1 - x$ and A gets $x$ while rejection means both get 0.

The game tree for the ultimatum game is represented in Figure 4.5. Notice that A can make a range of offers between $0 and $1 (represented for convenience by an arc). Working backwards, let's consider B's reaction to any offer by A. Notice that so long as $1 - x > 0$ or $x < 1$, B will want to accept that offer. This is because B gets more by acceptance than by rejection. Realising this, A maximises their own payoff by offering B as little as possible; that is, making $x$ very close to $1 (say 99c).

**Figure 4.5** Ultimatum game

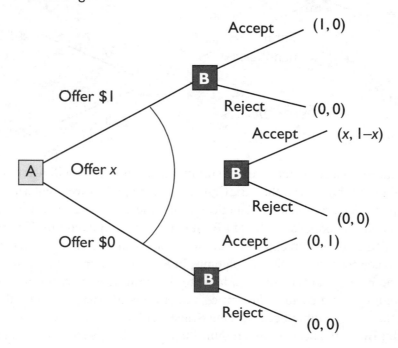

In the ultimatum game, an agreement is reached immediately and the offeror, A, obtains most of the surplus. This is a common feature of environments where one party is able to make 'take it or leave it' offers to another. Such offers allow that party to dictate terms and, not surprisingly, they do so in their favour. Of course, the opportunity to make such offers usually depends on there being some time sensitivity to reaching an agreement quickly.

As such, it is natural to ask what would happen if, following a rejection of A's offer, B could make a counter-offer? Suppose that following a rejection of A's offer, there is a 50% chance that B could make a counter-offer. Suppose also that B's counter-offer was the last available in that instance. This two-round negotiation is depicted in Figure 4.6.

**Figure 4.6** Two-round bargaining game

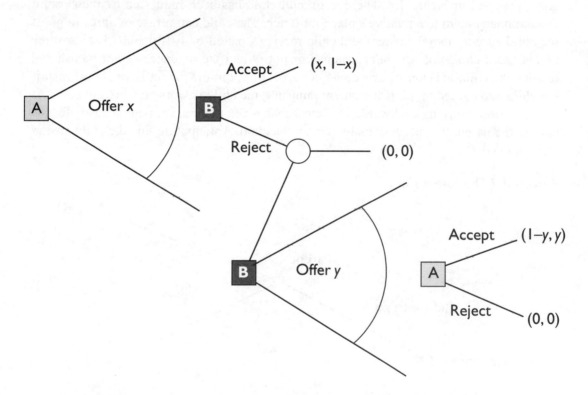

Working backwards, you can see that if B has a chance to make a 'take it or leave it' offer of $y$ to A, they will set $y = 99c$ and A will accept that offer. Anticipating this, B knows that there is a 50% chance that if they reject A's offer, they will make 99c. Thus, the expected payoff from rejection is approximately 50c. This means that B will not accept less than 50c from an initial offer from A. Given this, A's best option is to make an offer of $x = 50c$, which B will accept.

The possibility of a counter-offer changes the balance of bargaining power. By giving B an alternative option, B can credibly refuse offers from A that are too low. In addition,

A does not want to risk such rejection as, in this game at least, rejection can put A in a very poor bargaining position.

In reality, games of alternating offers – such as these – give a number of predictions regarding how much each party can expect to earn. Certainly, each party's patience will assist them in securing a greater share as would their alternative options should negotiations break down. We revisit some of these issues in Chapter 5 although we will consider a more free-form bargaining approach there than the non-cooperative one here.

## Commitment

Sequential games can also illustrate the value of commitment. A commitment is an irreversible but observable action taken by one player. To see its value, consider the game depicted in Figure 4.7. There a difficult child has been requested by their parent to accompany them to a relative's place for lunch. The child can refuse or agree to go. If the child agrees, both the parent and child receive a payoff of 1. If the child refuses, the parent has a choice of whether to punish or not. When the parent does not punish and relents, the child is better off, receiving a payoff of 2, but the parent is worse off than if the child had agreed to go. If the parent punishes, the child is worse off but the parent is worse off too. Working backwards, it is clear that, given that punishment is costly for the parent, the parent will never actually punish the child. Anticipating this the child always refuses to go.

**Figure 4.7** The rotten kid

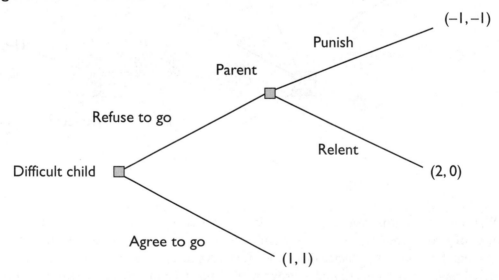

The problem for the parent would be solved if they could commit to punishing the child. Below we will show that if this game were repeated, then the parent's anticipation of future problems can provide them with an incentive to punish. Alternatively, the parent might change the game by finding a punishment that is less costly for them to implement.

If such a punishment could be found, the parent would be able to credibly commit to it and the child's behaviour would change.

We will see in coming chapters that commitment has a lot of value in business situations. However, this value is only realised if commitments are credible in that when an agent has the opportunity to take an action consistent with a commitment, they will actually have an incentive to do so.

## Simultaneous move games

When all agents cannot observe the actions taken by others prior to them having to take an action themselves, those agents are playing a simultaneous move game. It is called 'simultaneous' because we analyse this as if all agents are choosing their actions at the same time – a special case of being unable to observe one another's choices.

While it is possible to analyse these games with a game tree, it is easier to consider an alternative representation – called the normal form of a game. This puts the games in a matrix that illustrates all of the different possible payoffs for each distinct combination of actions by the players in the game. Such games can be analysed in several ways. One way – the elimination of dominated strategies – removes from consideration actions that an agent will never find it worthwhile to play. Another way – Nash equilibrium – looks for points of balance whereby if agents are playing those strategies no agent has an incentive to change what they are doing.

### *Representing simultaneous move games*

**Table 4.1** 'Rock, Paper, Scissors'

| | | Child B | | |
|---|---|---|---|---|
| | | Rock | Paper | Scissors |
| Child A | Rock | 0,0 | –1,1 | 1,–1 |
| | Paper | 1,–1 | 0,0 | –1,1 |
| | Scissors | –1,1 | 1,–1 | 0,0 |

To begin, let's consider a familiar game and how it might be represented in a matrix. The children's game of 'Rock, Paper, Scissors' involves each child counting to three and then revealing their hand in the form of a rock, paper or scissors. If both children have the same hand they tie but rock beats scissors, paper beats rock and scissors beats paper and one child wins while the other loses. Thus, if there are two children – Child A and Child B – then there are nine possible outcomes. Table 4.1 shows how this can be represented as a matrix where a 0 represents a tied payoff, 1 a win and –1 a loss.

Using the matrix, one can analyse what payoffs each agent will receive for each combination of choices. So if Child A chooses rock and Child B chooses scissors, this identifies the cell in the top right hand corner as the payoff outcome. By convention, the 'row' player's payoff is first and the 'column' player's is second. So in this case, Child A would receive 1 and Child B would receive -1.

But this type of representation is not useful only for children's games. Consider a typical business situation whereby two bidders are attempting to procure an asset from a seller. Suppose that bidder 1 values the asset at $4 while bidder 2 values it at $3. Suppose also that each can submit a bid – in a sealed envelope – in dollar increments and that the 'winner' of the auction will be the bidder with the highest bid when the envelopes are opened. This is a standard (first price) sealed bid auction or tender.

**Table 4.2** Sealed-bid auction

| | | 2's bid | | | | |
|---|---|---|---|---|---|---|
| | | $0 | $1 | $2 | $3 | $4 |
| | $0 | $2, $1.5 | $0, $2 | $0, $1 | $0, $0 | $0, –$1 |
| I's | $1 | $3, $0 | $1.5, $1 | $0, $1 | $0, $0 | $0, –$1 |
| bid | $2 | $2, $0 | $2, $0 | $1, $0.5 | $0, $0 | $0, –$1 |
| | $3 | $1, $0 | $1, $0 | $1, $0 | $0.5, $0 | $0, –$1 |
| | $4 | $0, $0 | $0, $0 | $0, $0 | $0, $0 | $0, –$0.5 |

Table 4.2 represents this as a game in a matrix. Notice that an agent's payoff is only positive if they win the auction (that is, their bid exceeds that of the other agent). If this occurs, then their payoff is their surplus – their value less their bid. Of course, it is also possible that a tie occurs. In this case, the asset is awarded randomly and so for those cells, we list agents' expected payoffs. For example, if both agents bid $1, then bidder 1 expects to receive surplus of $3 (= $4 – $1) with 50% probability and bidder 2 expects to receive surplus of $2 (= $3 – $1) with 50% probability. Hence, we write their payoffs as ($1.5, $1) to reflect these expected outcomes.

### Dominant strategies

Having represented simultaneous move games in a payoff matrix, how do we solve it to generate a prediction as to the game's outcome? A first approach is to recall that agents will be rational and only choose actions that maximise their payoffs. Conversely, a rational agent will not want to choose an action that will definitely result in a lower payoff no matter what. That is, no agent will want to take a dominated action:

> *A strategy or action is* dominated *for an agent if it results in a strictly worse payoff for that agent compared with another strategy for every alternative set of actions from other players.*

In 'Rock, Paper, Scissors' neither child has a dominated strategy. This is because it is conceivable that for a child either rock, paper or scissors could be a desirable action – that is, each is a possible winning strategy.

To see a game where players do have dominated strategies, we can consider the classic 'Prisoners' Dilemma'. Here is the scenario:

> Two people have been caught and arrested by the police. They are accused of armed robbery but there is no actual evidence that they did it. The prisoners are put in separate cells and offered a deal for evidence: 'Confess and admit that both of you are involved and you will be set free. Hold out and the other will accuse you and you will get a harsh sentence (10 years). If both confess, you will each get a light sentence (5 years). If both hold out, you will be held for a year.'

The resulting payoff matrix is represented in Table 4.3. Notice that in this case the 'payoffs' are years of jail time and so players want to get as low a payoff as possible.

**Table 4.3** 'Prisoners' Dilemma'

|  |  | Prisoner 2 | |
| --- | --- | --- | --- |
|  |  | Confess | Hold out |
| **Prisoner 1** | Confess | 5, 5 | 0, 10 |
|  | Hold out | 10, 0 | 1, 1 |

Examining this payoff matrix, notice that holding out is dominated by confessing for both prisoners. Consider Prisoner 1. If they confess while Prisoner 2 holds out, they are set free rather than having to serve one year. Moreover, if they confess while Prisoner 2 confesses, they receive 5 rather than 10 years. The same goes for Prisoner 2 and hence, in this game, both players confess and receive sentences of 5 years each.

The irony here is that if both could have held out, they both would have been better off. Notice also that this occurs regardless of whether one or both prisoners are actually guilty or innocent! For this reason, the 'Prisoners' Dilemma' game is often seen as a metaphor for many other issues where individual agents follow their own self-interest and cause an outcome that would not be in their collective interest had it been possible to coordinate their actions. In Chapter 9, we will see how 'Prisoners' Dilemma' can be useful in analysing price competition between sellers.

Nonetheless, 'Prisoners' Dilemma' does illustrate how eliminating dominated strategies can assist us in predicting the outcome of a simultaneous move game. Of course, this game was easier in the sense that both players had only two actions. What happens when they have many actions is something we consider next.

DIGGING

DEEPER

## Pricing of complements

It is useful to consider a business application where there may be a failure to cooperate just as in 'Prisoners' Dilemma'. Suppose that a pizza and video store are located close to one another. At present, the price of a pizza is $10 and the price of a video is $6 and there are 100 customers who purchase both. The pizza store owner believes that if either the pizza or the video store drops their price by $2 an additional 20 customers (of both pizza and videos) will be attracted. This could be achieved by the pizza or video store dropping their prices by $2 (we will suppose they cannot coordinate on a shared discount).

Table 4.5 is a payoff matrix illustrating the choices.

**Table 4.4** Failed cooperation

| | | Pizza Store's Discount | |
|---|---|---|---|
| | | $0 | $2 |
| **Video Store's Discount** | $0 | $600, $1000 | $720, $960 |
| | $2 | $480, $1200 | $480, $960 |

Notice that, for each store, dropping price by $2 is dominated by offering no discount. Hence, the unique equilibrium involves neither offering a discount. If either one were to offer a discount, total profits would be higher.

This illustrates a form of failed cooperation. Each store's discount impacts on its own profits but also positively on the profits of the other store. However, each chooses whether to discount or not only with regard to their own profits and, for each store, they judge a discount to be unprofitable. As such, when two firms have complementary goods, it pays to coordinate pricing in some way to ensure that prices are not too high and profit opportunities are not lost.

## Eliminating dominated strategies

Sometimes eliminating dominated strategies can help when each agent has many actions but cannot actually solve the game. For the sealed-bid auction considered earlier, notice that bidding $4 is dominated for Bidder 2. This is because compared with say, bidding $2, regardless of what Bidder 1's bid is, Bidder 2 would be strictly better off bidding $2 than bidding $4. Indeed, notice that bidding $0, $1 or $3 would also dominate bidding $4 for Bidder 2.

Given this, we can remove $4 as a bid from the game as Bidder 2 would never choose it. In this case, the reduced payoff matrix is as in Table 4.5. Notice that, in this reduced payoff matrix, bidding $4 for Bidder 1 is dominated by a bid of $3 (that is, for each of 2's bids from $0 to $3, 1 earns more by bidding $3 than bidding $4). Thus, we can also remove bidding $4 for Bidder 1 as a relevant strategy (producing Table 4.6).

This is, however, where, for this game, the elimination of dominated strategies stops. The reduced game in Table 4.6 contains some strategies that are weakly dominated (e.g., for player 2, bidding $3 is weakly dominated by bidding $2; earning a higher payoff for player 2 in every situation except where player 1 is bidding $3 where bids of $2 or $3 earn 2 a payoff of $0). However, there are no strategies that are strictly dominated. In this situation, we would need to use an alternative method to fully solve the game (e.g., Nash equilibrium discussed below).

**Table 4.5** Reduced payoff matrix

| | | 2's bid | | | |
|---|---|---|---|---|---|
| | | $0 | $1 | $2 | $3 |
| **1's bid** | $0 | $2, $1.5 | $0, $2 | $0, $1 | $0, $0 |
| | $1 | $3, $0 | $1.5, $1 | $0, $1 | $0, $0 |
| | $2 | $2, $0 | $2, $0 | $1, $0.5 | $0, $0 |
| | $3 | $1, $0 | $1, $0 | $1, $0 | $0.5, $0 |

| | $4 | $0, $0 | $0, $0 | $0, $0 | $0, $0 |
|---|---|---|---|---|---|

**Table 4.6** Reduced payoff matrix

| | | 2's bid | | | |
|---|---|---|---|---|---|
| | | $0 | $1 | $2 | $3 |
| | $0 | $2, $1.5 | $0, $2 | $0, $1 | $0, $0 |
| 1's | $1 | $3, $0 | $1.5, $1 | $0, $1 | $0, $0 |
| bid | $2 | $2, $0 | $2, $0 | $1, $0.5 | $0, $0 |
| | $3 | $1, $0 | $1, $0 | $1, $0 | $0.5, $0 |

Table 4.7 provides a game matrix that can be solved by eliminating dominated strategies. We won't go through all the details here but notice that (i) 0 is dominated by 1 for A and B; (ii) given this, 2 dominates 1 for both; (iii) given this, 4 dominates 5 for both; (iv) given this, 3 dominates 4 for both; and (v) finally, that given this, 3 dominates 2 for both. Thus, the outcome of the game will involve both A and B playing 3 and receiving payoffs of 9 each. We call games such as this, *dominance solvable*.

**Table 4.7** A dominance solvable game

| | | B | | | | | |
|---|---|---|---|---|---|---|---|
| | | 0 | 1 | 2 | 3 | 4 | 5 |
| | 0 | 0, 0 | 0, 8 | 0, 14 | 0, 18 | 0, 20 | 0, 20 |
| | 1 | 8, 0 | 7, 7 | 6, 12 | 5, 15 | 4, 16 | 3, 15 |
| | 2 | 14, 0 | 12, 6 | 10, 10 | 8, 12 | 6, 11 | 4, 10 |
| A | 3 | 18, 0 | 15, 5 | 12, 8 | 9, 9 | 6, 8 | 3, 5 |
| | 4 | 20, 0 | 16, 4 | 11, 6 | 8, 6 | 4, 4 | 0, 0 |

## Vickery or second price auctions

An alternative to the first-price sealed-bid auction is a second-price auction where each agent bids but the winner only pays the bid of the second-highest bidder. This auction was conceived of and analysed by William Vickery. What is notable about it is that its outcome is (weakly) dominance solvable.

To see this, suppose that there are $n$ bidders in this auction with a representative player, $i$, having a value for the asset of $v_i$. If the highest opposing bid of $B$ is made by $k$ bidders and $i$ bids $b$, $i$'s payoff is $v_i - B$ if $B < b$, $0$ if $B > b$ and $(v_i - B)/(k + 1)$ if $B = b$. Notice that (1) if $v_i > B$, then only bids greater than B earn the maximal payoff of $v_i$; (2) if $v_i < B$, then only bids less than B earn the maximal payoff of 0, and (3) if $v_i = B$, then all bids earns the same payoff, namely, 0. Thus, for each player, their expected payoff is maximised by setting $b = v_i$.

What is useful about this outcome is that each agent's bid reveals their true value and so the asset will end up going to the agent who values it the most. As such, it is an efficient outcome.

### Nash equilibrium

A dominance solvable outcome is a special case of another way of solving games called Nash equilibrium. It is named after John Nash – the Nobel prize-winner whose life was portrayed in the movie *A Beautiful Mind*. The benefit of Nash equilibrium is that, in one form or another (see the box on 'mixed strategies'), it exists in all games.

An equilibrium is literally a 'point of rest'. For instance, a pendulum has a natural equilibrium with the weight resting below the fulcrum. In games, a Nash equilibrium arises when, given the strategies being played by others, each player is playing their payoff-maximising strategy. In the 'Prisoners' Dilemma' game, each prisoner finds confessing preferable to holding out given that the other prisoner is expected to confess too. No player has an incentive to change what they are doing.

The 'Prisoners' Dilemma' game has a single Nash equilibrium (something that occurs when games are also dominance solvable). In many situations, games may have more than one Nash equilibrium. Consider the following scenario:

Two firms are considering simultaneously developing a new product for a market. The costs of developing the product are $10m but there will only be earnings in the market of $40m if one develops. If both develop the products, then those additional profits are competed away and each firm earns –$10m.

In this game, both firms have two options – to develop or not develop the product. Table 4.8 describes the resulting payoff matrix. In this game, there are two Nash equilibria, each involving only one firm developing. To see why this is the case, suppose that both firms develop. Then given what the other firm is doing, each can improve its payoff by not developing. Similarly, if neither are developing, each can earn $30m more by developing. However, if one firm develops while the other does not, neither has an incentive to change its strategy. The firm that develops earns $30m more by so doing given that the other does not. The firm that does not develop is $10m better off by not developing given that the other firm is developing the product.

**Table 4.8** Entry game

|  |  | Firm 2 | |
|---|---|---|---|
|  |  | Develop | Not |
| **Firm 1** | Develop | –$10m, –$10m | $30m, $0 |
|  | Not | $0, $30m | $0, $0 |

This example also highlights a way to find Nash equilibria in a game. Take each cell and examine whether one player or both would be strictly better off choosing another action than the one for that cell (given that the other player does not change what they are doing). If you find a cell where neither player would be better off you have identified a Nash equilibrium.

**Table 4.9** Nash equilibria in the sealed-bid auction

|  |  | 2's bid | | | | |
|---|---|---|---|---|---|---|
|  |  | $0 | $1 | $2 | $3 | $4 |
| **1's** | $0 | $2, $1.5 | $0, $2 | $0, $1 | $0, $0 | $0, –$1 |
|  | $1 | **$3**, $0 | $1.5, $1 | $0, $1 | $0, $0 | $0, –$1 |
| **bid** | $2 | $2, $0 | $2, $0 | $1, $0.5 | $0, $0 | $0, –$1 |
|  | $3 | $1, **$0** | $1, **$0** | $1, **$0** | $0.5, $0 | $0, –$1 |
|  | $4 | $0, **$0** | $0, **$0** | $0, **$0** | $0, **$0** | **$0**, –$0.5 |

Alternatively, when there are many cells, you might look at each action of one player and then ask which actions of the other maximise their payoff. For instance, in Table 4.9, this is done for the sealed-bid auction. If 2 bids $0, then bidder 1 maximises their payoff by bidding $1; hence, the boldface $3 highlighted in the relevant cell. If 2 bids $2, bidding

$2 and $3 gives 1 its maximal payoff, in that instance, of $1. Continue this for each strategy of each player and highlight as shown in Table 4.9. Then all of the cells for which both payoffs are in bold give you a Nash equilibrium. The coincidence means that each player is maximising its payoff given what the other is doing. Notice that in that game there are three Nash equilibria with 1 and 2 bidding ($2, $2), ($3, $2) and ($3, $3).

While all games have at least one Nash equilibrium, this does not always occur with agents picking a pure strategy. For instance, if you examine the cells in 'Rock, Paper, Scissors' you will find that, for each, at least one player will have an incentive to change what they are doing given the choice of the other player. In such games, the Nash equilibrium is in mixed strategies where agents randomise over the actions. In 'Rock, Paper, Scissors', the unique Nash equilibrium involves each child picking rock, paper or scissors with equal probability. This type of random outcome is common in games and sporting contests. The box on 'mixed strategies' shows you how to identify such outcomes.

## Mixed strategies

Consider the game – matching pennies – where two children simultaneously reveal a penny and can choose to reveal it with the heads or tails sides showing upwards. Child 1 wins if both coins show the same thing while child 2 wins if both coins show different things. The payoff matrix is depicted in Table 4.10.

**Table 4.10** Matching pennies

|  |  | Child 2 | |
|---|---|---|---|
|  |  | Heads (q) | Tails (1 − q) |
| Child 1 | Heads (p) | 1, 0 | 0, 1 |
|  | Tails (1 − p) | 0, 1 | 1, 0 |

Notice that, in this game, there is no pure strategy Nash equilibrium. However, it does have one mixed strategy equilibrium. Instead of picking a pure strategy such as 'heads', child 1 decides to play 'heads' with probability $p$ and 'tails' with probability $1 − p$. And child 2 decides to play 'heads' with probability $q$ and 'tails' with probability $1 − q$.

To solve the Nash equilibrium notice that, given child 2's choice of $q$, child 1 chooses $p$ to maximise their expected payoff of:

$$p(q.1 + (1 − q)0) + (1 − p)(q.0 + (1 − q)1) = 2pq + 1 − p − q$$

This implies that child 1 should choose $p = 1$ if $q > \frac{1}{2}$, $p = 0$ if $q < \frac{1}{2}$ and any $p$ between 0 and 1 if $q = \frac{1}{2}$. Similarly, child 2 would choose $q = 1$ if $p < \frac{1}{2}$, $q$

> = 0 if $p > \frac{1}{2}$ and any $q$ between 0 and 1 if $p = \frac{1}{2}$. The only time these coincide is when $p = q = \frac{1}{2}$. This is the mixed strategy Nash equilibrium of this game: where each child chooses 'heads' or 'tails' with probability $\frac{1}{2}$. At this point, each child is indifferent between playing either pure strategy or a mixture between them.

# Repeated games

The games we have analysed thus far have all been 'one shot' situations where players interact only once. In many economic environments, players interact repeatedly; playing the same game over and over again. When such repetitions are potentially infinite (or at least have no known end), this greatly enriches the strategies agents can play.

To see one example, consider the 'Rotten kid' game in Figure 4.7. In that game, the child misbehaved and the parent did not punish because punishment, after the fact, was costly. But if this game were repeated? If this case, the parent could play a strategy of punish if the child misbehaves and not otherwise. Moreover, the child could play a strategy of behaving if the parent punished them for the previous time they misbehaved and misbehaving otherwise.

Would this be an equilibrium outcome? In this case, following misbehaviour, the parent will choose to punish if the long-term returns from doing so outweigh the long-term payoff from not doing this. To evaluate the long-term returns, we have to consider how the parent discounts the future. In a business situation, the future discounting often depends on the interest rate. Here, we will suppose that the parent places only a $\delta < 1$ weight on the next period relative to the current period. This means that a unit of payoff tomorrow is only worth a fraction, $\delta$, of the same unit today. Thus, the parent's long-term return from punishment is $-1 + \delta.1 + \delta^2.1 + \ldots = -1 + \frac{\delta}{1-\delta}.1$.[3] The first term is the short-term cost of punishing while the remainder is the present discounted value of having the child behave well. This is compared with the long-term return from not punishing which is 0 as the child misbehaves in all future periods. Thus, the parent will choose to punish so long as $-1 + \frac{\delta}{1-\delta}.1 \geq 0$ or $\delta \geq \frac{1}{2}$. So long as the parent does not discount the future too much, the parent will punish.

For the child, they will behave so long as the long-term returns from so doing outweigh the short-term returns from misbehaving. Behaving nets the child $1 + \frac{\delta}{1-\delta}.1 = \frac{\delta}{1-\delta}$ while misbehaving for just one period (and then behaving again) nets them $2 + \delta(-1) + \delta^2.1 + \delta^3.1 + \ldots = 2 - \delta + \delta\frac{\delta}{1-\delta}.1$. Comparing these two payoffs, the child will behave if $\delta \geq \frac{1}{2}$. Thus, if this condition holds, it is a Nash equilibrium for the parent to punish and the child to behave.

Repetition can lead to a different outcome in many games so long as players are sufficiently patient. This includes 'Prisoners' Dilemma', which – if it were capable of repetition – could allow the agents to achieve a cooperative outcome, and the sealed-bid auction for which repetition might allow bidders to collude on a series of low bids. We will return to explore the concept of repeated games for competition (Chapter 9) and cooperation (Chapter 13).

## Summary

Strategic decision-making can be analysed in a similar manner to individual decision-making but with the twist that we need to carefully consider what agents can observe about the actions of others. When they can observe the actions of others, strategic decisions can be analysed using a game tree and then working backwards. This gives us insight as to what actions are credible and can really influence the choices others make.

When agents cannot observe one another's actions, we look for equilibrium points where no agent has an incentive to change what they are doing. This also allows us to reduce down the many potential outcomes into those that are more likely. We will see throughout this book that both sequential and simultaneous games can be fruitfully used to model many competitive and cooperative business situations.

## Endnotes

[1]  While the earlier case did not specify an actual number, here we do so for simplicity. In effect, this might be the value for $M$ in Chapter 2.

[2]  Recall that, in Chapter 2, TimeScape's entry cost was $c$ plus the $200 000 in development costs. This assumption, therefore, involves setting $c$ = $100 000.

[3]  This final step comes from a mathematical device called the geometric theorem. When adding an infinite series of compounding numbers, like $\delta$ here, $\delta + \delta^2 + \delta^3 + \delta^4 + \ldots = \delta/(1-\delta)$. This property is used often in finance and accounting in order to calculate net present values from investments.

# Part II

# Negotiations

A key aspect of business and how value is distributed involves negotiations between different economic agents. As already studied, by trading or cooperating, economic agents can create value. In a trading context, value is created when a customer's willingness-to-pay exceeds a seller's willingness-to-sell. Value is created by cooperation when more total value is created by engaging in the cooperative activity than by not engaging in it.

When there are only a few players engaging in a transaction, their respective shares of any value created are determined through negotiations. There are many different ways such negotiations could proceed and, for a given situation, one protocol may be more reasonable than another. Our intention here, however, is not to specify protocols per se but ask: *what outcomes are likely if negotiations are unrestricted and free form?*

It is in predicting the outcome of free-form negotiations where the concept of *added value* is very useful. This concept defines an agent's contribution to the creation of value and also how much they might reasonably expect to take from total value as their own surplus. The added value approach allows us to set a range of reasonable outcomes and, if we are happy to make assumptions about each player's relative sophistication as a negotiator, we can determine what the precise sharing arrangement may be.

This part of the textbook is devoted to describing the added value approach to negotiations and illustrating its usefulness for business decision-making. For this purpose, in Chapter 5, we will concentrate first on the case where there are only two players: i.e., bilateral negotiations. This will allow us to understand the principles of negotiated outcomes when there is no issue of competition among players. The issue of competition will be addressed in Chapter 6 when we consider multilateral negotiations. While more complex, the added value approach generates important insights into the nature of pricing when there are many parties to a set of transactions. Finally, Chapter 7 examines how agents' actions may change negotiations; in particular, how an investment may impact upon an agent's bargaining position. This gives a strategic rationale to certain decisions above and beyond the direct intention of such actions.

# 5 Bilateral negotiations

We begin our analysis of how prices are formed through negotiations by considering the case where there are only two parties to a transaction: that is, where negotiations are bilateral. This is a good starting point for two reasons. First, conceptually it is easier to consider how value created is divided between two agents rather than many agents – even though, as we will see, the principles upon which that division takes place extend to the multilateral case. Basically, with only two parties, there is no real issue of competition between players and only an issue as to how to divide the fruits of their cooperative decisions. Second, there are many business situations where there are only two parties that are relevant to a transaction; especially over the shorter term.

Here we will proceed as follows. Our first task is classificatory. We will consider two canonical types of two-player transactions: buyer-seller exchange and cost sharing arrangements. These two types represent the two most studied forms of cooperative decision-making that we outlined in Chapter 3 – cooperation via exchange and cooperation between complementors. Secondly, we will show how these transactions are related (you can conceive of each as involving a negotiation over price) but they are potentially distinguished by the fact that the former allows no difference in each player's contribution to value creation while the latter does.

## Classifying two-player transactions

Many transactions involve one player – the seller – who owns an asset, produces a good or provides a service, negotiating with another player – the buyer – who values that asset, good or service but must transact with that particular seller in order to realise value. These transactions we term a *buyer-seller exchange*. In such transactions, the key variable for negotiation is the selling or purchase price.

In contrast, some transactions involve two (or more) players who each wish to share an asset, good or service in order to realise some value. Indeed, sometimes it is possible for one or both players to realise sufficient value to cover the costs of the asset, good or service on their own. However, at other times, one or both players will not be able to generate sufficient value on their own and are forced to enter into a sharing arrangement. This will be possible so long as sharing is feasible – that is, both players can utilise the asset or consume the good or service without a diminution in the quality of its use. In this case, the two agents may be complementors in supply. We refer to these types of transactions as *cost-sharing arrangements*. Here negotiations are focused upon how much each player contributes to the costs involved.

### Examples of buyer-seller exchange

There are many examples of buyer-seller exchange. Every time you shop at a supermarket, purchase a car or acquire a stock, these transactions involve a seller exchanging something with a buyer in return for some monetary transfer or *price*. While a given transaction will only involve two players, the particular pricing outcome involves more than just those players. The other players provide other trading alternatives for the buyer, seller or both. As such, they involve competitive considerations that bring additional complications for the analysis of negotiations.

The effect of competition will be discussed extensively in later chapters. For now, it is easiest to introduce buyer-seller exchange for the special case where the buyer and seller involved have no other trading options; that is, if they are to trade at all, they must trade with each other.

Economists have a term for this type of trading relationship: *bilateral monopoly*. Recall that a monopoly is a situation where there is only a single seller of a product. A bilateral monopoly refers to a situation where there is only a single buyer as well. This ties the buyer and seller to each other.

Despite its special nature, there are many examples of bilateral monopoly:

- It is often much cheaper to locate an electricity generating plant near its fuel supply, for instance, coal deposits. Moreover, it is often the case that a single mine can service that plant and there are insufficient deposits to have two plants in that area. When different players own the generator and coal mine, they must negotiate over the price of coal. The coal mine, however, cannot easily sell coal to purchasers other than the generator and the generator cannot easily find other fuel sources.

- Many TV shows employ actors that become popular and integral to continued ratings success. Those actors also become well known for these roles and would find it difficult to land lead roles in another context. Therefore, in negotiations over what such actors may receive for another season for a TV show, TV networks and studios are forced to negotiate with those actors and those actors must negotiate with the TV studios in order to keep their current role. A similar tied relationship applies to sequels to popular movies.

- Pharmaceutical companies have their own research and development labs. They employ PhDs and other experienced researchers in those labs. While working at the company, those scientists develop expertise in a particular therapeutic category – such as cardiovascular or mental health – and the company itself generates patents and other key intellectual property in that area. Often companies achieve a competency in research in a therapeutic category that other companies do not have. As such, a scientist with skills in that category has limited alternative employment opportunities in which to utilise those skills. Similarly, the company itself cannot easily replace a scientist for their particular skills are not available elsewhere.

What these three examples have in common is that each of the parties to the exchange has made investments that are *relationship-specific*. That is, those investments have no value outside the relationship. In the case of the mine and generator, the key investments were the mine's development and the generator's choice of location. For actors and TV studios, the key choices were the actor's decision to play their TV role and the studio's decision to develop the actor as a popular character. Finally, for the scientist and pharmaceutical company, the key investments were the company's development of a research competency in a particular category and the scientist's learning and skill development in that category.

All of these investments share the property that they have no value outside the particular relationship they were developed for. Hence, the parties are forced to trade with each other in order to realise some value. You might wonder how the parties came to invest in such a manner and we will examine that issue closely in Chapter 7. For the moment, however, we want to concentrate on the pricing outcomes in such bilateral monopolies without regard to the decisions that placed the parties in that situation.

### Examples of cost-sharing arrangements

People share costs all of the time. Sometimes this is explicitly recognised while at other times it is implicit. An excellent example of implicit cost sharing decisions are the decisions of couples to have and raise a child. It is obvious that, by biological necessity, some costs will be vested with just one person. Nonetheless, each partner derives benefits from child rearing and without explicitly identifying all of the costs they arrive at some allocation of them by assigning different tasks to each other.

Here we will concentrate on explicit cost-sharing arrangements that potentially involve monetary transfers. Nonetheless, you should keep in mind that the considerations involved will apply to implicit arrangements as well.

There are many examples of explicit cost-sharing arrangements. Consider:

- Research and development costs can often be large but nonetheless research outcomes can benefit more than a single company. Moreover, even when duplicate research effort can be individually profitable, two companies (even if they compete against each other elsewhere) might benefit from forming a joint venture to avoid resource waste. Such joint ventures might be a separate company funded by the firms involved or a jointly owned and operated lab. In either case, the parties must agree upon what share each will contribute to the costs of the joint venture.
- Some companies have come to recognise that certain back office functions can be shared. Typically, these involve data processing and information technology resources. These companies have moved to integrate those back office functions while retaining separate downstream or retailing arms. Once again, while each company could have its own, separate back office, each recognises that they could economise on these resources by integrating their functions and sharing the costs involved.

What these examples have in common is that the costs involved do not rise considerably when more than one player is involved. The players are, therefore, *complementors on the supply side*. That is, the sum of opportunity costs of supplying the resource to each player individually is greater than the opportunity cost of joint supply. In research and development and back office integration, costs were lower because the duplication of certain resources and effort would be avoided by a joint venture or integration arrangement.

### Relationship between buyer-seller exchange and cost-sharing arrangements

Our two broad cases of two player transactions – buyer-seller exchanges and cost-sharing arrangements – are related in many ways. A buyer-seller exchange always involves negotiation of a monetary transfer or price that the buyer pays to the seller. Cost-sharing arrangements involve some allocation of costs. However, this allocation could also be viewed as a price if we viewed one player as the owner of the asset or resources that comprises the costs to be shared. That player could be seen as selling a service to the other player.

An excellent example of this potential equivalence is that of a business school. A business school utilises its lecture theatres and other facilities when classes are in session. At other times, such as during weekends or over summer recess, they do not need these facilities or, indeed, their faculty(!).[1] At these times, it makes sense to sell the use of those facilities to other players; for example, conference organisers or company in-house training programs.

Equally, however, the use of school facilities by the school itself and other parties can be viewed as a cost-sharing arrangement. This is particularly the case if the school would not find it profitable to invest in those facilities without the possibility of selling the use of those facilities to others. Prior to investing, therefore, it may negotiate cost-sharing arrangements. This might be a contribution to investment costs or commitments for later use.

Nonetheless, as we will see below, a cost-sharing arrangement is very different from a buyer-seller exchange when one or either party can go it alone. That is, in the absence of an agreement, each party might just bear their own costs rather than share them. As we will see, a party's ability to bear their own costs and still be profitable is an important determinant of what constitutes the value created by their joint relationship and, hence, their added value and their outlay towards the shared costs.

## Price formulation in buyer–seller exchange

We now turn to consider how prices are actually formed in buyer-seller exchange. Having identified a potential value-creating trade or cooperative activity, agents then need to negotiate over how that value is divided between them. In many situations, negotiations will focus on the price that must be paid from one agent to another. Suppose a customer values a good at $100 and it costs a supplier $40 to produce. So $100 is the customer's willingness-to-pay and $40 is the supplier's willingness-to-sell. If willingness-to-pay is WTP, willingness-to-sell is WTS and the price paid by the customer to the seller is $p$, then the customer receives WTP – $p$ while the supplier receives $p$ – WTS. The amount WTP – $p$ is called the *consumer surplus* while the amount $p$ – WTS is the *supplier surplus*. The total surplus is the sum of consumer and supplier surplus.

Trade will be valuable if the total surplus when trade occurs exceeds $0. In this case:

$$\text{Total surplus} = \underbrace{\text{WTP–}p}_{\text{Consumer surplus}} + \underbrace{p\text{–WTS}}_{\text{Supplier surplus}} = \text{WTP–WTS}$$

In this case, WTP – WTS = 100 – 40 = 60. Thus, a value of $60 is created by producing the good for the customer's use. Notice that trade is desirable here regardless of what the price, $p$, is. In principle, even if $p$ were very low (close to $0) or very high (greater than $100), it would still create value for trade to take place.

However, in practice, not only must value be created by trade but the customer and supplier must individually prefer trading to not trading; that is, both consumer and supplier surplus must be greater than $0. For the customer, this means that $p$ must be lower than their willingness-to-pay of $100 while for the supplier, $p$ must be greater than their willingness-to-sell of $40. So long as $p$ lies between $40 and $100, both consumer and supplier surplus will be positive. Figure 5.1 summarises this situation.

**Figure 5.1**

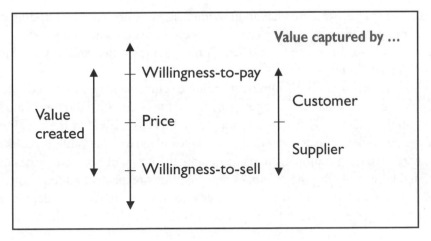

### Added value

You have now seen how, in trading situations, for trade to occur not only must value be created but it must be divided in a way that leaves all agents that are parties to trade with more surplus as well. In the above trading example, we saw that for trade to occur, price must lie below the customer's willingness-to-pay and above the supplier's willingness-to-sell.

An alternative and more generally applicable way of looking at the outcomes of negotiations is to use the notion of added value. Adam Brandenburger and Barry Nalebuff define added value as:[2]

> *YOUR ADDED VALUE =*
> *The size of the pie when you are in the game*
> *Minus*
> *The size of the pie when you are out of the game*

When they talk about the 'size of the pie', they are talking about the total surplus and when they talk of being 'in the game', they are talking about being a party to the trade or cooperative venture. Thus, another way of defining added value in a trading context is:

> *YOUR ADDED VALUE =*
> *Total surplus when you are engaged in the trade*
> *Minus*
> *Total surplus when you are not engaged in the trade*

Added value is a measure of what an individual agent is bringing to a trading situation; that is, how much additional surplus or value is being created when you participate in the transaction. It is a useful concept because it defines the most that an individual agent can obtain from a trade in terms of their own surplus.

When there is only a single customer and a single seller, each agent's added value is very easy to derive. In that situation, an agent's added value is equal to the total value created by the potential exchange. The reason is simple: in this case, if either the supplier refuses to sell or the customer refuses to buy, no trade takes place and no value is realised.

In our earlier trading example, we can calculate the range of possible prices that could be negotiated by calculating the customer and supplier's respective added values.

- *Customer's added value*: If the customer were not to engage in trade, i.e., refuse to purchase the service from the supplier, it would lose $100 and the supplier would save $40. In effect, there would be no surplus. Therefore the customer's added value is $60 (= $60 – $0).
- *Supplier's added value*: If the supplier were not to engage in trade, i.e., refuse to provide the service to the customer, it would save costs of $40 and the customer would not get $100 in value. Again, there would be no surplus. Therefore the supplier's added value is also $60 (= $60 – $0).

In this trading example, the customer and the supplier have the same added value. This is because each is *essential* to the value being created from trade. If either party did not participate, a valuable trade would not be made. We can state this result as a basic principle:

> *When every player is essential to a value-creating activity, each player's added value is identical and equal to the total value created.*

How does this determination of added values translate into a price range? The customer cannot pay a price that would allow them to obtain a consumer surplus greater than their added value. Thus, $p$ must be such that $\$100 - p < \$60$ or $p > \$40$. This makes sense as a price less than \$40 would leave the supplier with a negative surplus from trade and they would not participate in it.

Similarly, the supplier cannot be paid a price that would allow them to obtain a supplier surplus greater than their added value. Thus, $p$ must be such that $p - \$40 < \$60$ or $p < \$100$. Again, if the supplier was to earn a price that gave them more than their added value, ie, a price greater than \$100, the customer would have a negative surplus from trade and would refuse to participate in it.

Thus, the added value approach gives the same outcome in terms a price range as willingness-to-pay and willingness-to-sell. You will see, however, that the added value concept will be easier to apply in other situations, especially when there are more than two parties to the transaction.

## The BATNA approach

Another way of looking at this range of outcomes is to consider the 'Best Alternative to a Negotiated Agreement' or BATNA approach to bargaining. In contrast to the added value approach, the BATNA approach asks what would a player realise if they walked away from the negotiations: this is a player's **outside option**. In our example, the buyer would not receive anything if they walked away, so their outside option is \$0. If the seller walked away, they would recover their opportunity cost, so their outside option is \$40.

A seller would not accept a price less than their outside option, while a buyer would not pay a price for which their consumer surplus (i.e., willingness-to-pay less that price) was negative. In notation:

$$p > O_S$$

and

$$v_B - O_B - p = \text{WTP} - p > \$0 \text{ or } \text{WTP} > p$$

Where $O_S$ is the seller's outside option, $v_B$ is the buyer's value, $O_B$ is the buyer's outside option, WTP is the buyer's willingness-to-pay (or $v_B - O_B$), and p is the price. In our example, price must therefore, exceed \$40, the seller's outside option and must not be greater than \$100 or the buyer's consumer surplus would be negative. As in the added value example, this implies that prices may range from \$40 to \$100.

One thing that is easy to see from both analyses is that if the buyer's willingness-to-pay rises (falls) the highest possible price rises (falls) while if the seller's opportunity cost rises (falls) the lowest possible price rises (falls). Indeed, if total value falls (rises) the range of prices available will fall (rise).

## Specific price predictions

Added value analysis can determine the range of possible prices in a trading situation. To make our pricing predictions more precise, we need to impose additional assumptions on the relative negotiating abilities of the customer and supplier.

To see this, suppose that the customer had far superior negotiating abilities than the supplier. This might occur, for instance, when the customer can make a take-it-or-leave-it offer to the supplier. The customer names a price that the supplier can either take, in which case trade takes place at the price, or leave, in which case no trade will take place. In choosing a price, the customer first puts itself in the position of the supplier and asks: what is the lowest price the supplier will accept? In our example, the supplier will not accept a price lower than its willingness-to-sell of $40, so the lowest price is $40. The customer will then announce this price (or a cent more than it). The supplier, faced with a choice of a very small amount of surplus or no surplus, chooses to accept the price. Because the customer ends up appropriating all of the value created in this case, we can refer to this situation as one where the customer has all of the bargaining power.

On the other hand, it is conceivable that the supplier has all of the bargaining power. This may occur if the supplier can make a take-it-or-leave-it offer to the customer. This time, the supplier considers the customer's decision and asks: what is the highest price she can demand and still have the customer agree to purchase the service? By definition of willingness-to-pay, this price must be $100 (or a cent less than it). Therefore when the supplier has all of the bargaining power, her surplus is equal to the total value created.

In reality, such extremes are not likely. Counter offers are possible and, in many situations, both customer and supplier will be equally sophisticated. In this case, an *equal bargaining power* solution would be a reasonable outcome. This would leave the customer's consumer surplus equal to the supplier's surplus.

In an equal bargaining power solution, $p$ is such that

$$\underbrace{\text{WTP}-p}_{\text{Consumer surplus}} = \underbrace{p-\text{WTS}}_{\text{Supplier surplus}}$$

or

$$\text{Consumer surplus} = \text{WTP} - p = \frac{\text{WTP} - \text{WTS}}{2} = p - \text{WTS} = \text{Supplier surplus}$$

In the example, WTP + WTS is $140 and a price of $70 would be likely.

When, in Chapter 6, we consider the effect of competition, you will see how this changes each agent's added values but we will still assume that an equal bargaining power solution is a reasonable bargaining outcome.

# Sharing costs

In cost-sharing arrangements, the basic principles of how value is divided remain the same as in a trading situation, except that the calculations become more difficult. This is because, in many situations, the underlying basis for the total value created can change dramatically depending on the particular situation. While agents may jointly benefit from sharing costs, it may be possible for some agents to go it alone and bear their own costs. Hence, value created may, in some situations, involve an avoidance of cost duplication while in others a joint relationship may be the only way in which one or more players can earn value.

## *Added value*

As in the trading situation, we will demonstrate the application of added value using a simple example. Suppose there are two agents A and B. If they have access to an asset, each agent can earn some revenue. For A, this revenue is $100 and for B it is $200. The asset is, however, costly to acquire. It may cost $50, $150 or $250. Nonetheless, for each level of costs, the asset can be easily used by both A and B. Hence, it would not be efficient for the asset to be duplicated.

The key issue in any negotiation is: how much of the asset's cost should A and B pay respectively? Their respective shares of the asset's cost will be determined by their added value. However, before calculating these, we have to consider what the total value created by the relationship is. This is not a trivial matter because, for some level of costs, without a joint acquisition, it may be still worthwhile for one or both players to go it alone. In this case, the total value created by the relationship is the avoidance of duplication in the investment costs.

## (a) High asset costs

Nonetheless, to build intuition, we will begin with the case where investment costs are high, equal to $250. Notice that here, neither A nor B can go it alone. Individually, the costs of acquiring the asset exceed the revenue they might earn. In this case, the only way to make a positive profit is to agree to a joint acquisition of the asset. That is, their joint revenues of $300 will exceed the asset's cost of $250. Total value created by the relationship in this case is $50 because neither player would earn a positive profit outside the game.

The high costs mean that both A and B are essential to the relationship. No profits will be earned if either decides not to participate. We know from the trading situation that when players are essential, their respective added values are identical and equal to the total value. Given the revenues each expects to earn, the highest contribution A could make would be $100 (leaving B with $150 to contribute) and the highest B could make would be $200 (leaving A with $50 to contribute). So the range of cost allocations for A would be $50 to $100 and $150 to $200 for B.

## (b) Medium asset costs

Turning now to the case where the asset cost is $150, while A would still not find it profitable to go it alone, B would. So if either A or B were to decide not to enter into a joint relationship, B would earn a value of $50. Hence, given that the total profits of a joint acquisition would be $150 (= 100 + 200 − 150), A and B's added value would each be $100 (= 150 − 50).

Another way of looking at the total value created is from a buyer-seller perspective. We can do this because B would acquire the asset regardless of whether A is involved or not. Hence, we can consider the relationship from the point of view of B selling access to the asset to A. Note that such access has the potential to allow A to earn $100 in revenue. In this light, $100 represents A's willingness-to-pay for access to the asset. If B owns the asset, it faces no opportunity cost in allowing A access to it, hence the total value created is $100. As this is akin to a buyer-seller exchange and both A and B are essential to the creation of the $100, their respective added values will be identical and equal to the total value created.

In either case, the focus on A's revenues mean that the maximum it can contribute to the asset's costs is $100 and the minimum is $0. Thus, B's contribution will lie from $50 to $150.

## (c) Low asset costs

When the asset costs are low (= $50), then it becomes profitable for both A and B to go it alone in the absence of a joint relationship. If they do not use the asset jointly, then A will earn $50 and B will earn $150. The profits from a joint relationship, however, would be $250. This exceeds the sum of profits each would earn on their own, i.e., $200. Hence, a joint relationship is valuable. If either player left the relationship, the total value would fall by $50 as a duplication of the asset's costs would occur. Hence, both A and B's respective added value is $50.

Once again, A and B are both essential to the creation of value from a joint relationship. As such, each has identical added values equal to the total value created. Given this, each would end up contributing between $0 and $50 depending on their respective bargaining power.

The difference between the three cases lies in the source of the value from a joint relationship. Here, when asset costs are low, that value is in the avoidance of a duplication of those costs. On the other hand, for medium levels of asset costs, the value of a joint relationship was in the ability it afforded for A to earn revenue of $100. Finally for high asset costs, a joint relationship was the only way for both A and B to earn their respective revenues.

### Equal bargaining power cost-sharing rules

In many situations, people choose cost-sharing rules that are fair, i.e., each person contributes an equal amount to the costs involved. For A and B, this would mean splitting an asset's costs evenly. This would be fine if the asset's cost were less than $200 but when it is higher than this, say, $250, A would not find it worthwhile to enter into the arrangement as 50% of $250 exceeds A's revenue of $100. Without A to share costs, B would not find it profitable to go it alone as the cost of $250 exceeds B's revenue of $200. So to insist upon fairness would lead to no value created at all.

In other situations, cost-sharing rules are proposed that are 'equi-proportional' to each person's relative benefit. This would mean that B would contribute two-thirds of the asset's cost since it would receive 50 per cent more value than A. As such, both A and B would earn some positive value from the project. However, this rule still might not be the best solution for A. Regardless of the asset's cost, A's surplus is always less than that earned by B.

These rules do not reflect the economics of a cost-sharing situation. Therefore, while they might be desirable for fairness reasons, such rules are unlikely to be good predictors of actual bargaining outcomes.

Economic analysis suggests that the shares of costs paid will be determined by each player's relative bargaining power, i.e., their relative sophistication as negotiators. If they have equal bargaining power, then this will lead to cost-sharing rules that equate the surplus each player earns from a joint relationship. As such, A would expect to come away with the same surplus as B, not less. Table 5.1 below summarises the contributions we would expect A and B to make if they had equal negotiating abilities.

**Table 5.1** Contributions expected from A and B when negotiating abilities are equal

| Cost | A's contribution | B's contribution |
| --- | --- | --- |
| 50 | 25 | 25 |
| 150 | 50 | 100 |
| 250 | 75 | 175 |

Notice that when costs are low, A and B share equally in their contributions. This is because the value created by their relationship is an avoidance of the duplication of those costs. When costs are at a medium level, the bargaining solution mirrors an equi-proportional rule. Finally when costs are high, the sharing rule does not reflect equality or equi-proportional outcomes. In that case, B contributes relatively more because A can prevent it from earning its high revenues if A walks away from the joint arrangement.[3]

While this will be discussed at length in a later chapter, it is interesting to note that there is a sense in which an added value outcome is not a good thing. An equi-proportional rule had the benefit of encouraging all projects that were value creating to go ahead. This is especially the case if A and B had to make some sunk investments before beginning negotiations. When bargaining takes place after such investments, and A and B expect that outcome, by sometimes 'under' rewarding A and other times 'over' rewarding B, some desirable investments may be deterred.

## Summary

This chapter has introduced bilateral negotiations and the use of the added value approach. As you can see, for bilateral transactions – whether it be buyer-seller exchange or cost-sharing – the main issue is to work out what value is created by the transaction and then to assess how an equal division may impact on each agent's surplus. While useful in some contexts, it is often the case that transactions are not simply isolated and between two parties. It is to such multilateral contexts – involving more than two agents – that we turn to next.

### Endnotes

[1]  Actually, faculty requires this down time to prepare additional classes and undertake research that keeps it up to date. These activities are more difficult to achieve in-session.

[2]  Brandenburger, A. & Nalebuff, B. (1996), *Coopetition*, Harper Collins: New York.

[3]  Actually, A and B will contribute equally to all costs ranging from $0 to $100. However, A's contribution will be equal to $50 for cost ranges between $100 and $200. Finally, for costs between $200 and $300, for A's surplus to equal B's, A's contribution will be $p = (\text{cost} - 100)/2$ (where this is the $p$ that solves: $200 - \text{cost} + p = 100 - p$). Above $300, no joint relationship will create positive value.

# Multilateral negotiations

**6**

The previous chapter looked at price formation when there were only two parties to a transaction. There we noted that, since each party was essential to the creation of value from that transaction, each party had the same added value equal to the total value created. This meant that the key issue in any analysis was to determine what was the precise source of the value created.

In this chapter, we introduce the effects of competition; something that can be studied when there is more than just a single buyer and seller. Not surprisingly, competition reduces the added values of agents on the same side of the market but increases the relative added value of those on the opposite side of the market.

The chapter builds in two parts. In the first, we consider a situation where there is only a single seller (a monopolist) but many buyers. We look at when this situation may realistically arise and then at the outcome of negotiations when there is a single seller. The second part then considers situations where there are many buyers and sellers. The chief insight of this extension is that the range of possible negotiated prices becomes smaller as you add buyers and sellers. Indeed, when there are large numbers of these, the outcomes of negotiations will resemble the market equilibrium (i.e., supply and demand models) traditionally explored in economics textbooks.

## How do monopolies arise?

We begin with the case where a market is a monopoly with just one seller. In that market, the same player controls all of the substitutable products. However, what are substitutes for one type of buyer may not be substitutes for another. Hence, it is rare that a particular market can be unambiguously classified as a monopoly.

To see this, consider Sony Playstation 2 games. These games are disks developed to work with the Playstation game console and no other. As such, if you own this console and you wish to purchase a game, you have little choice but to consider a Playstation game. When you consider substitutes, therefore, you will trade off buying the game with engaging in another mode of entertainment. However, to you, Sony is a monopolist in the gaming market.

On the other hand, if you have not bought a Playstation game console but are considering buying a computer game, your options are wider. You could purchase a Nintendo Game Cube, Microsoft X-Box or even a PC. If you are a buyer in this position, Sony hardly has a monopoly on your gaming options. Your willingness-to-pay for any given game machine will depend more on the pricing and quality of a similar machine rather than your alternative entertainment options.

This type of analysis often applies in situations where you, as a buyer, make choices that lock you into a particular set of choices later on. Consider software choices, such as PC operating systems, word processing packages, email address books, or company accounting software. Consider also car purchase decisions and the availability of spare parts, textbook adoption choices, or when you train an employee in your organisation. In each of these situations, while there is competition at the time of an initial decision, later on a buyer's choices are constrained and potentially limited to dealings with a single player.

Each of these instances of *lock-in* is the result of a buyer's purchase of an asset that is complementary with other components that are controlled by a single seller. There are instances of lock-in that can arise from other decisions. For example, there are many goods that exhibit *network effects*. These effects mean that your willingness-to-pay for a particular firm's product is higher when there are more consumers of that product. A good example of this is the Windows Operating System for PCs. One reason why Microsoft's software is on 85% of all PCs in the world is because of the importance of interchangeability. Buyers of operating systems are concerned that, if they purchase another system, such as Mac OS or Linux, they will have difficulties swapping data with other users. In this case, buyers are locked into choosing Microsoft, not because of their own past decisions necessarily, but because their co-workers or colleagues have chosen Windows.

## Ownership or control of key assets

Lock-in is one example of how a monopoly can arise. Essentially, the seller comes to own or control a key resource through the choices of buyers. There are, however, other examples of monopoly that arise when a firm owns a key resource.

- *Government licensing*: Sometimes governments create monopolies. Patent laws vest monopoly rights with an innovator for a period of time. Copyright laws ensure that others do not expropriate a firm's brand. Government-run services are often under the control of a single firm, e.g., the Post Office or public transport. In each of these cases, the government vests the ownership of a key asset with a single player.
- *Cartels*: Monopolies are sometimes formed when previous competitors get together and form a cartel. Two prominent examples are the OPEC cartel of oil-producing nations and the De Beers diamond cartel. In many nations, such cartels are made illegal precisely because they give rise to monopolies. Unions are also an example of a cartel. While they face restrictions, unions are legal associations of groups of workers. They act like a monopolist because unions engage in collective negotiations with individual employers and employer groups.

- *Ownership of raw materials*: When a single firm owns a key raw material, this can allow them to monopolise an industry. An example of this is the ESSO-BHP joint venture on gas that comes from fields in Bass Strait between Tasmania and mainland Australia. Up until recently, this joint venture was the only supplier of gas into the Australian state of Victoria. Hence, users of gas had no alternative but to purchase gas that came from ESSO and BHP.

By owning a key asset, an agent can prevent others from entering the market for goods that rely on that asset for production.

## Natural monopoly

Another reason why a monopoly may arise is technological in nature. It is sometimes the case that a good or service can be produced at a lower per unit or average cost if there is a single supplier. If there are economies of scale, i.e., falling long-run average costs, over the entire range of possible demand, then to have two suppliers would generate inefficient duplication. In this case, we say that production takes place using a natural monopoly technology.

There are many examples of natural monopoly production technologies. For example:

- *Networks*: Distribution networks are common in transportation, communications and energy transmission. They have the quality that, for any desired capacity, costs are lower on average if a given set of customers use a single network. For example, in telecommunications, it is inefficient to have two systems side by side that allow any caller on one network to call another. This simply duplicates switching effort and the costs involved in keeping track of call connections.
- *Mass production*: Some manufacturing and service industries require large sunk investments in order to generate low marginal production costs. As demand grows, such investments become more and more desirable allowing all potential users in a region to be supplied at the lowest possible marginal cost. Therefore if there are two firms, these sunk investment costs are duplicated.
- *Information*: Once produced, information can be distributed relatively cheaply. As such, fixed production costs form a large component of the average costs of information provision. If two different suppliers produce the same information, this simply duplicates those fixed costs.

Natural monopolies are natural because to have a single supplier is best if your objective is to minimise costs. As such, in the past, governments have vested monopoly rights with a single supplier so as to ensure those scale economies are reached.

However, natural monopolies can also be natural because it is difficult for market forces to sustain more than a single supplier. As we will see in a later chapter, a potential entrant to an industry with an incumbent using a natural monopoly technology may fear a price war. Hence, that entrant may think twice about incurring any sunk-investment costs that it may not recover in more competitive circumstances. The resulting outcome is that the incumbent maintains its monopoly position and profits despite the possibility of entry.

## Monopsony

Finally while we focus here on the case of a single seller in a market, there are situations in which there is a single buyer and many sellers. This situation is called monopsony.

There are many examples of monopsonies. Consider a large employer in a small town, a national supermarket or department store chain dealing with wholesalers, electricity or gas supply onto their respective networks, or digital switch suppliers to a telecommunications network. In each of these cases, there are many potential suppliers but only one customer. Nonetheless, the type of price negotiations examined here easily carry over to these types of cases.

# Negotiations with a monopolist

We now turn to consider the outcome of negotiations between several buyers and a single seller. Analysing this requires us to calculate each player's added value and also to make assumptions regarding each player's relative sophistication as a negotiator. However, in this context, it is also important that buyers are not able to trade with one another.

## Added value in a monopoly

For example, suppose there are four potential buyers of a good but only one producer of that good or any good that would be considered a substitute by the buyers. That producer is therefore a monopolist.

To start with, we assume that the monopolist can produce an unlimited number of units of the good at a cost of $200 per unit. This is its opportunity or marginal cost of production. Our four buyers only wish to purchase a single unit of the good each and have willingnesses-to-pay of $1000, $800, $600 and $400, respectively. Notice that since each buyer has a willingness-to-pay greater than the seller's opportunity cost for that unit, the total value created will be maximised by having the seller provide each buyer with the good. In this case, the total value created will be $2000 (= 1000 + 800 + 600 + 400 – (200 x 4)).

Graphically, this situation is depicted in Figure 6.1. The stepped line comprising the descending ordered willingnesses-to-pay of buyers represents consumer *demand* for the product in this market. The flat marginal cost curve represents producer *supply*. The shaded area between these two lines represents the total value created where all four buyers receive one unit of the good each.

**Figure 6.1** Total value created with unlimited supply

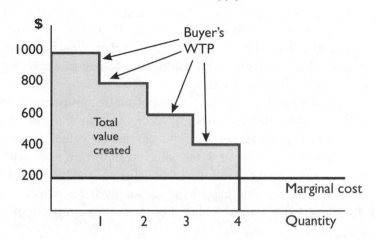

We can use this information to calculate each player's respective added values. These are summarised in Table 6.1.

**Table 6.1** The players' respective added values

| Player | Added value | Likely price | Expected surplus |
|---|---|---|---|
| Buyer 1 (WTP = $1000) | $800 | $600 | $400 |
| Buyer 2 (WTP = $800) | $600 | $500 | $300 |
| Buyer 3 (WTP = $600) | $400 | $400 | $200 |
| Buyer 4 (WTP = $400) | $200 | $300 | $100 |
| Seller | $2000 | $450 on average | $1000 |

Recall that an agent's added value is the difference in the total surplus when that agent participates in a trade compared with the total surplus when they do not participate. The seller is essential to the production of the good. Hence, when they do not trade, there is no surplus. As such, the seller's added value is equal to the total value created. This is a characteristic of their monopoly and we can state it as a general principle

> *A monopolist is essential to the creation of value in a monopoly situation and, as such, its added value is always equal to the total value created.*

In a monopoly, individual buyers are not necessarily essential to the creation of value. For the buyers here, however, because supply is unrestricted, i.e., the monopolist is able to produce four units, each is essential to their own particular transaction. Take, for example, buyer 3 who has a willingness-to-pay of $600. If that buyer leaves the game, i.e., refuses to purchase the good, then the monopolist will only be able to sell goods to the remaining three buyers; creating a value of $1600. Hence, buyer 3's added value is $400 (= 2000 − 1600). Notice that this is not an artefact of the fact that each buyer has a different willingness-to-pay. If all four buyers had a willingness-to-pay of $600, each individual buyer would have an added value of $400.

The reason for this outcome is that buyers are not really competing with each other. While there is only a single seller, that player is forced to deal with each buyer in order to realise value from that trade. Hence, each buyer's added value is equal to the total value created from that trade. For buyer 3, the value created from trade with the seller is $400. That buyer is essential to the creation of that value so its added value is also $400. In the next section, we will see what happens when supply is restricted. In that case, an individual buyer's added value will be reduced because they must compete with other buyers.

The above table also lists the likely price and expected surplus that each player may receive. These outcomes assume, as we did in Chapter 5, that the seller and individual buyers are equally sophisticated negotiators. To see this, consider the extreme outcomes that occur if the seller or a buyer had all of the bargaining power, i.e., could make take-it-or-leave-it offers in negotiations. If the seller could make a take-it-or-leave-it offer to each buyer, it will offer a price equal to each buyer's willingness-to-pay. As such, it would receive prices of $1000, $800, $600 and $400, respectively, and appropriate all of its added value. On the other hand, if an individual buyer can make a take-it-or-leave-it offer, they will offer a price of $200. This is equal to the seller's opportunity cost of producing the good for that buyer. So the sale price could range from $200 to each buyer's willingness-to-pay. In each individual negotiation, with equal bargaining power, the price will lie halfway between these bounds. Hence, in negotiations between the seller and buyer 3, the likely price will be $400 (= (600 + 200) ÷ 2).

**Figure 6.2** Price and value division with unlimited supply

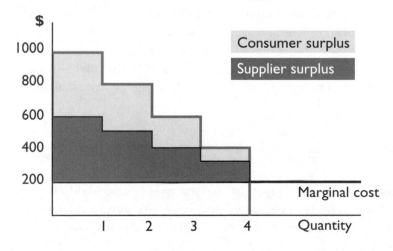

The expected surplus is calculated using the likely price. For the seller, this is his or her supplier surplus or profit. It is equal to half of the total value created. For each buyer, surplus is their willingness-to-pay less the price they negotiate. This outcome is depicted in Figure 6.2. While a buyer with higher willingness-to-pay will pay a higher price for the good, they will nonetheless earn a greater surplus than a buyer with a lower willingness-to-pay. In this example, the consumer surplus, i.e., the total value realised by all buyers, is $1000.

### The no re-sale condition

An implicit condition underlying this analysis is that buyers are not able to re-sell the good to each other. Consider what might happen if this was possible. Because a buyer, such as buyer 1, is only able to negotiate a relatively high price of $600, while buyer 4 can negotiate a lower price of $300, this creates an incentive for buyer 4 to sell its good to buyer 1. Buyer 4's profits from that transaction would be potentially as high as $300, in contrast to his own surplus of $100. Even if this was not the case, buyer 4 could simply purchase two units of the good and sell one unit to buyer 1.

Anticipating this possibility, buyer 1 would not accept such a high price from the seller. Ultimately, this would undermine the seller's ability to negotiate different prices for each buyer. Hence, in order for our analysis here to be valid, we must assume that re-sale is not possible.

We will consider what happens when re-sale is possible in Part III. There, we will look at mass markets where it is harder to imagine that a seller can control re-sale by buyers. For the moment, however, we will continue to make the assumption that re-sale is not possible.

## Competition among buyers

A key assumption for the above analysis was that supply was effectively unlimited. The monopolist could produce any number of units for the same marginal cost of $200. This meant that our four buyers were not really competing with each other and, as such, were essential for their particular trade with the seller.

In contrast, when supply is limited, buyers do compete with one another. Suppose that the previous example is as before but that the seller now only has three units of the good to sell. This might be because the seller only can produce three units of the good or, alternatively, because producing a fourth good involves a very high marginal cost. In contrast to the previous analysis, this simple change alters the relative added values of the buyers and the seller.

### Added value under limited supply

To examine the negotiated outcomes under limited supply, we first need to consider what the maximal total value created is when there are only three units available. Whenever there is a scarce commodity, it is best allocated to those buyers who value it the most. In our example, buyers 1, 2 and 3 would receive the good while buyer 4 would be left out. This would create a total value of $1800 (= 1000 + 800 + 600 – (200 x 3)). Not surprisingly, this value is less than the situation with unlimited supply.

In terms of added value, the changes are more dramatic with each player's added value lower than before. These are summarised in the following table:

**Table 6.2** Values added with limited supply

| Player | Added value | Likely price | Expected surplus |
|---|---|---|---|
| Buyer 1 (WTP = $1000) | $600 | $700 | $300 |
| Buyer 2 (WTP = $800) | $400 | $600 | $200 |
| Buyer 3 (WTP = $600) | $200 | $500 | $100 |
| Buyer 4 (WTP = $400) | $0 | No trade | $0 |
| Seller | $1800 | $600 on average | $1200 |

The seller is essential to all trades and hence his added value is equal to the total value created. Each buyer, however, is no longer essential. If any buyer left the game, the seller would sell that unit to buyer 4. For instance, for buyer 3, the total value created when she is not in the game would be $1600. Hence, her added value is only $200. Buyer 4 is effectively competing with every other buyer. This gives the seller a stronger bargaining position. So even if buyer 3 was able to make a take-it-or-leave-it offer to the seller, she could not ask for a price lower than $400 as the seller would be able to convince buyer 4 to pay up to that amount.

To look at this another way, with a limited number of units available, the seller's opportunity cost of supplying a given buyer is now different from his marginal cost of production. As buyer 4 would be willing to pay up to $400 for a unit, the seller's cost of supplying any other buyer is $400. So this, rather than their production cost of $200, is the lower bound on the price the supplier would accept in negotiations.

The result is likely to be higher prices on average for the monopolist. Figure 6.3 depicts the new division between buyers and the seller. Notice that even though the total value created is smaller than before, as is the added value of all players, the seller's expected profit is higher. This is because the sum of the buyer's added values is not equal to the total value created but, rather, is $1200. This leaves $600 that the seller can claim of the total value created without *competing* with any buyer. Hence, the seller can expect to claim that and half of the remaining $1200.

**Figure 6.3** Price and value division with limited supply

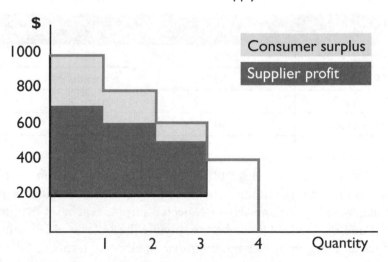

Competition among buyers means that a seller's outside option in negotiations becomes the willingness-to-pay of the *just-excluded* buyer. If any other buyer tries to negotiate a price less than the just-excluded buyer's willingness-to-pay, the seller knows that he will be able to elicit a higher bid from that buyer. This strengthens the seller's bargaining position, and hence raises his expected surplus from any given trade.

### Further limitations on supply

What happens when there are only one or two units available? Basically, the total value created, and hence the added values of each player, continues to fall but the average price negotiated rises.

The negotiated outcomes with two and one available units are calculated in Tables 6.3 and 6.4 below respectively.

**Table 6.3** Negotiated outcomes with two available units

| Player | Added value | Likely price | **Expected surplus** |
|---|---|---|---|
| Buyer 1 (WTP = $1000) | $400 | $800 | $200 |
| Buyer 2 (WTP = $800) | $200 | $700 | $100 |
| Buyer 3 (WTP = $600) | $0 | No trade | $0 |
| Buyer 4 (WTP = $400) | $0 | No trade | $0 |
| Seller | $1400 | $750 on average | $1100 |

**Table 6.4** Negotiated outcomes with one available unit

| Player | Added value | Likely price | Expected surplus |
|---|---|---|---|
| Buyer 1 (WTP = $1000) | $200 | $900 | $100 |
| Buyer 2 (WTP = $800) | $0 | No trade | $0 |
| Buyer 3 (WTP = $600) | $0 | No trade | $0 |
| Buyer 4 (WTP = $400) | $0 | No trade | $0 |
| Seller | $800 | $900 on average | $700 |

Figure 6.4 summarises the average price and surplus the seller can expect to receive under the various scenarios regarding available supply. Notice that while the price rises as supply becomes more limited, the seller's expected surplus reaches a maximum at three available units and then falls. This is because, while the seller's added value relative to the buyers rises as supply becomes more limited, in absolute terms, it falls as the value created is reduced.

**Figure 6.4** Expected price and seller profit

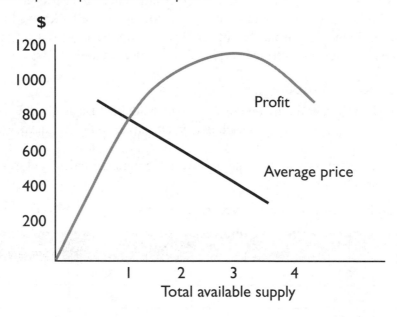

## Many buyers and sellers

Having competition on both sides of a market creates additional complexity in terms of analysis. However, the added value approach to negotiations can be readily applied to this case. What becomes more difficult is to pin down the actual prices. Despite this, as you will learn here, in situations where there is a large number of buyers and sellers, it becomes fairly straightforward to make clear pricing predictions.

## Extending the example

As in the monopoly case, it is best to illustrate the application of added value analysis by way of a simple example. In this regard, we continue to assume here that there are four potential buyers of a good with willingnesses-to-pay of $1000, $800, $600 and $400, respectively, for one unit of the good. On the supply side, it is now assumed that there are four sellers each holding one unit of capacity. To begin, it will be assumed that the cost of production of each seller is $200 per unit (as in the monopoly case). Thus, all that has changed from the earlier example is that capacity is diversely held rather than consolidated into a single entity.

The first thing to note about this change is that the total number of units sold in the market will not be any different from the single seller case. Recall that the first step in analysis is to work out what trades maximise total value created. In this case, since each buyer's willingness-to-pay exceeds each seller's willingness-to-sell of $200, then total value created is $2000 (= $1000 + $800 + $600 + $400 – 4 x $200). If one seller does not sell to, say, buyer 4, total value created falls to $1800 (= $1000 + $800 + $600 – 3 x $200). As such, we would expect all buyers to purchase a good.

Turning now to added value, each buyer's added values are the same as they were in the single seller case. If buyer 1, say, were to leave the game and not trade, then three sellers would end up trading to the remaining buyers; creating value of $1200. Thus, buyer 1's added value remains $800 (= $2000 – $1200). Put simply, in terms of their contribution to total value created, no buyer's role has changed.

The situation for sellers is very different. When a seller is a monopolist and chooses not to trade, no value is created; so a monopolist's added value was $2000. Here, however, if one seller chooses not to trade, the remaining three sellers will still trade to three buyers. Which three buyers? As with all negotiations, trades will be naturally organised to maximise total value created. In this example, this means that buyers 1, 2 and 3 will continue to be supplied with a good each but buyer 4 will not as their willingness-to-pay is the lowest. So, in the absence of one seller, total value created falls to $1800.

Note here that if buyer 4 did trade when there were only three sellers total value created would be even lower (e.g., if buyer 3 did not obtain a good, total value created would only be $1600). This would be unsustainable because, regardless of the prices agreed upon, buyer 3 would be able to offer buyer 4's seller more than their willingness-to-pay of $400 and still obtain some buyer surplus. It is precisely in this sense that an outcome that does not maximise total value created is not sustainable. Put simply, for any such outcome, at least one buyer and seller could make each other better off by coming to a trade that increased total value created. It is only when total value created is maximised that all such opportunities for trade are exhausted.

We can use this logic to calculate each player's respective added values. These are summarised in the table below.

**Table 6.5** Each player's respective added value

| Player | Value if do not trade | Added value | Surplus range |
|---|---|---|---|
| Buyer 1 (WTP = $1000) | $1200 | $800 | $600 to $800 |
| Buyer 2 (WTP = $800) | $1400 | $600 | $400 to $600 |
| Buyer 3 (WTP = $600) | $1600 | $400 | $200 to $400 |
| Buyer 4 (WTP = $400) | $1800 | $200 | $0 to $200 |
| Each Seller | $1800 | $200 | $0 to $200 |

That table calculates a range of surplus that each player might receive. In each case, recall that no player can receive more than their added value; as such each player's added value is also the highest surplus each could receive. On the other hand, the lowest surplus that a player might receive can be calculated by assuming that they have recieved take-it-or-leave-it offers. For each seller, if each receives a take-it-or-leave-it offer from each buyer of a price of $200, each is left with no surplus. For Buyer 4, the highest price they would accept would be $400. Note, however, that this means that no other buyer will pay more than $400. If, say, Buyer 3 were made a take-it-or-leave-it offer of $600, he could safely refuse this offer and make an offer to Buyer 4's seller of $400 or above and have that accepted. This means that the highest price that could prevail would be $400; placing a lower bound on the surplus of each buyer as depicted in the table.

What this implies is that while in a monopoly market each buyer might potentially be left with no surplus, in a competitive market that is no longer the case. Competition between sellers means that all but the 'marginal' buyer will earn a positive buyer's surplus even if they were particularly unsophisticated negotiators and faced sellers who could credibly make take-it-or-leave-it offers. As such, we can see here that competition among sellers will deliver benefits to buyers – shifting the division of value created in their favour.

### Law of one price

This analysis also yields another important insight: when there are competing sellers, all goods trade at the same price. This is called the 'law of one price'.

The way to see this is to consider what pricing outcomes are *stable*. An outcome will be stable if no buyer and seller pair has an incentive to abandon their current trades in favour of trading with others. So suppose that all four sellers negotiate a price of $200 (leaving each with no surplus). In this case, buyers are obtaining their added values and could not do any better by switching to another seller. So this outcome is stable. But what if all prices were $400 a unit? In this case, it is the sellers who are obtaining their best outcome (i.e., their added values) and so no buyer will be better off by offering any of them a higher price. Even if all prices were some intermediate price, like $300, the outcome would be stable. In this case, expecting to pay a price of $300, no seller could attract an alternative buyer and still earn a higher price. Similarly, no buyer could attract an alternative seller with a lower price.

But what about a situation where different buyers are paying different prices? For instance, suppose that one seller has negotiated a price of $300 with buyer 1 while all remaining sellers have negotiated a lower price, say $250, with their respective buyers. In this case, buyer 1 could approach any of those sellers with a price between $250 and $300 and that seller would prefer that offer to their current potential trade. Thus, this outcome is not stable. Indeed, it is relatively straightforward to see that for any pricing outcome where buyers pay different prices, that those paying higher prices can approach sellers receiving a lower price and negotiate a mutually beneficial alternative trade.

What this means is the following:

> *In a market where the products of sellers are all identical in the eyes of consumers and each seller has unit capacity, all trades will occur at the same price.*

So while we might not be able to pin down the precise price that will be negotiated for each transaction, we can say that they will all be the same price in any stable outcome.

### Additional sellers

One situation where prices in multilateral negotiations become easier to pin down is where there is sufficient competition on one side of the market. To see this, suppose that there was an additional fifth seller with one unit of capacity. As there are still four buyers, this means that should one seller refuse to trade, the remaining sellers would still be able to supply all of the buyers and total value created will be unchanged.

What this small change means is that sellers have no added value. For a buyer, should they leave the game, value created would fall by their willingness-to-pay. In contrast, no one seller can change value created by becoming unavailable. As such, the price per unit will fall to $200 leaving sellers with no surplus and the buyers with their respective added values.

### Upward sloping supply

In reality, however, this extreme situation – where adding another seller creates intense competition – does not often occur. What is usually the case is that some sellers are more efficient than others; i.e., they have different production costs. In this case, while they compete against one another, some sellers, at least, can earn a positive surplus. This type of surplus is sometimes called a *quasi-rent* in the business strategy literature.

To see this, suppose that the marginal costs of the five sellers in our example are $50, $150, $250, $350 and $450. Let's also suppose that our four buyers' willingnesses-to-pay are unchanged but there is also a fifth buyer with a willingness-to-pay of $200. Figure 6.5 depicts the value maximising outcome in this case.

**Figure 6.5** Value maximising outcome

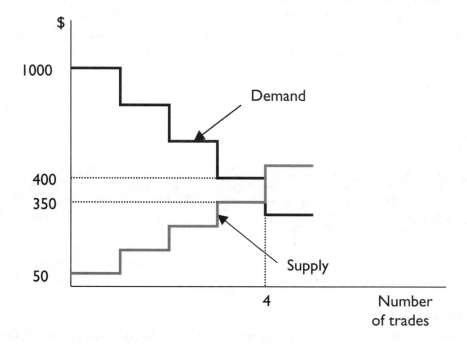

It is instructive to reflect on why this is the value maximising outcome. First of all, notice that total value created is $2000 (= $1000 + $800 + $600 + $400 – $50 – $150 – $250 – $350) and that it is generated by having the four sellers with the lowest marginal costs sell to the four buyers with the highest willingnesses to pay. The fifth buyer and seller do not trade. Second, if only three buyers and sellers were to trade (say, buyer 4 and seller 4 do not trade), then total value created will fall (to $1950) because that buyer's willingness-to-pay exceeds the seller's willingness-to-sell. Finally, if the fifth buyer and seller do trade, then total value created is reduced by $250 to $1750. This is because the fifth buyer's willingness-to-pay is less than the fifth seller's willingness-to-sell.

To look at this another way, one might wonder why not all trades occur as it is always possible to find some buyer with a willingness-to-pay greater than any individual seller's willingness-to-sell. For instance, have buyer 1 purchase from seller 5 and buyer 5 purchase from seller 1. If this were to happen, then the *lowest* price seller 5 could offer buyer 1 would be $500 while the *highest* price buyer 5 could pay for seller 1's product would be $400; this would be the outcomes most favourable to buyer 1 and seller 1 in this situation. However, even at these prices, buyer 1 and seller 1 could strike a deal for a price lower than $500 and higher than $400 and make each other better off. Hence, this type of outcome – that does not maximise value created – is not stable. Buyer 1 and seller 1 would be better off by striking an alternative deal. This, in turn, would leave buyer 5 and seller 5 out in the cold.

So at the value maximising outcome, what prices will emerge? Because buyer 4 has a willingness-to-pay of $400, if she is able to trade, it will be at a price less than $400. By the logic of the law of one price, this means that all prices must be below $400. Similarly, seller 4 will only trade at prices above $350, constraining all prices to be above this level. Thus, there is a range of possible prices from $350 to $400.

This division is depicted in Figure 6.5. Notice that despite the presence of an alternative fifth seller (who isn't engaged in trade), for any price the first three sellers earn some surplus. This is because each has a cost advantage over some other sellers and each need not accept a price below $350, the marginal cost of seller 4. If they are offered a lower price (say $300), each could go to buyer 4 (or some other buyer) and offer to trade at a price between $300 and $350. Buyers will always compete in this circumstance until the price rises to at least $350. This gives some sellers at least some positive surplus.

## Competitive advantage

The comparison between the cases where all suppliers are identical and where some have lower costs than others demonstrates that suppliers will earn a positive surplus or profit in the latter case only. In this situation, some suppliers are able to do better than just earning an amount equal to their next best alternative (or willingness-to-sell) because buyers effectively compete for their trade.

To see this, consider seller 1. While any buyer can go to other sellers and purchase the same product, seller 1 can potentially supply the product at a lower price than those sellers. However, seller 1 can insist on a price higher than their costs of $50 because if any one buyer were to insist on a price of $50, seller 1 could find another buyer who would pay more than this. After all, if they are not purchasing from seller 1, the lowest conceivable price any other buyer could receive would be $150 and they would surely be happy to pay a lower price to purchase from seller 1.

Of course, in the end, seller 1 benefits from the fact that there are many buyers and competition among them drives all prices up to $350. So it is not simply the fact that seller 1 has lower costs than seller 2 but the fact that there are four active buyers and seller 1 has lower costs than seller 4 that drives the profits they end up earning.

The notion that competition among buyers can give sellers surplus above their willingness-to-sell has been termed *competitive advantage*.

> *A supplier's* competitive advantage *is the level of surplus that they can earn solely from the results of competition for their product.*

When a supplier has (i) lower costs than other firms and (ii) there is more than one buyer, that supplier has a competitive advantage. Note that both of these conditions are required. If a supplier has the same costs as all other firms it has zero added value and so no competitive advantage. Similarly, if there is a single buyer, even if the supplier has lower costs than others and hence positive added value, it may not have a competitive advantage. This is because that buyer can conceivably insist on a price equal to the supplier's willingness-to-sell and leave it with no additional surplus. In reality, that supplier may have some bargaining strength that allows it to earn a positive surplus. However, this surplus is not guaranteed by competition as there is no competition among buyers.

We will return to consider competitive advantage and its drivers in the next chapter when we examine how pre-emptive actions on the part of agents can change negotiations.

### Large numbers of traders

The outcomes in all of the cases thus far in this chapter – from single seller to many sellers – all share in common that the number of trades in a market is determined at the point where demand and supply intersect. Take Figure 6.5. There the demand 'curve' is a representation of the willingnesses-to-pay of buyers in descending order while the supply 'curve' is a representation of the willingnesses-to-sell of suppliers in ascending order. They intersect at four trades. The same is true of Figure 6.2 where the demand curve intersects a flat supply curve.

In Figure 6.3, there is limited supply. In this case, the supply curve has a backwards L-shaped form. It is flat until the capacity constraint of three units is reached, in which case production of four units or more is not possible. In effect, it is infinitely costly to produce these units and so the supply curve becomes vertical at that point. You can see that the vertical part of the supply curve intersects the demand curve at three units.

The idea that the expected volume of trades is determined by supply and demand is one of the long-standing economic notions. However, it holds for price as well when there are many buyers and sellers and the law of one price operates. In Figure 6.5, the expected price is determined by the point or range corresponding to the intersection of the supply and demand curves from the perspective of the vertical axis. In this case, there is a range of intersecting points, and hence a range of possible prices between $350 and $400. The basic idea is that if prices in a market were above this range, then there would be a *surplus* of suppliers wanting to sell and too few buyers wanting to purchase. If prices were below this range there would be a *shortage* with many buyers wanting to purchase at that price but too few suppliers willing to sell for that price. Thus, prices tend to be in a range so that the quantity suppliers wish to supply equals the quantity buyers demand.

Economists refer to this situation as a *market equilibrium*. We encountered the notion of equilibrium in Chapter 4 when we discussed the outcomes of games. In a market, equilibrium is similarly a point where no agent wants to change their actions – in this case, who they are trading with and at what price. As it turns out, in markets the intersection of supply and demand curves corresponds to an equilibrium outcome.

Using demand and supply curves becomes more straightforward when there are large numbers of buyers and sellers (as might occur in a stock market). In this case, it is often the case that demand and supply curves are smooth lines rather than steps and the equilibrium price is not a range but a single number. This type of situation is depicted in Figure 6.6. Notice that if the prevailing price for any trade was above P*, that buyer would have an incentive to trade with another seller. Similarly, if the price for any proposed trade was below P*, the seller involved would have an incentive and would be able to find another buyer to trade with at a slightly higher price. It is only when all trades are at P* that no buyer or seller can find another seller or buyer, respectively, to trade with on better terms.

**Figure 6.6** Market equilibrium

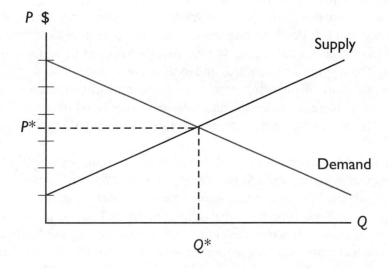

This type of demand and supply model is useful because it can be used to assess how broad changes in the market impact on total volumes and price. There are many factors that may have an impact on the willingnesses-to-pay of many consumers. These include:

- *consumer income*: should consumer income rise (fall), consumers will be more (less) likely to purchase some goods and their willingness-to-pay will rise (fall). This will cause the demand curve to shift upwards (downwards) and to the right (left).
- *prices of related goods*: some goods are consumed in conjunction with one another (e.g., milk and cookies) while others are only consumed in lieu of other goods (e.g., Coke versus Pepsi). The former goods are complements while the latter are substitutes. If the price of a related good should change, this will impact on willingness-to-pay of some or many consumers and cause a shift in the demand curve.
- *advertising and consumer preferences*: if something should occur that raises a consumer's intrinsic desire for a good, their willingness-to-pay may change. An example of this may be advertising that can increase demand by changing the tastes of many consumers.

- *population*: the more consumers there are the more demand there will be for a product. Population growth (decline) can cause demand to shift upwards (downwards) and to the right (left).

Similarly, there are many factors that might have an impact on suppliers' willingnesses-to-sell. These include:

- *input prices*: a primary driver of the willingness-to-sell of a supplier are the costs of production it faces. Should the prices paid for inputs (capital, labour and resources) rise, then willingness-to-sell will rise as suppliers require greater payments to cover these costs. If these changes are widespread, this could cause a decrease in supply, shifting the supply curve downwards and to the left.
- *technology*: on the other hand, technological change can increase productive efficiency. If this is done, willingness-to-sell will be reduced as suppliers can bring goods to market at a lower cost. In this case, there would be an increase in supply, shifting the supply curve upwards and to the right.
- *number of firms*: firms bring both capital and human resources into industries. In this case, more firms means an increase in supply (shifting the supply curve downwards and to the right) as there are more suppliers willing to sell at any given price.

By identifying whether broad changes impact on supply, demand or both, you can then use the supply and demand model to predict what this will do to prices.

Figure 6.7 on the following page summarises the impacts of various changes on equilibrium price and quantity. Note that what this can tell you is the direction of any price and quantity change. It is more difficult to determine the magnitude of such changes. However, if you had more detail regarding the exact nature of supply and demand curves (notably their slopes) such predictions would be possible. Details on how to achieve this are something you may encounter in more advanced economics courses.

## Summary

When there are more than two relevant players in an industry, how value is divided becomes more complex to analyse. In particular, in some situations, some players are essential for the creation of any value; the primary example being that of a single seller or a single buyer. However, even an essential player will not be able to claim a large share of total surplus unless it is a good negotiator or there is some competition among other players in terms of their value creating ability.

When no player is essential, then it is also possible to analyse market outcomes. In many situations, when there are many buyers and sellers, the outcomes of multilateral negotiations can be easily analysed using supply and demand diagrams. This can provide you with a useful tool for predicting how prices and also the division of total surplus changes as key cost or demand conditions change.

**Figure 6.7** Changes in market equilibrium

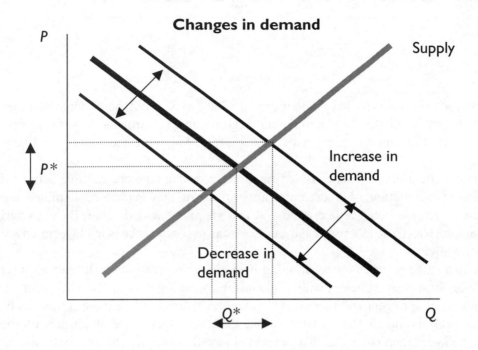

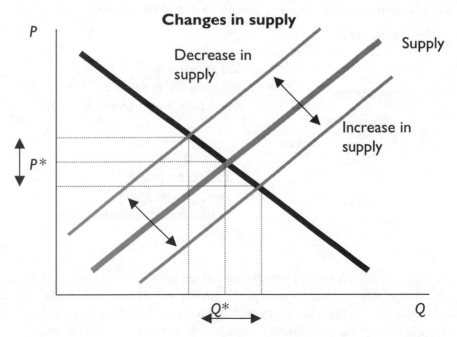

# 7  Changing negotiations

The previous two chapters have demonstrated what types of outcomes economic theory predicts regarding bilateral and multilateral negotiations. In particular, it has highlighted added value as an important driver of what share of value created agents are likely to receive.

In many situations, agents consider investments or can take pre-emptive actions that can change negotiations. For example, an investment may reduce a supplier's costs, and hence increase both value created and that supplier's added value. By considering situations such as these as a two-stage game, we can assess whether such investments will be worthwhile.

The two-stage games we have in mind here can be represented as a tree; see Figure 7.1. We analyse such games as with all games, by working backwards. This means first assessing what our agent will receive in negotiations that take place if the action has been taken, as well as the alternative negotiations that take place if the action has not been taken. The agent then compares these expected payoffs from negotiations with any costs that the action may involve in order to determine whether the action is worthwhile.

**Figure 7.1** Two-stage game

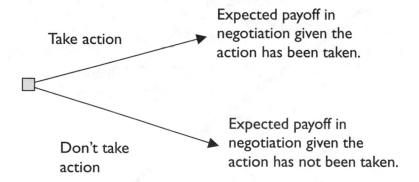

In this chapter, we focus on two types of two-stage games to demonstrate how certain actions can change negotiations in an agent's favour or against it. The first considers how an agent may take actions to create scarcity and enhance their bargaining position. Specifically, we look at the conditions under which competition among buyers serves to alter their added value and the added value of a single seller, or a monopolist. If a monopolist can engender competition among buyers, they are able to exercise monopoly or market power. We will demonstrate that, in general, the effect of the exercise of market power is to reduce the total value created from exchange and increase the added value of the monopolist. Therefore a monopolist, who can exercise market power, will do so because it is likely to increase his or her own payoff.

The second considers the risks associated with some value creating investments whose costs are not factored into subsequent negotiations. Those negotiations can 'hold-up' an agent from receiving full value from their investments. Nonetheless, by recognising this, there may be actions an agent may take to avoid the problem.

## Scarcity and market power

In Chapter 6, we examined a single seller who had capacity to produce four units of a good for four potential buyers. We also noted how the situation changed if there was more limited capacity (as summarised by Figure 6.4). In that example, the total value created is higher when there are more units available. However, if it was up to the seller, they would prefer a situation where supply is limited to three (or even two) units to the case of unlimited supply. That is, creating scarcity assists the monopolist. This highlights the tension between social incentives to create value and a monopolist's private incentives.

### Choosing production capacity

It is sometimes possible for the monopolist to choose the number of units available. For instance, prior to any negotiations, the monopolist may be considering investing in a plant to produce this good. In so doing, the monopolist will make a choice regarding the plant's capacity. Let us consider the simple, but admittedly unrealistic, case where a plant of any capacity costs $500, but having chosen its capacity, it is prohibitively costly to expand the plant at a later date. At this investment cost, regardless of capacity chosen, the monopolist will earn a positive return on that investment. As these sunk investment costs do not depend on the size of the plant, the monopolist will have an incentive to choose a capacity of three. In so doing, the monopolist creates conditions of limited supply and is therefore able to force buyers to compete with one another. This results in a maximal level of profit for the monopolist.

The monopolist's choice of plant capacity is made on a very different basis from the usual trade-offs in these decisions. The usual concern is with plant utilisation. Hence, if it is costly to produce plants with greater capacities, the concern will be the chance of unused capacity with the possibility that some sales may be lost if the firm underbuilds. On the other hand, a monopolist, with an eye on subsequent negotiations and their added value, is concerned that overbuilding will give buyers power in those negotiations. Hence, a monopolist favours underbuilding so as to limit each buyer's added value.

By restricting plant capacity to raise its subsequent added value and price, the monopolist is *exercising monopoly* or *market power*. It is this type of action that gives monopolists a bad name. Socially, a plant of unlimited capacity would be desirable.

However, the monopolist, considering only his private interest, restricts available supply. The total value created from the investment is, therefore, not at its maximum.

## Market power and commitment

By choosing plant capacity, the monopolist can exercise his market power and ensure that supply is limited. The reason why this works for the monopolist is that the limited capacity commits him to not being able to expand supply after he has sold his intended three units of the good.

To see why this is important, suppose that such capacity expansion was not costly. Initially, the monopolist chooses a capacity of three units with the intention of playing buyers against one other. Suppose, therefore, that they bargain successfully with buyers 1, 2 and 3 for the prices of $700, $600 and $500, respectively. Having done this, given the low cost of expanding capacity, the monopolist would find it worthwhile to produce another unit for buyer 4 and negotiate with him. Had buyers 1, 2 and 3 anticipated this, they could have bargained harder. The monopolist's actual opportunity cost was not $400 but $200 as in the case of unlimited supply.

In economics, we suppose that buyers, such as 1, 2 and 3, are sophisticated enough to anticipate the monopolist's later deal with buyer 4. They will take this possibility into account during negotiations and this will weaken the monopolist's bargaining position. The result is that if supply is really unlimited, the negotiated prices will be determined on that basis, despite the monopolist's intention to convince them otherwise.

The difference between simply intending to restrict supply and actually doing it by making it costly to expand supply is an important one. The former intention is *not credible*. Buyers will anticipate the monopolist's later incentive to sell to buyer 4 and alter their bargaining positions accordingly. If it is actually costly to sell to buyer 4, the monopolist is able to *commit* to limiting supply. This commitment gives the monopolist credibility in negotiations and allows them to negotiate higher prices with the first three buyers.

Thus, we see that while the monopolist has an incentive to exercise monopoly power, they may not have the ability to do so. This is because limitations on supply must be credible. The monopolist must be able to commit to not expanding supply later on to take advantage of value-creating trades. They must be able to convince buyers that one or more will be excluded in order to create competition among them. Unless this is a real commitment, then an intention to exclude will not be credible and the monopolist will not be able to exercise market power.

## Committing to exclude buyers

Limitations on productive capacity are one way of committing to exclude buyers. There are, however, other mechanisms. Note that the primary way a monopolist can commit to exclude is by raising the opportunity cost he faces in expanding production at a later date. A capacity commitment does this directly by raising physical production costs.

But it is also possible to raise the monopolist's opportunity cost of subsequent expansions in other ways. Here are three broad mechanisms that are used by sellers:

1. *Reputation*: When a seller deals continuously, it may be possible for them to develop a reputation for not flooding the market. This strategy is adopted by collecting houses, such as the Franklin Mint. Disney has also tried to develop a reputation for not discounting its video releases at a later date by announcing short production runs. A firm with such a reputation faces higher opportunity costs of subsequent output expansions. While output expansions might yield returns on their current product choices, they will lose their reputation for future product offerings.

2. *Leasing*: Rather than sell a product, some firms favour leasing. IBM followed this approach in the 1970s with its mainframe computers. It claimed that leasing would insure buyers against technological risk. However, it was also concerned that potential buyers might wait for its prices to fall rather than purchase a computer immediately. By leasing rather than selling these computers, IBM made a commitment to offer the same pricing terms to early and later purchasers. In so doing, it raised its opportunity cost of offering discounts towards the end of a given computer's product life cycle.

3. *Most favoured customer clauses*: Some firms offer buyers a contract that guarantees them the best price they offer any buyer. This means that a firm contemplating discounting to some of its customers must discount to all of them.

Each of these mechanisms is a credible means of reducing the monopolist's ability to expand output. Hence, they can be employed to commit to supply restrictions and foster competition among buyers. How the most favoured customer clause works to change negotiations is worthy of some additional elaboration. Suppose that our previous example with unlimited supply remains the same except that each buyer has a willingness-to-pay of $600. It is easy to see that offering only three units for sale results in the greatest profits for the monopolist, who would earn $1200 in this situation. To see why, notice that if the monopolist offered four units, their added value would be $1600 (= (600 − 200) x 4). Given that the buyers would not compete, the monopolist would only claim $800 of this. If the monopolist offers three units, each buyer's added value falls to zero as the just-excluded buyer's willingness-to-pay is the same as the others'. Hence, the monopolist would have an added value of $1200 and could appropriate all of this. If the monopolist reduced output further, this would not be profitable. The monopolist would not enhance his average price of $600 but would lose sales. Therefore, the monopolist would wish to commit to three units of output.

With unlimited capacity, the monopolist might be tempted to sell to all four buyers. However, suppose he offered each buyer a contract that specified that they would receive the lowest price offered to any buyer. Then, if he made sales to three buyers for a price of $600 a piece, the willingness-to-sell to a fourth buyer would be the marginal cost of $200 plus the reduction in revenue that would result from the other buyers. The monopolist may still expand output – so long as this does not result in a price lower than $500 for the fourth buyer, he benefits from an output expansion. However, the use of this clause allows the monopolist to appropriate a greater proportion of the added value.

### Market power in general

It is worth remarking that the ability of a firm to exercise market power does not necessarily rely on them being a monopolist. While it is true that when there are many sellers this ability will be limited, when a seller has a product that is not a perfect substitute for products sold by others, they will be able to raise the price by restricting their output somewhat. Nonetheless, in order to do this, that output restriction must be credible. So even in more competitive markets, some of the above practices will be employed as a means of raising a firm's relative added value and creating competition among buyers.

It is useful to consider what would happen if a competing seller was (potentially) available. Suppose that buyers in our example face a monopolist who has limited capacity to three units. In order for another plant to be built, another firm will have to pay $500. However, it will have to recoup these costs upon entry. This may be problematic.

If a competitor invests in a plant with unlimited capacity and a constant marginal cost of $200, this reduces the added value of the incumbent seller to zero as the entrant can easily replace his output. The added value of the entrant is higher because of the incumbent's limited capacity. They have an added value of $200 because of their unique ability to supply the fourth buyer. Nonetheless, even if they had all of the bargaining power in negotiations and received $200 in profit, the entrant could not expect to recoup their investment costs of $500. Hence, no entry would occur.

Thus, the entry decision is also a form of two-stage game where an action is taken prior to negotiations. We can see from this example that, anticipating the outcomes of those more competitive negotiations, the entrant chooses not to enter. This arises even though buyers would benefit from such entry.

## Hold-up problems

IMPERIAL OFFICER: Skywalker has just landed, my lord.

VADER: Good. See to it that he finds his way here. Calrissian, take the princess and the Wookiee to my ship.

LANDO: You said they'd be left in the city under my supervision.

VADER: I am altering the deal. Pray I don't alter it any further.

(From *The Empire Strikes Back*)

One way parties may be able to achieve outcomes that maximise total value created is by including all of the relevant variables and decisions as part of the negotiations. That is, the negotiated outcome in effect yields a contract that specifies, in a manner enforceable by a court of law, all the rights and obligations of parties to the contract. Nothing is left to chance and, if there is any uncertainty (say, about market conditions), what each party would do in every contingency is still specified.

In reality, while there are many contractual relationships for which most relevant variables are included in the (formal) contract, there are just as many that leave important decisions and obligations outside of any negotiations. In effect, those contracts are incomplete. If an action is not specified within the contract, it will be taken if the agent able to take it has an incentive to do so. Importantly, that agent will have to bear the full costs of those actions and may only be able to partially appropriate any resulting value created in subsequent, or *ex post*, negotiations.

Consequently, the outcome from the contract may not maximise total value created. This is because these actions have an effect on the payoffs, and sometimes the incentives, of other agents. When such effects are positive, an action may not be undertaken even though it may have increased overall value. This is because a single agent bears all of the costs but receives only part of the benefit. Alternatively, an incomplete contract may leave room for some agents to take actions that, while personally beneficial, confer negative effects on other agents. In this case, contractual incompleteness prevents an agreement being reached that compensates one agent for refraining from an action that would impose a negative effect on others. Once again, total value created may be less than it could be.

As an example, consider the manager-worker relationship and the problem of worker skill acquisition. The manager wants the worker to become familiar with some new technical procedures. Those procedures are only used within the worker's current firm and so any skills acquired would not be valuable elsewhere. If the worker expends personal effort in acquiring those skills, it will be valuable to the manager, and hence the firm, as it increases productivity. For this, the manager agrees to compensate the worker by a promotion and pay increase. This promise is not written down in a formal contract because it is difficult to specify the worker's obligations objectively in a way that could be verified by a third party.

The worker now faces a problem. While the skills are clearly value enhancing, the worker is concerned that a lot of effort may be expended and the manager, ultimately, may not keep the promise of a promotion and pay rise. While the worker may trust the manager somewhat, circumstances may change and it may be difficult for the manager to keep the promise. Nonetheless, the worker will be more valuable to the company if those skills are acquired. In this respect, the worker will have some bargaining power. The problem, for the manager and the worker, is that the worker may still face some risk that the skill acquisition will not be personally worthwhile. Consequently, the worker does not put as much effort into the task as would be desirable.

In this example, the worker is concerned that new investments, such as skill acquisition, may be subject to 'hold-up'. In economics, 'hold-up' is a term that originated in particular contracting contexts whereby one party may delay payment until the other renegotiates payment terms. Now it refers to any situation whereby one party may not be paid a previously agreed price for a service or may not supply a service and ask for a new price. For the worker, a promise of rewards that are not easily contractible, is in turn not credible. Without a clear contractual commitment, the worker may not realise sufficient returns to justify effort spent. What this means is that total value created from the worker-manager relationship is not at its maximal level.

Here, we analyse this type of 'hold-up' problem that arises when contracts are not complete. We describe how contractual incompleteness can reduce the incentives of agents to take actions that improve value and may increase their incentives to take actions that lower value. The solution to 'hold-up' problems requires parties to find ex-contractual means of committing to rewards and prices. In general, these involve improving the bargaining power of the agent taking the non-contractible action. Such mechanisms include commitments to inflexibility, group bargaining, increased competition and changes in asset ownership.

## Importance of contractual commitments

Possibly the primary benefit of being able to agree to a contract is its commitment value. Because it specifies all of the rights, obligations and payments to parties, a contract creates an environment in which agents can rely on others to take certain actions and refrain from others. The resulting outcome is one that potentially maximises total value created.

In contrast, without clear contractual commitments, some rights and obligations are either not specified, or the payments for them will arise only after later rounds of negotiation. Recall that what gives an agent power in negotiations is the amount they can take away from value created if they leave the game: that is, their added value. However, when they have already taken an action, they cannot threaten to undo it. This reduces an agent's bargaining position.

To see this, let's put some numbers to the manager-worker relationship described earlier. Assume that to the manager (and firm) the benefits from an increase in the worker's skills would be $100. If the worker expends the necessary effort to acquire these skills, this will cost the equivalent of $60 in monetary terms. As this is less than the benefit of those skills to the firm, it would increase value by $40 (= $100 − $60) if those skills were acquired.

Suppose first that the worker and the manager can write a contract that specifies what the worker will receive if the skills are acquired. In negotiations over this payment, a failure to agree results in no skills being acquired. As such, the worker's added value is $40. This is also the manager/firm's added value, as the worker cannot acquire those skills and use them elsewhere. Under our usual assumption of equal bargaining power, the worker and manager may agree to a payment of $80 to the worker if the skills are acquired. With this price, it is indeed worthwhile for the worker to acquire the skills.

If such a contract cannot be written, this value maximising outcome is unlikely to arise. Suppose that the worker and manager agree to the payment of $80 if the skills are acquired but that this cannot be committed to in a formal contract. The worker will then consider what might happen after the skills have been acquired. At that point, because there is no legal obligation to pay anything, the manager may want to negotiate a new payment to the worker. By threatening not to work, the worker still has some bargaining power. However, the skill acquisition costs cannot be recovered as part of this threat. They are sunk. In this respect, the worker and manager are now negotiating over $100 of potential value created, rather than $40. The worker has a diminished bargaining position, even though their added value appears to be higher (also $100 rather than $40).

If the worker anticipates this *ex post* bargaining, no skills will be acquired. This is because, if both parties have equal bargaining power at that stage, the worker will only receive a payment of $50. This will not justify the initial investment. In general, by not being able to commit to a contract price before skills are acquired, the worker has a diminished ability to negotiate a price that covers the costs incurred. The worker must bear all of the costs at the risk of not recovering them later on.

The importance of contracts is that they provide commitments to certain payments after valuable actions are taken. As such, during initial negotiations, parties can assure themselves that, at the very least, any personal costs associated with those actions will be recovered. Without such a contract, those agents will be subject to a risk of **post-contractual opportunism** and, as a result, a diminished bargaining position. This will, in general, reduce their payments and, consequently, lower their incentives to take otherwise value-creating actions.

CASE

## Coal supply contracts for electricity generation

A canonical example of the types of problems that can arise as a result of contractual incompleteness concerns the location decisions of coal-fuelled electricity generating plants. Coal is expensive to transport from the mine mouth. It is low in weight but high in volume. In contrast, it is relatively easy to transmit electricity for longer distances.

Consequently, many coal-fired generating plants are located near the mine-mouth. Those mines that are not owned by the utility have long-term contracts to supply coal to the plant. These contracts are invariably long and complex. They include escalator-pricing clauses that automatically adjust coal prices to take into account cost conditions and international price changes. Thus, they are examples of how contracts can be written – not to resolve uncertainty – but to automatically take it into account and prepare for various contingencies.

The need for such complex contracts arises because the mine and plant both face the possibility of hold-up by one another. A plant may refuse to take all of its fuel from a particular mine and a mine may refuse to supply a plant. To protect against such hold-up risks, the mine and plant engage in lengthy negotiations, resulting in a very detailed contract. This gives each a level of commitment that assists in improving their incentives to undertake their respective investments.

## Sources of contractual incompleteness

Having demonstrated the consequences of contractual incompleteness, it is worth considering why it may be difficult to write complete contracts. In general, there are three broad reasons why contracts may be incomplete. Those reasons are: the complexity of the operating environment; costs associated with third party verification; and the potential for renegotiation.

1. *Complexity*: Perhaps the simplest reason contracts are incomplete is the costs associated with identifying and negotiating all of the possible consequences and obligations that might fall on agents under every possible contingency. Some contingencies may simply not be foreseeable or are of sufficiently small probability that it is not worth negotiating rights and obligations for that event. Agents may have insufficient experience and not realise that certain rights and limitations need to be clearly specified. As a result, parties to a contract may not negotiate some important aspect of their relationship.

2. *Verifiability*: There is a sense in which complexity is simply a difficult fact of the contracting environment and may not lead to hold-up problems per se. That is, to the extent that it is difficult to forecast contingencies, it is also difficult to foresee the outcomes of subsequent negotiations and alter one's actions to confer a bargaining advantage at that time. Of greater potential concern in contracting, therefore, are issues of verification. That is, while the rights and obligations of parties may be understood by them, it may be difficult for those parties to commit to actions and rewards because those actions cannot be verified by a third party.

   To see this, consider the worker/manager problem discussed earlier. In that transaction, if the manager could commit to pay the worker $80 if the skills were acquired, the worker would find it worthwhile to undertake the investment. However, it may be difficult for a court or third party to determine whether the skills were actually acquired. If this is the case, the worker faces a real risk: the manager/firm may hold-up the worker. They may refuse to employ the worker for a payment of $80. Instead, the manager may try to negotiate a new payment. For the worker, at that stage, it may be better to agree to a new round of bargaining than to face unemployment.

   As demonstrated earlier, the likely payment in this eventuality would be $50. If the worker anticipates the possibility of a new round of negotiations with this outcome, no skills will be acquired. It is verifiability that makes the initial promise of $80 a credible one. Without verifiability, the worker faces a real risk of 'hold-up' and the manager acting self-interestedly has an incentive to re-open negotiations in an opportunistic manner.

3. *Renegotiation*: The above problem of verifiability could be mitigated if the parties could simply commit not to engage in any further rounds of negotiation. However,

under most legal environments concerning contracts, it is difficult to see how this could be achieved. For example, while the worker's investment in skills may not be verifiable, a court could verify if the agreed payment is renegotiated. One could imagine the manager committing not to renegotiate by offering a large sum (say, in the millions of dollars) if any further negotiations took place. However, this commitment could be undermined as any new contract could include a term waiving such penalties. If the penalty were to be paid to a third party, that party could be included in subsequent negotiations (i.e., some reduced payment to them could be negotiated). As a result, it may be difficult to commit not to renegotiate.

### Renegotiation and final exams

If the primary goal of education is learning, exams are inefficient. On the day of a final exam, the student has done all the learning they are going to do. Therefore, both student and teacher alike would benefit by not having an exam. The student saves the time cost of sitting the exam and the teacher saves time spent in writing and grading. Consequently, on the day of the exam the student and teacher have an incentive to 'renegotiate' and cancel the exam.

The problem with this is that if the student anticipates that the exam may not be held, this reduces incentives to study hard. Consequently, in terms of the teacher's goals, there may be insufficient learning. Therefore, despite their immediate incentives to do so, teachers do not renegotiate assessment arrangements with students.

## Relationship-specific investments

An incomplete contract means that agents must bear the costs of some action prior to any negotiations over value created taking place. As a consequence, agents may change their actions and investments in order to avoid being held up in those later negotiations. Ultimately, the reason why this situation may not lead to maximum value created is because of the relevant agent's weaker bargaining position in *ex post* negotiations. If the agent could recover the costs of the actions in another way, the incomplete contract problem would be mitigated.

Perhaps the primary reason why an agent has a poor *ex post* bargaining position is a lack of outside options. In many situations, the actions an agent is considering taking only generate value if the agent trades with a particular person who may be the only holder of key assets. As such, any investments are **relationship-specific**.

We already encountered the concept of relationship-specific investments in Chapter 5. In that chapter, three examples of relationship-specific investments were considered, including: the location decisions of electricity generating plants near to fuel sources, the choices by movie studios of particular actors for movie sequels, and the specific learning made by scientists in pharmaceutical companies. Our worker's choice regarding skill acquisition was relationship specific because those skills were assumed to be only of use to the firm in question. All of these investments were potentially desirable because they improved value created. However, in each case, after the action was taken, the relevant agent was tied to the relationship. That is, they could not realise any value from their actions unless they dealt with a particular party.

When an agent considers making a relationship-specific investment, it is important to realise that a 'fundamental transformation' occurs in terms of their bargaining position with the other party. While the agent may have many potential agents it can trade with prior to any investment taking place, after those costs have been sunk, the negotiating environment turns into a bilateral monopoly. From the agent's perspective, while they had many trading partners prior to investing, having done so they must negotiate with a single agent in order to appropriate some value.

There are, of course, degrees of specificity to many actions. For some non-contractible actions, agents may be able to realise all or some value if they are forced to transact with another party. In others, the agent has some choice about the degree of specificity. For example, an MBA student who is funded by their employer may choose subjects that would be more valuable if the student were to work for another company having completed the degree. In such cases, the main transaction cost associated with the potential for hold-up is not diminished investment but investment of a type that may not maximise total value created.

CASE

## Ownership of domain names

In the early years of the World Wide Web (around 1995!), domain names that identified the web sites of businesses and organisations (e.g., www.amazon.com; www.cnn.com; www.nike.com; www.sony.com) were allocated on a first–come, first-served basis. Enterprising people realised that some established companies would be slow to realise the potential of the Internet and snapped up some important brand names. The end result was when those businesses wanted to use those domain names they had to pay (sometimes millions) for them.

On one level, there is a sense in which the effects of this were distributional only. That is, those who were quick to stake a claim to a domain name reaped rewards but eventually the name ended up with the business that could use it most effectively. No harm was done, as value created was the same regardless.

However, while that may be true in a static sense, taking a longer-term viewpoint the loss in surplus to established brands sets a poor precedent. New technologies are always emerging that increase the value of a brand. One of the reasons firms invest in quality is to be able to reap the rewards when they are forthcoming; and those rewards may depend on new technologies. So when those brands see part of their rewards going to third parties, this potentially diminishes their incentives to build a brand name. The Internet is but one example of a technology that impacts on brand value. The future could hold others and if the allocation of property rights over those new complementary assets does not recognise prior ownership of trade marks, this can have a detrimental effect on investment incentives.

## Solving hold-up problems

When contracts are incomplete and do not cover the costly actions of key decision-makers, there is potential for hold-up. In some circumstances, this potential may not be realised. For instance, an investment that is not relationship-specific may take place regardless of whether a return on the investment is guaranteed by the contract terms or not. In other circumstances, however, the investment may not take place or may be made in an inefficient way. This is because the investor may choose to avoid the hold-up problem or expend resources in minimising it. Ultimately, the end result is that valuable trading opportunities may not be realised.

There is a sense in which hold-up problems are a necessary part of business life. Nonetheless, awareness of them could improve contractual terms that are negotiated early on. For example, a franchisee of a fast food outlet may be concerned about stories that franchisors were allowing further franchises in a location that had proved to be highly profitable. The solution to this may be to explicitly include a term in the franchise agreement restricting the franchisor's ability to expand the number of franchises or, alternatively, to stipulate damages that could be paid to the franchisee if such an expansion took place.

However, awareness of potential hold-up may not always suggest a contractual solution; especially where renegotiation is possible. Consequently, parties may look for ways to substitute for the commitment value that a contract might otherwise give. As we will see in Chapter 11, changes in ownership (i.e., vertical or horizontal integration) – by increasing the added value of the asset owner – may be such a mechanism. And, in Chapter 13, we will examine how relational contracting may resolve some hold-up problems by allowing hold-up itself to be punished. For the moment, we will look at some alternative ways of resolving hold-up problems. Each has in common that it improves the added value of the players whose investment may be subject to hold-up and diminishes the added value of other players that may have a claim on any value created.

1. *Increased bargaining power*: One direct means of mitigating hold-up problems is to find a way of improving the bargaining power of the player making the investment. An improvement in bargaining power will mean that that player would expect to appropriate more value in negotiations after the investment takes place. For instance, if the worker in our previous example appropriated 80% rather than 50% of the bargaining surplus, this may have given them a sufficient return to acquire skills regardless of whether there was an explicit contract or not.

   Collective or group bargaining is another way of improving the added values of investors. When a group of workers forms a union, their average added value is increased because when there is a breakdown in bargaining, all workers leave the firm. Hence, unions may be desirable organisations when a firm wishes to encourage workers to make relationship-specific investments. For example, the incentive of a worker to relocate in a 'company town' may be greater if that company has a strong union that would protect workers from downward wage pressure after they have moved.

2. *Competition and substitutes*: Another way of raising a player's payoff is to reduce the added value of others. If a player taking a non-contractible action has many substitute players whom they could transact with, this improves their bargaining position. They can use competition among those players to increase their expected outcome. In a sense, if there is sufficient competition, this can substitute for contractual commitments on price; allowing the player to capture more value and justify bearing the costs of any non-contractible actions. In our earlier worker-manager example, if the worker's skills were of value to other employers, the worker could use competition among them to prevent excessive hold-up. In many respects, this is just another way of saying that the worker's investment is not specific to a particular firm.

   Another example of this comes from the licensing of new technology. Sometimes patent holders, as well as producing a new product innovation themselves, license the rights to sell the product to another manufacturer. This practice is called 'second sourcing'. This practice may be seen as strange as the patent holder is effectively giving up its monopoly rights to the new technology. However, this is exactly the goal because it wants to convince users to make their own complementary investments that enhance the innovation's value. For example, a computer chip manufacturer may second source so as to encourage the development of software for that chip. The idea is that by creating competition, the patent holder reduces the possibility that it may hold-up the investments made by complementors.

3. *Burning bridges and inflexibility*: A final way in which hold-up problems can be mitigated is if one player reduces their relative added value by making it costly to break existing arrangements. This can be achieved if that player cuts off their own outside options; that is, they burn their bridges. If this occurs, then that player will

find it more difficult to hold-up other players who may be making non-contractible investments. Their reduced bargaining position necessarily enhances the bargaining position of the investor after they have made any investments.

An example of burning bridges occurred in 1984 when Apple built its plant for its new Macintosh computer. Despite the general uncertainty over the nature of information technology, Apple built and publicly announced that the Macintosh plant would be highly specialised to that product and would not be sufficiently flexible to produce any other type of computer. While such inflexibility may often be seen as a weakness, in this case it could also be viewed as a commitment to users and complementors. The inflexible plant meant that Apple would face less incentive to discontinue the Macintosh line in the future. This sent a signal to users and complementors that they could invest in Macintosh with less risk of those investments becoming worthless in the future.

## Summary

The pre-emptive actions of agents and firms can change subsequent negotiations in an industry. In particular, in anticipation of such negotiations, agents may take actions that increase the surplus they expect to receive but do so by reducing total surplus available to all players. The creation of scarcity by a monopolist is an example of this.

In other situations, when agents face upfront costs on investment, they may fail to take those value-enhancing investments for fear of not being able to recover those sunk costs in subsequent negotiations. Hold-up problems arise when key decisions cannot be contracted upon as part of an all-encompassing negotiation. To overcome this, substitutes for contractual commitments need to be found. An important substitute is a change in ownership of key assets. This will be discussed in more detail in Chapter 11.

# Part III

# Pricing

As consumers, most of us are familiar with the practice where you simply look at a posted price and then decide whether or not to purchase a particular good or service. There is little thought given to whether the store you are in is offering their lowest possible price and if there is 'room to move,' so to speak. You simply take whatever prices are posted as given, and make your choice based on that fact.

This type of market behaviour stands in contrast to the negotiations we considered in Part II of this book. In those chapters, buyers did not react passively to seller price offers but negotiated to a mutually agreeable outcome. This type of negotiation occurs not only over employment or large supply contracts but also at a consumer level. For instance, it is rare for consumers to simply look at the listed price of a new Lexus and decide to buy or walk out of the dealership based on that offer alone. Car purchasers will give counter-offers and, indeed, it is common for dealers to recognise this and reduce price right away based on their own perceptions as to a consumer's willingness-to-pay. In this situation, prices are not simply posted but arise from the process of negotiation.

This part of the book is about what happens when such negotiations do not occur; that is, prices are posted. This practice is most common in mass markets where firms have many potential buyers. As we will see, it is rare for firms to know or even guess as to the individual willingnesses-to-pay of consumers in this situation. Instead, they have information about the *average* preferences of consumers. Setting prices on the basis of average preferences is a difficult problem for firms to solve and analysing how they tackle that problem gives us insight into the determinants and efficiency of mass market pricing.

The immediate consequence of a lack on information on the part of sellers is that individually tailored pricing is not possible (nor profitable from a seller's perspective). Hence, in mass markets, generally sellers offer the same pricing to all customers. This means that sellers will face a tension between the margins earned in each unit sold and the number of units sold. As a consequence, sellers will end up setting their price too high and some valuable trades will be lost. This loss in total value created means that sellers and buyers will have an incentive to find methods of overcoming the information problem at the heart of mass market pricing.

But such pricing practices also have implications for the nature of competition between firms. When firms set a single posted price, they will have regard to the prices set by other firms. This becomes a non-cooperative game. What is important is that competition may be strong or weak depending upon whether firms are focused on maintaining their prices or sales quantity in the face of changes in their rivals' price. This, in turn, impacts upon their attitudes towards strategic investments such as product differentiation and cost reduction. Moreover, in some situations strategic pricing is part of an ongoing game that itself is disciplined by the fear of potential price wars.

Finally, we explore how prices can provide information for firms and agents regarding their economic activities. Specifically, we focus on the decisions of firms to enter an industry. The nature of entry barriers is critical both for whether an entrant is able and has the necessary information to enter but also whether it has the incentive to do so.

# 8 Mass market pricing

This chapter considers what price a firm should set in a mass market if it wishes to maximise profits. Upon setting a price, consumers will purchase the product or not based on the price offered to them. All consumers with a willingness-to-pay in excess of the price will buy and all those with a willingness-to-pay less than the price will not. This behaviour will ultimately determine the firm's revenue and the costs it incurs.

Setting a price based on this notion that consumers form a mass market, rather than buyers that can be individually negotiated with, is a common decision faced by firms operating in retail markets. Economics has developed a well-defined approach to this type of price setting that identifies the way that price should relate to costs and market conditions as well as the potential loss in value creation that comes from a 'one size fits all' pricing strategy. This chapter will give you an understanding of that approach; and also how it can inform more innovative pricing strategies that allow firms to create value by targeting additional consumers, whose willingness-to-pay for a product is more than the firm's willingness-to-sell and in this way improve the total profits received by the firm.

## Simple pricing

Most posted prices are the same regardless of the identity, or any other characteristic, of the consumer. In particular, regardless of the quantity of a good or service a consumer purchases, the per unit price is the same. When there is a constant per unit price we say that firms are posting a *simple* price. This stands in contrast to prices that depend on the quantity purchased (such as bulk discounts) or prices that depend on the type of consumer (such as student concessions). Those, more complex, prices are discussed later in the chapter.

### Private information and pooled prices

In mass markets, sellers have good information about the statistical properties of the market but poor information regarding the individual willingnesses-to-pay of consumers. As a consequence, they are restricted in the type of prices they can offer; basing prices only on broad market characteristics rather than tailoring them to an individual.

When sellers are so restricted, they must offer the same pricing terms to each potential consumer. This is sometimes called a *pooled* price as all consumers are effectively pooled together and treated as identical from the perspective of the firm. Of course, consumers are not identical. Therefore, even when they are treated the same, they will not behave the same.

To see how pooled prices work, consider the following example regarding a seller of the latest Madonna CD. Suppose that there are 100 consumers of two types. There are diehard Madonna fans and moderate fans. Your market research is summarised in Table 8.1. Notice that diehard fans have a higher willingness-to-pay for the CD but are fewer in number than moderate fans.

**Table 8.1** Market research on Madonna CD buyers

|  | Diehard | Moderate |
| --- | --- | --- |
| **Willingness-to-pay** | $30 | $15 |
| Proportion of buyers | 40% | 60% |

To make things simple, suppose that the wholesale price of a CD is $10. This cost-side information can be placed alongside demand-side information on a graph, as in Figure 8.1.

**Figure 8.1** Demand and cost information

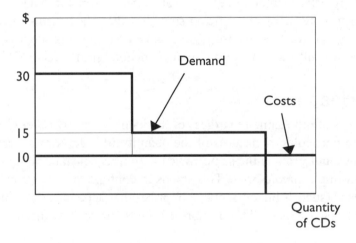

Taking into account this market information, the CD seller has to determine a price to post for the Madonna CD. Notice that to post a price less than $15 is to give away revenue with no visible benefit; for instance, in terms of increased volume. Hence, the seller would not post a price less than $15. Also, notice that to post a price less than $30 but above $15 would also not be profit maximising for the seller. Once again, this would involve a sacrifice in revenue as compared with setting a price equal to $30. This means that the seller is effectively choosing between a low price of $15 or a high price of $30.

The choice between a low as opposed to a high price involves a trade-off for the seller in terms of low margins ($5 per unit) and high volume (all potential consumers) versus a high margin ($20 per unit) but low volume (only 40% of potential consumers). This trade-off, in terms of profits, is illustrated in Figure 8.2. Regardless of the price it sets, the seller earns area A. However, if it sets the high price it earns an additional amount given by area H, while setting a low price gives it the additional profits of area L. What it should do depends upon whether area H is greater than area L or not.

**Figure 8.2** Trade-offs in pricing

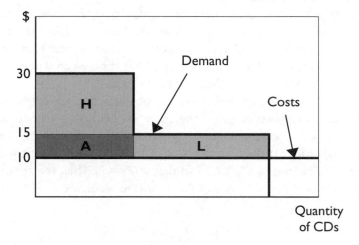

To see this numerically, suppose there are 100 potential consumers. If the firm sets a price of $30 it earns $800 (= ($30 – $10)40) while by setting a price of $15 it earns $500 (= ($15 – $10)100). In this case, area H exceeds area L, so that the seller will opt for a price of $30.

In this case, the seller has decided to sacrifice volume for high margins. Essentially, the high proportion of diehard fans makes it worthwhile for the seller to decide to target them exclusively in pricing. If a smaller proportion of fans (say 20%) were diehard, the seller may in fact choose to price low and sell a greater quantity of CDs.

The lack of sales to moderate fans represents a loss in the overall value that could be created. Those fans are willing to pay more than it would cost to supply them with CDs. However, because the seller is restricted to offering a single price to all consumers, it maximises profits by setting that price high rather than low. As we will see below, this loss in value also gives sellers an incentive to find another way of eliciting information on willingness-to-pay from consumers and make it possible to implement pricing strategies beyond the simple pricing described here.

### Representing demand with statistical information

In reality, there are many consumers who have different characteristics. From the seller's perspective, the key characteristic of interest is a consumer's willingness-to-pay. Let us make the simplifying assumption that each consumer demands at most a single unit of the seller's product and denote the willingness-to-pay of a given consumer for that unit by *v*. *v* can range from 0 to *V*. This number also describes fully a consumer's 'type' in terms of the willingness-to-pay information the seller is interested in.

There may be many consumers of a given type, *v*. However, the seller cannot observe a given consumer's type at all. What the seller does know is the probability distribution of types of potential consumers. This probability distribution is represented by a function *n(v)* (that is between 0 and 1) that has the quality that summing over *v*, these numbers total 1.

Taking this information together – the probability that any single consumer has a particular willingness-to-pay – the seller knows that if it posts a price *P*, only consumers with a willingness-to-pay greater than or equal to *P* will purchase its product. Suppose that the type of the consumer for whom willingness-to-pay just equals *P* is denoted by *v\*(P)* (i.e., so that *v\*(P) = P*). Then the total quantity that would be demanded if a price of *P* was posted would be:

$$Q(P) = \sum_{v-v^*(P)}^{v} n(v)$$

Notice that the higher is *P*, the lower is *Q* as fewer consumers are likely to purchase the product.

An interesting special case is where there is a just a single consumer of each type. In this case, *n(v)* = 1/*V* for all *v*. Then:

$$Q(P) = V - v^*(P) = V - P$$

Writing this in terms of price we have, *P* = *V* – *Q*. Moreover, graphically, the seller's demand function is linear as depicted in Figure 8.3.

**Figure 8.3** Linear demand

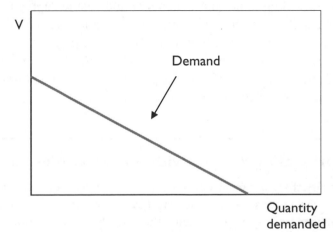

### Price versus quantity

When a seller posts a price, it is making an offer to all potential consumers. That offer is to sell to consumers any number of units they may demand at that price. The seller then has the job of making sure there is sufficient production to meet that demand. In effect, it is as if, by posting a price, the seller is implicitly choosing quantity demanded and supplied as well. This is because, for any given demand function faced by the seller, the choice of a price determines the quantity demanded.

For this reason, we can also view the seller as directly choosing the quantity it produces. In that case, the seller is saying to consumers: 'here is the quantity I have to sell and I will accept the maximum price that allows me to sell all of it'. In this respect, by choosing a quantity to produce, the seller is implicitly setting a price.

The relationship between price and quantity is determined by the demand function facing the seller. Therefore, when analysing the setting of simple prices by seller, we can take the perspective of the seller choosing price or choosing quantity. Moreover, in many situations, it is convenient to take the quantity choice perspective even as we talk about the seller setting a price. We will do so here.

One caveat is important to emphasise, however: while sellers can in principle choose both price and quantity, market constraints and their own incentives will drive them to a point where a choice of one determines the choice of another. Consider Figure 8.4. Notice that a seller always would like to have both a higher quantity and higher price. However, it cannot make an offer such as point H because, at that price, there would be insufficient quantity demanded. Market conditions make a point like H infeasible. On the other hand, if the seller were to make an offer such as point L, it would not be maximising profits. This is because it could always increase its price offer at that point without sacrificing total sales. Hence, for feasibility and profit maximisation reasons, we always view the seller as choosing an offer along the demand curve it faces.

**Figure 8.4** Choices of price/quantity offers

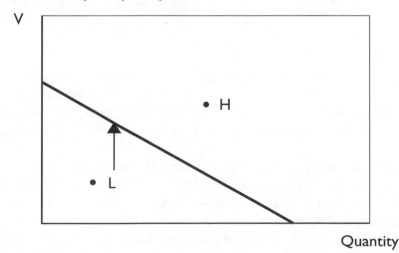

## Prices and revenue

The basic trade-off for a seller in simple pricing is between setting a high price and earning a high margin on each unit sold or setting a lower price and thereby sacrificing margins for a greater quantity sold. That is, higher prices do not always translate into higher revenue, because at some point the additional margin earned is not worth the volume of sales sacrificed.

This basic trade-off is represented in Figure 8.5. There a seller who sets a price equal to 0 earns no revenue. By increasing price a little, the seller earns positive revenue as that small change in price will deter only a few consumers while allowing the seller to earn a margin on each unit sold. On the other hand, a seller setting too high a price will drive all of its customers away. In this case, lowering price and attracting some customers will generate some revenue. In actuality, the price that will maximise revenue generated lies somewhere in between. Nonetheless, sellers to mass markets always face the trade-off between higher margins and greater sales volume.

**Figure 8.5** Price and revenue

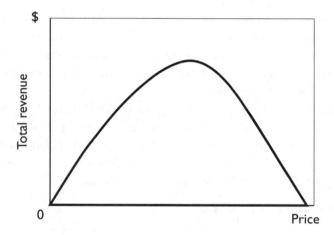

## Marginal revenue

A key concept in a seller's decision regarding price is the concept of *marginal revenue*. That is, when a seller is considering raising quantity by a unit (conversely, lowering price), marginal revenue is the increment to total revenue generated. Marginal revenue is a measure of the benefit a seller receives from deciding to sell an additional unit of output.

As was observed, however, it is not always the case that an additional unit of output will actually improve a seller's total revenue. That total revenue is defined as price multiplied by quantity. If we suppose that a seller's quantity is denoted by $Q$ while its price is $P(Q)$, a function of quantity as derived from the seller's demand curve, then total revenue is price multiplied by quantity; i.e., $TR = P(Q)Q$. If, starting from $Q$, the seller were to produce an additional unit of output, revenue would change to $TR_1 = P(Q+1)Q+P(Q+1)$. In this case, marginal revenue is:

$$MR(Q) = TR_1 - TR = \underbrace{\left(P(Q+1)-P(Q)\right)Q}_{\text{inframarginal effect}} + \underbrace{P(Q+1)}_{\text{volume effect}}$$

Thus, marginal revenue is comprised of the loss of margins on existing quantity (the *inframarginal* effect) and an extra unit of sales (the *volume* effect). The inframarginal effect is negative while the volume effect is positive, reflecting the seller's trade-off in terms of margins and volume when choosing its quantity.

Marginal revenue can be depicted graphically. Consider Figure 8.6. That graph depicts an increase in quantity by a unit. Area I is the inframarginal effect while area V is the volume effect. Marginal revenue is, therefore, V − I. This is depicted in Figure 8.7. Performing these calculations repeatedly for each quantity, we can draw the marginal revenue curve; as in Figure 8.8.

**Figure 8.6** Marginal revenue

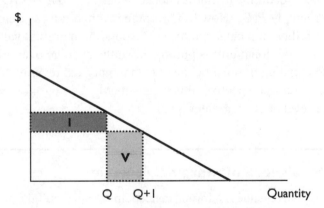

**Figure 8.7** Marginal revenue

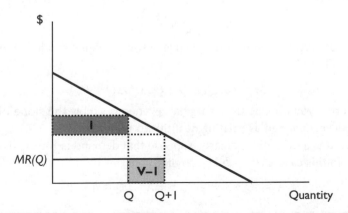

**Figure 8.8** Marginal revenue

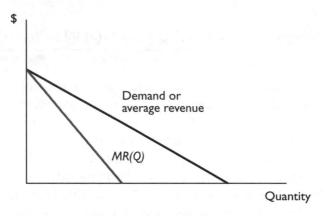

Notice that, in Figure 8.8, the marginal revenue curve lies below the demand curve. This is because that demand curve is actually a graph of the *average revenue* that the seller receives at each quantity it might choose. That is, if *TR* = *P*(*Q*)*Q*, then average revenue is *TR*/*Q* or simply *P*(*Q*). However, average revenue falls as quantity rises. When an average value is falling, it means that the corresponding marginal value must be below that average (i.e., the additional unit is pulling down the average over all units). So, here, as average revenue is falling, it must be the case that marginal revenue lies below average revenue. From the seller's perspective, this means that by selling more, a seller is always sacrificing average revenue for a greater quantity sold.

### The algebra of marginal revenue

Marginal revenue is a formal concept in economics. Take any increment to quantity, $\Delta Q$, that might be chosen by a seller. This will induce a corresponding change in the price the seller changes of $\Delta P$. Then the change in total revenue is:

$$\Delta TR = Q.\Delta P + P.\Delta Q$$

Marginal revenue is simply the change in total revenue divided by the change in quantity. That is,

$$MR = \Delta TR/\Delta Q = Q.\Delta P/\Delta Q + P$$

From this, you can see that marginal revenue is simply the slope of the total revenue curve, depicted as relating quantity to revenue.

To see this a little more clearly, suppose that demand is linear; that is, $P(Q) = A - bQ$. In this case, $\Delta P = -b\Delta Q$, so that

$$MR = -Q.b + P = -Q.b + A - bQ = A - 2bQ.$$

That is, marginal revenue has the same intercept but twice the slope as demand.

Sometimes, however, it is easiest to analyse quantity choices using calculus. In this case, marginal revenue is the derivative of total revenue with respect to price:

$$MR = Q\frac{\partial P}{\partial Q} + P.$$

## Determining profit-maximising output

The concept of marginal revenue tells you how much your revenue will increase by increasing quantity. However, to determine the impact on profits, you have to consider the impact on costs as well. The concept of marginal cost refers to the additional cost the firm incurs when it produces one additional unit of output; it is simply the change in total costs: $TC(Q + 1) – TC(Q)$.

You can put the marginal revenue (MR) and marginal cost (MC) together to determine the profit-maximising or loss-minimising output for the firm. First of all, given any output, $Q$, note the following marginal rules that specify whether a firm should or should not expand output from $Q$ to $Q+1$:

- MR > MC at output $Q+1$: firm should increase output from $Q$ to $Q+1$
- If MR < MC at output $Q+1$: firm should not increase output from $Q$ to $Q+1$

MR is the additional revenue generated if the firm increases output by one unit from $Q$ to $Q+1$. MC is the additional cost of producing this one unit of output. If MR > MC, then the additional revenue generated from selling unit $Q+1$ is greater than the additional cost. Therefore, it is profitable for the firm to produce and sell this unit of output. If, on the other hand, MR < MC, then producing and selling this unit of output loses money for the firm; therefore, this unit of output should not be produced.

Graphically, the quantity that equates marginal revenue and marginal cost is depicted in Figure 8.9. In that figure, $Q^*$ is that quantity that equates MR and MC while $P^*$ is the resulting price; found by looking at the demand curve to consider the price that would generate that quantity of sales. That figure also depicts the resulting profit that is the area $(P^* – MC) \times Q^*$.

**Figure 8.9** Profit-maximising price and quantity

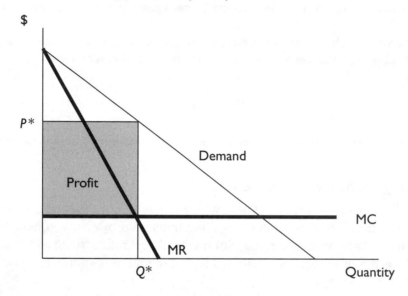

### Algebraic derivation of the profit-maximising price

Continuing on from the algebra of marginal revenue, suppose that there is a constant marginal cost, $MC = c$ (that is, marginal cost does not change with quantity, $Q$). Total cost may be of the form $TC = F + cQ$ where $F$ is the firm's fixed costs. In this case, marginal cost is simply

$$TC_1 - TC = F + c(Q+1) - (F + cQ) = c.$$

Using this we can consider what determines the profit-maximising quantity. Profits are $TR - TC$ which changes to $TR_1 - TC_1$ if output is increased by one unit. This one unit increase will increase profits if:

$$TR_1 - TC_1 > TR - TC$$

or, equivalently,

$$TR_1 - TR > TC_1 - TC$$

That is, MR > MC.

In our linear demand example, where $P = A - bQ$, $MR = A - 2bQ$. So equating MR and MC, we have:

$$A - 2bQ = c \text{ or } Q^* = (A - c)/2b.$$

Plugging this value of $Q^*$ into the demand function gives:

$$P^* = A - bQ^* = (A + c)/2.$$

More generally, using calculus:

$$MR = MC \text{ or } Q\frac{\partial P}{\partial Q} + P = c$$

gives

$$\frac{P^* - c}{P^*} = \frac{-1}{e} \text{ or } P^* = \frac{c}{1 + \frac{1}{e}}$$

where $e = \frac{P}{Q}\frac{\partial Q}{\partial P}$ is the price elasticity of demand. The concept of elasticity is explained next.

## The inverse elasticity pricing rule

While it may be possible to determine profit-maximising prices and quantity by carefully examining information on marginal revenue and costs, sometimes the information required for that exercise is not available. The algebra of profit-maximising pricing yields a simpler formula for the optimal price. That formula is:

$$P^* = \frac{MC}{1 + \frac{1}{e}}$$

where e is the *price elasticity of demand*.

Elasticity is a useful concept as it summarises the statistical information about the demand curve that is most relevant to price setting; namely, if price were to increase by a per cent what percentage decrease in sales would this cause. Mathematically,

$$e = \frac{\% \text{ change in } Q}{\% \text{ change in } P}$$

Thus, it is a measure of the sensitivity of your sales to changes in price. If demand is highly elastic, this means that a small increase in price would lead to a large percentage drop in sales. In contrast, if demand is highly inelastic, a relatively large increase in price may only cause a small percentage drop in sales. Figure 8.10 depicts some demand curves with different elasticities.

The inverse elasticity pricing rule suggests several important principles about pricing:

- *Base mark-ups on marginal costs*: prices should be set to be a mark-up over marginal costs only. Fixed costs and overhead should not matter in pricing decisions. The reason for this is that in selecting the profit maximising quantity, fixed and overhead costs do not change. They are incurred as soon as it is decided to produce some positive output. Recall from Chapter 2, that optimal decisions should ignore costs that are not impacted upon by the decision. In this case, those fixed or overhead costs do not change as a result of different price levels and hence, the pricing decision should not be guided by them.

- *The size of the mark-up depends on price elasticity*: the more sensitive is your firm's quantity demanded to changes in price, the lower should be your mark-up. This is because a high mark-up and hence higher price will generate a large loss in volume and this will impact negatively on your profits. In contrast, when quantity is less sensitive to price, the firm can increase its mark-ups and capture higher margins without sacrificing as much in terms of quantity.

**Figure 8.10** Demand curves with different elasticities

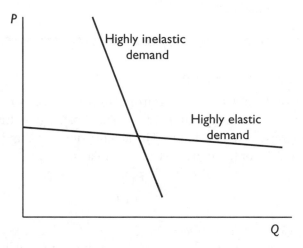

DIGGING

DEEPER

### Drivers of elasticity

What makes a firm's demand more sensitive to price? The quantity sold will fall by a large amount when there are many consumers who will reduce their purchases in response to a price increase. This suggests that at the current price, the surplus they are receiving from purchasing the firm's product is low; so that a small price increase leads to their willingnesses-to-pay being below that price.

A key driver of this type of sensitivity is the *availability of substitutes* for the firm's product. This may come from similar products sold by other firms or from products that have a similar function in the eyes of consumers.

Also, driving price elasticity is how important the product is in consumer budgets. For example, the price of shoelaces may vary by a large amount and a typical consumer will not give it much thought. The price of the shoes themselves is of considerably more interest to most buyers. Similarly, consumers will be more sensitive to price changes in goods purchased frequently, such as milk or cheese, than in goods purchased infrequently, such as gourmet mustard. Consumers, in other words, tend to be more sensitive to price changes in large-budget items because these small percentage differences translate into significant amounts of money.

Finally, time can change elasticity. A petrol price rise does not necessarily do much to change consumer choice over whether to drive to work or not in the short-run. If it persists, however, habits can change and more fuel-efficient cars can be purchased, for example. This leads to a long-run reduction in quantity demanded. In this case, while demand is relatively inelastic in the short-run, in the long-run it becomes more elastic.

# Pricing strategies

Thus far, this chapter has examined how firms should set prices if they are constrained to charge the same per unit price to all consumers. The reason why a firm might be constrained to treat all consumers the same is that it cannot differentiate among them according to their respective willingnesses-to-pay. Here we show how that constraint creates lost opportunities for mutually beneficial trade, leaving total value created short of its maximum possible level. At the same time, this gap in value created gives rise to the potential to use more innovative pricing strategies. Those strategies – sometimes referred to as *price discrimination* by economists – entail being better able to match prices to consumer willingness-to-pay and potentially not only raise firm profits but overall value created as well.

## Lost opportunities in simple pricing

When using simple pricing, the firm sets a price above its marginal cost of production and consumers purchase the product on the basis of that price. What this means is that there are some consumers with willingnesses-to-pay above the firm's willingness-to-sell to them (as represented by their marginal cost) who do not end up trading with the firm. This is a loss in total value created.

Figure 8.11 depicts this lost trading opportunity. If the firm was negotiating with each consumer and knew their respective willingnesses-to-pay, those trading opportunities could be realised as the firm could engage in personalised pricing. However, because the firm does not have that information, it sets a pooled price to all consumers – a single offer. It, therefore, considers the profits it would make and chooses that price accordingly. If that price were set equal to marginal cost, in Figure 8.11, the firm would make no profits. More generally, when marginal cost is rising (say, due to diminishing returns), the firm would still earn some profits from pricing at marginal cost. However, even in that case, if the demand it faces is not perfectly elastic, the firm will want to set its price as a mark-up above marginal cost; as per the inverse elasticity pricing rule. This mark-up creates the shaded triangle representing lost trading opportunities.

This lost opportunity creates a potential for moving beyond simple pricing to more complex arrangements that may allow more trades to occur but also for the firm to capture some value from that and some of the consumer surplus as well. We now turn to explore these pricing strategies.

**Figure 8.11** Lost trading opportunities

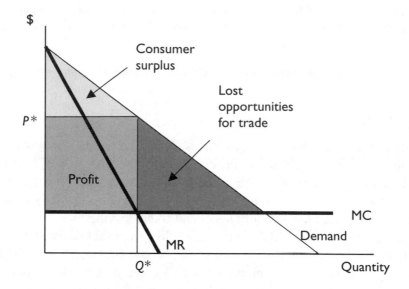

## Group pricing

In some situations a firm is able distinguish between people as members of broad classes or groups. This enables the firm to tailor a price to each group. Examples of this include:

- *Country-specific pricing*: firms often set different prices in different countries. This happens with books, DVDs, computer games and even cars.
- *Student discounts*: software is often set at a discount for students compared with normal retail prices.
- *Institutional pricing*: publishers set different subscription rates to consumers based on whether they are universities, libraries, companies or individuals. It is often the case that an institutional rate is 10 times that for an individual.

In each case, different groups have different average willingnesses-to-pay for products and by using group pricing a firm can charge a higher price to the group likely to have a higher willingness-to-pay. In each case, however, the differences in willingness-to-pay come not so much because of the group itself but because that group is associated with something that is a key driver of willingness-to-pay. This might be location, age or income.

To understand the challenges posed by group pricing, consider the case of a dealer selling cars in two distinct markets. The dealer knows that, with greater disposable incomes, the consumers in market 1 are less sensitive to price increases than those in market 2. If the dealer has procured a fixed quantity of cars, profit is maximised by maximising revenue in both markets.

When allocating the number of units to sell in each market, the dealer must decide whether to charge the same price in both markets. As the demand functions in both markets are different, marginal revenue also differs. So if the dealer charges the same price in both markets, it will be the case that at this price, the marginal revenue of one market will exceed that of another; say $MR_1 < MR_2$.

As figure 8.12 shows, the demand function in market 1 is steeper, indicating that customers in this market are less sensitive to price increases. Therefore, the marginal revenue to the dealer from the sale of the last unit in market 1 is less than in market 2. Hence the dealer can increase revenue by selling fewer units in market 1 and more in market 2.

As marginal revenue in market 2 is greater than in market 1, the dealer should continue to allocate cars to market 2 and away from market 1. By allocating more cars into the market where the marginal revenue is greater, revenue is increased. The dealer should continue reallocating cars from market 1 to market 2 until the marginal revenue in both markets is equal. Once this occurs, there are no additional gains in revenue to the dealer from reallocating cars. The price charged in market 1, $P_1$, is higher than that charged in market 2, $P_2$. This makes sense, as customers in market 1 are willing to pay a higher price.

**Figure 8.12** Group pricing

Reallocation should continue until $MR_2 = MR_1$.

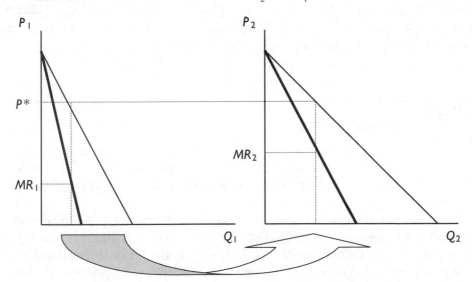

At a common price of $P^*$, $MR_2 > MR_1$, so quantity should be shifted from market 1 to market 2.

Reallocation should continue until $MR_2 = MR_1$.

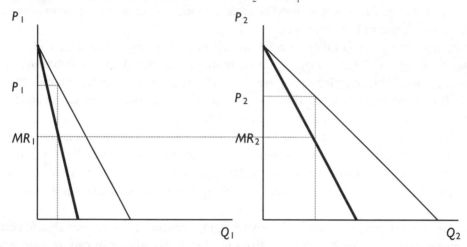

Of course, to sustain different prices across the two markets, it must not be possible, or at least not easy, for consumers in those markets to trade with one another. If consumers in market 2 could purchase cars at a low price of $P_2$ and then sell them to consumers in market 1, who would otherwise face a high price of $P_1$, then group pricing would be unsustainable. By attempting to charge different prices, the dealer would end up losing (at the extreme at least) all of its higher margin sales in market 1. The end result would be that it would sell only in market 2; effectively all of its sales would be at a single price.

Transportation and transaction costs can prevent such arbitrage. But a fundamental requirement for group pricing to succeed is that arbitrage is relatively difficult for consumers or third parties. This is why firms who sell at lower prices also try to restrict the total quantity any one consumer can purchase in those markets.

### Ramsey pricing

In group pricing, the price in each market should be based on the common marginal cost of the firm and the price elasticity of demand in each market. This outcome is sometimes referred to by economists as Ramsey pricing.

To see this, suppose that price in market 1 is a function $P_1(Q_1)$ and price in market 2 is represented by $P_2(Q_2)$. The cost to the firm of producing $Q_1$ and $Q_2$ is represented by $C(Q)$ where $Q = Q_1 + Q_2$, so that the firm's costs depend on the *total* production across both markets. The firm chooses its quantities in each market to maximise its profits of:

$$P_1(Q_1)Q_1 + P_2(Q_2)Q_2 - C(Q_1 + Q_2)$$

In this case, there are two conditions stating that marginal revenue in each market should equal marginal cost.

$$\frac{\partial P_1}{\partial Q_1}Q_1 + P_1 = \frac{\partial C(Q)}{\partial Q_1} \text{ and } \frac{\partial P_2}{\partial Q_2}Q_2 + P_2 = \frac{\partial C(Q)}{\partial Q_2}$$

However, since costs come from a common source, marginal costs are the same for Q1 and Q2 (equal to $\frac{\partial C(Q)}{\partial Q}$), and hence marginal revenue in each market should be the same. This implies that the price in each market will satisfy:

$$P_1^* = \frac{\frac{\partial C(Q)}{\partial Q}}{1 + \frac{1}{e_1}} \text{ and } P_2^* = \frac{\frac{\partial C(Q)}{\partial Q}}{1 + \frac{1}{e_2}}$$

where $e_1 = \frac{P_1}{Q_1}\frac{\partial Q_1}{\partial P_1}$ and $e_2 = \frac{P_2}{Q_2}\frac{\partial Q_2}{\partial P_2}$ are the price elasticities of demand for the product in market 1 and market 2 respectively. Notice that $P_1 > P_2$ if $e_1 > e_2$. Thus, the principle behind group pricing is to base price in any market on price elasticity in that market, while the market with a more elastic demand will have a lower price.

## Versioning

Group pricing is a direct way in which firms can charge different prices to different groups. An indirect way is via versioning. With versioning, the firm does not offer group-based pricing but instead offers more than one product or differential supply terms (say by changing price over time). Consumers then choose their desired product and, in this way, sort themselves into different groups. A good versioning strategy will allow this sorting to take place on the basis of willingness-to-pay, effectively meaning that the firm receives higher prices from the higher willingness-to-pay consumers.

To see how versioning works, let's return to our CD example from the beginning of the chapter. In that example, it would be very difficult for the firm to identify and charge diehard fans a different price from moderate ones. However, what if the firm chose to change its price based on time? For instance, the firm could charge a high price upon release of the new CD and then lower that price later on.

To see how this works, let's call the two prices $P_{now}$ and $P_{later}$. Let's also suppose that all consumers – regardless of their type – discount consumption later by the same factor, $\delta < 1$. This says that a dollar of surplus consumed later is worth only $\delta$ of a dollar consumed now. In this case, given the prices $P_{now}$ and $P_{later}$, each consumer faces a decision tree as depicted in Figure 8.13.

**Figure 8.13** Consumer decisions

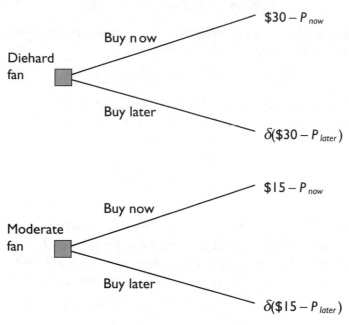

Consumers will sort into different purchases if it is the case that diehard fans buy now while moderates buy later. From Figure 8.13, it is easy to see that for diehard fans to buy now:

$$\$30 - P_{now} > \delta(\$30 - P_{later}) \text{ or } (1 - \delta)\$30 > P_{now} - P_{later}.$$

What this says is that the value gained from buying now must be greater than the price saving from waiting to buy later. Similarly, for moderates to want to wait, it must be the case that:

$$\$15 - P_{now} < \delta(\$15 - P_{later}) \text{ or } (1 - \delta)\$15 < P_{now} - P_{later}.$$

So for moderates, the value gained from buying now would have to be insufficient compared with the price discount from buying later.

Putting these two inequalities together means that the price discount $(P_{now} - P_{later})$ must satisfy:

$$(1 - \delta)\$30 > P_{now} - P_{later} > (1 - \delta)\$15.$$

Notice also, that while $P_{now}$ must be strictly less than \$30 (otherwise diehards would never purchase now), $P_{later}$ could equal \$15 and moderates would still buy later. So setting $P_{later} = \$15$, the above inequality becomes:

$$(1 - \delta)\$30 > P_{now} - \$15 > (1 - \delta)\$15 \text{ or } P_{now} < \$15 + (1 - \delta)\$30.$$

Indeed, the firm can set $P_{now}$ just under $\$15 + (1 - \delta)\$30$ and the diehards would still buy now. Thus, with these prices (and recalling that a CD costs the firm \$10) the firm's profits are:

$$40 \times (\$15 + (1 - \delta)\$30) + 60 \times (\$15) - 100 \times \$10$$

$$\text{or } 100 \times (\$15 - \$10) + 40 \times (1 - \delta)\$30 = \$500 + (1 - \delta)\$1200$$

Notice that as long as $\delta < 0.75$, then these profits will exceed the profits from simple price (where the firm charged one price of \$30 to all customers but only sold to diehard fans). What this says is that versioning can work to increase firm profits if diehard fans are sufficiently impatient (as measured by a low $\delta$).

It is also important to note in this example that total surplus also increases as a result of this version. Whereas under simple pricing, the firm charged a high price so that fans either didn't purchase (the moderates) or were left with no surplus (the diehards), here all consumers purchase and diehards are left with surplus of $\$30 - P_{now}$ or $\delta\$30 - \$15$. Of course, had it been the case that under simple pricing all consumers purchased the CD, a move to versioning would make diehard fans worse off.

Firms use many different methods to achieve a versioning outcome. They offer deluxe and 'lite' versions of products, they offer differential classes of service (e.g., first and economy), and they use sales or coupons to sort among consumers. In each case, versioning is designed to overcome the firm's informational problem in identifying customers on the basis of willingness-to-pay. A thoughtful pricing strategy based on versioning allows them to achieve a similar outcome by playing a game with their consumers and letting the consumers sort themselves into different groups.

## Bundling

A similar outcome to versioning can occur when firms bundle more than one product together. Bundling refers to a situation where the firm charges less if consumers purchase both of two products than if they were to purchase them separately. Here we can describe how bundling can allow firms to earn greater revenue than by opting for independent pricing of their product lines.

To see this, consider how a software-development company could benefit by bundling new versions of its two best-selling software programs: a graphics illustration program and a digital image-editing program. From market research, the company knows its potential customers are either graphic artists or digital photographers.

Graphic artists value the illustration program highly, but they would find the image-editing program less useful. They would pay \$500 for the illustration program but only \$100 for the image-editing program. On the other hand, digital photographers would have the opposite valuations. They would pay \$500 for the image-editing program but only \$100 for the illustration program. The company knows a lot about its potential customers, but it cannot effectively price discriminate as it cannot distinguish between graphic artists and digital photographers when they make a purchase.

Assume there are equal numbers of graphic artists and digital photographers in the potential customer base. Also, assume that the marginal cost of producing an additional copy of each of the programs is zero. Under the company's current strategy of selling its products individually, what price should it charge to maximise profits?

If the company charged $500 for each program separately, only graphic artists would buy the illustration program and only digital photographers would buy the image-editing program. For each pair of potential customer types, the company would make $1000.

Could the company improve its profits by, in addition, selling the programs as one bundled product? The answer is yes. Notice that each potential customer is willing to spend a total of $600 for both programs. Therefore, if the company offered only a bundle, priced at $600, both potential customer types would buy it (over just buying one program or the other), and the company would make $1200.

Bundling is successful because both consumer groups exhibit a pattern of negative correlation in how much they would pay for each component, sold separately rather than bundled. In other words, graphic artists would pay more for the illustration program than for the image-editing program, whereas digital photographers would pay more for the image-editing program than for the illustration program.

What would happen if the company decided to bundle the illustration program with an animation program instead of the image-editing program? Assume that if it were sold separately, graphic artists would pay $500 for the animation program, but digital photographers would pay only $100.

By charging $500 for the animation program and $500 for the illustration program, the company receives a profit of $1000. This is because graphic artists are the only consumers likely to buy the programs at these prices. Even if both were bundled, the price that would maximise profits would be just $1000. In this case, bundling would not increase profits.

In summary, the company will not benefit from bundling two components with positively correlated values. But bundling components with negatively correlated values will extract as much consumer surplus as possible from a potential customer base.

## Two-part tariffs

Thus far, we have considered pricing strategies that work to increase total value created and profits by allowing the firm to charge different prices to different consumers on the basis of their willingness-to-pay. This could increase value created as it means that the firm does not have to set prices too far above marginal costs for low willingness-to-pay consumers.

But in some situations a loss in total value created comes not because simple prices exclude consumers but because they cause all consumers to reduce their total volume of consumption. For most consumers, the additional value they receive from consuming a unit of a good falls as they consume more and more of that good. Think about the value you place on one ice cream as opposed to two. When prices are above marginal costs, consumers only purchase limited quantities and thus, there is a loss in total value created as there may be opportunities for all consumers to consume more.

In this situation, the best pricing strategy is not necessarily to charge different per unit prices to consumers but instead to alter the pricing structure so that the unit price better reflects the firm's marginal costs. One popular way of doing this is to charge consumers a fixed or subscription fee for a service and then charge them a per unit rate for what they consume. It is as if the very first unit of consumption attracts a very high unit price while subsequent units attract a low price.

To see how a two-part tariff can work to increase total value created consider a luxury golf course and its pricing. Figure 8.14 depicts the demand and marginal revenue (MR) curves for a typical consumer. Marginal cost (MC) in this case refers to the cost of supplying an additional round of golf. If the golf course charges a simple price, that price is generated from the intersection of the MR and MC curves and is set at $60 per round of golf. At this price, a typical member would play 40 rounds each year, and the course would make $1600 in profit.

**Figure 8.14** Golf course simple pricing

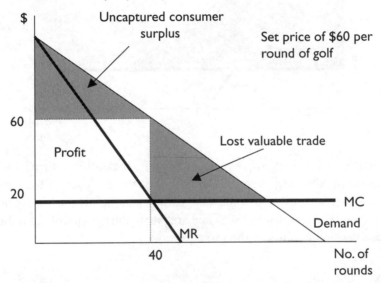

But pricing in this way does not capture profits from two additional sources. First, customers would pay more than $60 for 40 rounds of golf. The triangle above the rectangle of profits is $800 of consumer surplus that the course could obtain.

Second, the course is selling fewer rounds of golf than it could. If it set its price as low as possible (at its MC), it would sell 80 rounds. The triangle to the right of the rectangle of profits is another $800 of consumer surplus that the course could obtain from selling these additional rounds.

Many courses use a two-part tariff to capture these additional consumer surpluses. The fixed fee is the annual membership fee. The variable fee, called a green fee, is paid each time members play a round of golf. The challenge is to find the prices to charge for these fees.

The answer lies in Figure 8.15. By setting the green fee equal to its MC, the course supplies the maximum number of rounds that make economic sense. Furthermore, by setting the membership fee equal to the total consumer surplus from purchasing 80 rounds of golf, the course can capture the profits that it would have had, plus the two additional sources of consumer surplus. By setting the fees optimally, the golf course can earn a total of $3200 in profits.

**Figure 8.15** Two-part tariff

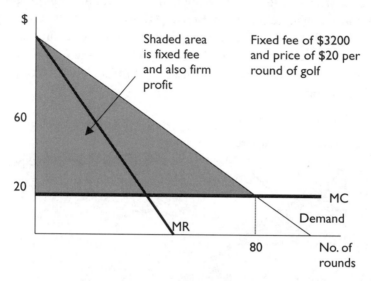

Two-part tariffs are a form of non-linear pricing that allows firms to capture and create more value by allowing them to charge a unit price closer to their marginal cost of production. Other examples include congestion pricing where unit prices rise and volume discounts where unit prices fall. They are particularly valuable in industries where consumers purchase many units of the same product.

## Summary

In mass markets, firms face an information problem when setting their prices. They know some statistical properties of their consumers but cannot identify the willingness-to-pay of any single one. In the end, this creates a game between them and their consumers as they try to find prices that give them information and in so doing enhance total value created.

This chapter has illustrated the implications of that type of game. Firms setting simple prices face a trade-off in terms of maximising total value created and maximising their own profits. This results in lost opportunities for trade. By utilising group pricing, versioning, bundling or two-part tariffs, some of these lost opportunities are recovered. What this chapter demonstrates is the innovative potential of such pricing strategies and how you should think about their usefulness in creating and capturing value in your industry.

# 9 Strategic pricing

The previous chapter examined firm choices about pricing strategies when they face limited information about their consumers' willingnesses-to-pay. However, the discussion considered firm pricing in isolation from the pricing behaviour of other firms. While this might be reasonable for a monopolist in a given market, in most industries the pricing behaviour of competitors will constrain the pricing options for firms.

This chapter looks at mass market pricing in a strategic context. For the most part, we will focus on simple pricing and examine how such pricing is constrained by the activities of competitors. Not surprisingly, the focus will be on the game played among competitors with mass market consumers treated as passive agents. Also, not surprisingly, when that competition is more intense, it is those consumers who are the primary beneficiaries, although total value created is enhanced as well.

## Strategic pricing and competition

To understand the behaviour of a firm in an oligopoly, consider a duopoly market for flowers with two sellers, Bill and Ben. The market demand curve is depicted in Figure 9.1. Suppose they are initially producing 40 flowerpots each, so that the market price is $40 per pot. Suppose also that neither Bill nor Ben face any costs in supplying flowerpots.

**Figure 9.1** The market demand curve

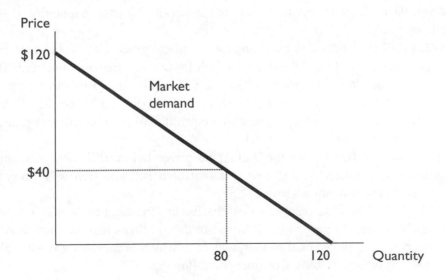

Bill is considering producing more than 40 pots. However, this will be profitable only if price does not fall by too much. This depends on how Ben might react to Bill's increased production. Bill conjectures that there are two ways Ben may react:

- *Reducing price to maintain quantity sold.* Ben might be concerned about the reduction in his sales quantity as a result of Bill's increased production. In order to maintain his existing volume, Ben could reduce his price.
- *Reducing production to maintain market price.* Alternatively, Ben might be worried about the potential drop in the market price of flowers when Bill increases his output. He realises that, if he cuts back production, he can maintain the existing price in the market.

It is possible that Ben's reactions might be more complicated. Economists, however, have found that focusing on reactions that maintain price or quantity simplifies the analysis of oligopoly. In effect, they define two distinct theories of competition – price competition and quantity competition. We will examine each in turn. As we will see, because Bill anticipates price matching by Ben under quantity competition but not price competition, the former results in higher equilibrium prices than the latter.

## Tough price competition

Suppose first that Bill believes that Ben will always maintain his current price. That is, he believes that Ben will let his sales decline rather than reduce his price in the face of a changed price by Bill.

To see what happens in price competition, imagine that Ben currently sells flowers at $40 per pot. He will sell as much or as little as he needs to maintain this price. Now if Bill sets his price at, say, $50, he will find himself unable to sell any flowers. This is because flowers, from the point of view of consumers, are a homogenous product. Hence, consumers will purchase from the firm that sells at the lowest price. With Bill setting his price at $50, Ben is able to capture the entire market (in this case, a quantity of 80 pots). Bill earns no profits.

Can Bill do better than this by changing his price, given that he believes that Ben will maintain his price at $40? Suppose that Bill lowers his price and undercuts Ben. For example, Bill could lower his price to $30. As Bill is selling flowers more cheaply than Ben, he will capture the entire market. Bill will sell 90 pots and make $2700 in profit. Ben, in contrast, will make no sales and earn no profit. Bill is better off undercutting Ben than by pricing above him.

What is true for Bill is true for Ben. If he prices below Bill, he earns more than if he prices above him. What this means is that both Bill and Ben will always find it advantageous to lower their own price.

When Bill and Ben have reactions that involve undercutting each other's price, what will be the Nash equilibrium prices? It turns out that, in this situation, there is one Nash equilibrium price – a price equal to marginal cost, which is zero. To see why this is the case, we need to reason in steps. Consider the following:

1. It cannot be a Nash equilibrium for Bill to charge a different price than Ben. If this were to occur, the person with the higher price could always earn more profits by lowering price and undercutting their rival.

2. It cannot be a Nash equilibrium for Bill and Ben to charge the same price at some level above marginal cost. If this were to happen, then either Bill or Ben could gain the entire market by charging a slightly lower price. By making a small price cut, either Bill or Ben can steal all the other flower seller's customers and increase his own profit.

3. It cannot be a Nash equilibrium for Bill or Ben to charge a price lower than marginal cost (in this case, zero). They would make a loss by selling at such a price and would prefer not to produce at all.

Given these three steps, we must conclude that the only Nash equilibrium is where Bill and Ben charge the same price for flowers equal to marginal cost – in this case, zero.

In our example, price competition leads to a startling conclusion. Even with only two firms, each firm in equilibrium will set a price equal to marginal cost. This result holds whenever production involves constant marginal costs. This is a tough competitive outcome because, from this point, if either firm believes the other will maintain its price, then raising their own price will result in a loss of all of their sales.

### Softer (Cournot) quantity competition

The issue with tough price competition is that when you drop your own price you do not believe the other firm will drop theirs. Hence, you go for a small discount to grab a large share of the market. The end result is a very competitive outcome.

But what if you did believe the other firm would react and change their price? To see what happens, suppose that Bill believes that Ben will always maintain his current level of output. That is, he believes that Ben will let the price of flowers fall rather than reduce his output.

This belief is the basis of Cournot quantity competition. This competition is named after Augustin Cournot who, in 1838, was the first person to attempt to model oligopolistic competition. It is called quantity competition because each firm believes that its rivals will always act to maintain their current quantity.

The following table highlights the decision facing Bill. If Ben is producing 20 pots of flowers, then Bill knows that demand for his flowers is simply the market demand less a quantity of 20 pots. This is because for every level of production he chooses, Ben will adjust his price so that the difference between market demand at that price and Bill's production is exactly 20 pots. The individual demand schedule for Bill's flowers is simply the market schedule less 20 pots.

**Table 9.1** Bill's profit maximisation decision when Ben produces 20 pots.

| Ben's quantity (pots) | Bill's quantity (pots) | Market quantity (pots) | Price ($) | Bill's total revenue (and total profit) ($) |
|---|---|---|---|---|
| 20 | 0 | 20 | 100 | 0 |
| 20 | 10 | 30 | 90 | 900 |
| 20 | 20 | 40 | 80 | 1600 |
| 20 | 30 | 50 | 70 | 2100 |
| 20 | 40 | 60 | 60 | 2400 |
| 20 | 50 | 70 | 50 | 2500 |
| 20 | 60 | 80 | 40 | 2400 |
| 20 | 70 | 90 | 30 | 2100 |
| 20 | 80 | 100 | 20 | 1600 |
| 20 | 90 | 110 | 10 | 900 |
| 20 | 100 | 120 | 0 | 0 |

To maximise profits, Bill will follow the same rule we discussed in Chapter 8 – he will choose a quantity that equates his marginal revenue and marginal cost. As Bill's marginal cost is zero in this example, he will maximise profits by maximising total revenue. From the above table, if Ben is producing 20 pots, Bill will produce 50 pots to maximise his profit.

What if Bill believes that Ben will produce 60 flowerpots? This is shown in the following table.

**Table 9.2** Bill's profit maximisation decision when Ben produces 60 pots

| Ben's quantity (pots) | Bill's quantity (pots) | Market quantity (pots) | Price ($) | Bill's total revenue (and total profit) ($) |
|---|---|---|---|---|
| 60 | 0 | 60 | 60 | 0 |
| 60 | 10 | 70 | 50 | 500 |
| 60 | 20 | 80 | 40 | 800 |
| 60 | 30 | 90 | 30 | 900 |
| 60 | 40 | 100 | 20 | 800 |
| 60 | 50 | 110 | 10 | 500 |
| 60 | 60 | 120 | 0 | 0 |

Because Ben is producing more, Bill has to produce less to maintain a given market price. The individual demand schedule facing Bill is lower and Bill's profit maximising output level is now only 30 pots of flowers.

Notice that when Bill believes that Ben is going to produce more, he will react by producing less. The more Ben is going to produce, the smaller the share of the market available to Bill. So Bill reacts by limiting his own output to maintain the market price and maximise his own profits.

**Figure 9.2**

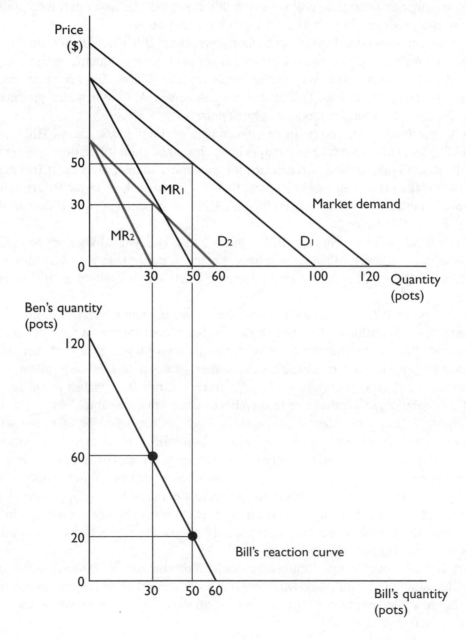

Figure 9.2 shows how Bill's output choice will alter with Ben's production decision. The upper part shows how Bill's individual demand curve depends on Ben's output choice. If Ben produces 20 pots, then Bill's individual demand curve is given by $D_1$ – the market demand shifted left by 20 pots. Bill will maximise profits by producing 50 pots of flowers. This is where the relevant marginal revenue curve $MR_1$ intersects with marginal cost. Remember that marginal cost is zero in this example. The lower part then plots this decision. Bill produces 50 pots when Ben produces 20 pots.

If Ben increases production to 60 pots, then this reduces Bill's individual demand curve. This is shown by curve $D_2$. Again Bill maximises profits by producing where marginal revenue equals marginal cost. But because Ben is producing more, Bill's marginal revenue at each level of output is less. This is shown by the curve $MR_2$. When Ben produces 60 pots of flowers, Bill wants to produce only 30 pots.

Bill's *reaction curve*, shown in the lower part of Figure 9.2, shows Bill's profit-maximising level of output for every output level chosen by Ben. If Ben produces nothing, then Bill is a monopolist and will produce the monopoly output, 60 pots. If Bill expects Ben to flood the market and sell 120 pots, then it is not worthwhile for Bill to produce anything. In between, if Ben produces 20 pots, Bill will produce 50, and if Ben produces 60 pots, Bill will produce 30.

If Ben holds similar beliefs to Bill – that is, that Bill will always act to maintain his existing output level – then he will have a reaction curve with a similar property to Bill's. That is, Ben will always want to decrease (increase) his output as Bill increases (decreases) his.

We can place Bill's and Ben's reaction curves on the same diagram. This is done in Figure 9.3. This allows us to determine the Nash equilibrium in Cournot quantity competition. Recall that the choice of strategies for two players is a Nash equilibrium if neither player can gain by changing to another strategy. In this case, in the choice of quantities, a Nash equilibrium occurs if neither Bill nor Ben wishes to change their output, assuming that the other acts to keep his or her output the same.

In Figure 9.3, the only Nash equilibrium is where Bill and Ben both choose 40 pots of flowers each. If Bill were to choose 20 pots, Ben will want to choose 50 pots – the corresponding point on his reaction curve. However, these choices of output are not a Nash equilibrium because, while Ben is happy with his choice, Bill can improve his profits by changing his output to 35 pots. This corresponds to a point on his reaction curve. Unless both Bill and Ben are choosing outputs on their reaction curves, each is not maximising profits given the choice of the other. Hence, only points where reaction curves coincide represent a Nash equilibrium.

Note that the Cournot equilibrium involves total production of 80 pots, more than the monopoly output of 60 pots. It also involves less production than under price competition. In this example, the output under price competition would be 120 pots with a price equal to the marginal cost of zero.

## Figure 9.3

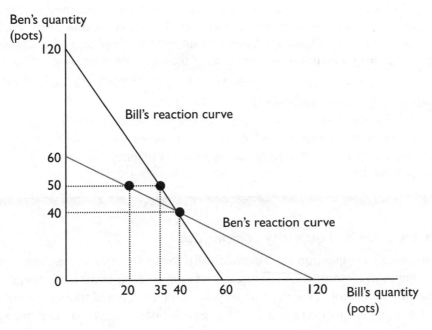

Ben's quantity (pots)

Bill's reaction curve

Ben's reaction curve

Bill's quantity (pots)

---

## The mathematics of oligopolistic competition

It is useful to illustrate the mathematics of oligopolistic competition. We will do this with the same market demand curve $P = A - bQ$ that we used in Chapter 8 for monopoly. In this case, if there are $n$ firms labelled $i = 1$ to $n$, then $Q = q_1 + q_2 + \ldots + q_n$. Each firm has a marginal cost of $c$.

Under price competition, the unique Nash equilibrium will involve each firm setting a price equal to $c$ so that $P = c$. This means that $Q = (A - c)/b$. This is in contrast to the monopoly situation were $Q = (A - c)/(2b)$.

Under quantity competition, firm 1 chooses its quantity, $q_1$, to maximise profits of $(P - c)q_1 = (A - bq_1 - b\sum_{j=2}^{n} q_j - c)q_1$. Holding the quantities of other firms as constant, maximising this involves setting marginal revenue equal to marginal cost; that is:

$$\underbrace{(A - b\sum_{j=2}^{n} q_j) - 2bq_1}_{\text{Marginal Revenue}} = c$$

This implies that:

$$q_1 = \frac{A - b\sum_{j=2}^{n} q_j - c}{2b}$$

> Notice that for each individual firm, as other firms increase their quantity, it is optimal for a given firm to reduce its quantity. This gives the downward sloping reaction curves as in Figure 9.3. A similar result follows for all other firms. Indeed, since each firm is identical, we can set all of their quantities equal $q_i = Q/n$ and solve. This gives $q = \frac{1}{(1+n)b}(A-c)$ or $Q = \frac{n}{(1+n)b}(A-c)$ where $P = \frac{1}{(1+n)}(A+nc)$. Thus, an individual firm's profit is $\frac{1}{(1+n)^2 b}(A-c)^2$.
>
> Notice that this price and total quantity lies between the monopoly and price competition levels. Indeed, if $n = 1$, it becomes the monopoly price and quantity but as $n$ gets very large (i.e., approaches infinity) it becomes the price competition level.

## Comparing price and quantity competition

Price and quantity competition yield markedly different outcomes. Price competition leads to very competitive outcomes with price driven to cost. In contrast, pricing outcomes under quantity competition are in between price competition and monopoly pricing.

Both types of competition are theoretical possibilities. Which one is more applicable depends on the situation. Remember that each involves firms having a different type of belief about their competitors. In quantity competition, firms believe rivals will act to maintain output, whereas in price competition, they believe that their rivals' price will remain fixed.

It will be more appropriate to have beliefs that quantity will be maintained in industries where it is difficult for firms to actually change their output levels. This could occur when firms have limited production capacities, face rigid production technologies or manufacture to maintain an inventory stock rather than to supply customers' orders.

Price competition is more likely when firms compete directly over price before setting output. For example, when tendering for a one-off project, like building a major highway in a large city, competitors face a situation like price competition. The firm with the lowest bid wins the tender and gets to build the project while the losers get nothing.

## Product differentiation

The previous example of how competition between firms operated assumed that each firm was selling the same product: specifically, each firm's product was perfectly substitutable in the eyes of consumers. In many situations, however, firms have differentiated products. For one firm, there may exist a collection of consumers who are willing to pay a premium to purchase from them. This might simply be a matter of taste although it could also reflect locational advantages (e.g., the closest store to a consumer), desirable features or brand appeal. Here we explore how product differentiation changes the nature of price competition (very similar conclusions would flow from quantity competition).

### Niche markets

To begin, let's consider an alternative scenario for Bill and Ben. Suppose that there are 120 potential consumers of flower pots and that Ben is pricing at $0 (as per a price competition Nash equilibrium). Bill has the opportunity to invest in an alternative pot design that will appeal to one-third of all consumers, making those consumers willing to pay a premium of $5 per pot for Bill's pots; that is, Bill could price his pots at $5 and still retain those consumers. However, suppose also that this new design makes pots more expensive to produce. So Bill's costs of producing such pots would be $2 per pot. Finally, we suppose that if Bill chooses to go with the new design, all of his pots would have to be produced with that design.

In this situation, it is easy to see that Bill will find it desirable to produce the new design. In so doing, he will be able to charge a price of $5 per pot and make a margin of $3 (= $5 − $2) on each pot. Given that 40 consumers will pay this premium, his profits become $120. Clearly, this is better than the $0 profits he made before.

While this is good for Bill, we haven't considered Ben's reaction. Notice that if Bill is charging $5 per pot, Ben can get away with charging more too. Indeed, if Ben charges $1 per pot, he earns profits of $80 as two-thirds of the market continues to purchase from him.

But what is the Nash equilibrium of this more complicated game? Notice that if Ben charges $1 per pot, Bill would actually make more by charging $6 per pot (in which case he would make $160). So this isn't a Nash equilibrium. Moreover, Ben cannot charge a price too close to Bill's – such as $4 – or Bill would want to undercut Ben and take the entire market.

This illustrates that finding a Nash equilibrium in this type of environment can be difficult. Instead, suppose we impose a simpler condition: that each firm sets a price that maximises their profits but that their rival will not want to undercut to capture the entire market; thus, we look for an outcome that is *undercut-proof*. For Bill and Ben this means the following conditions must hold:

1. The difference between Bill and Ben's price must be $5 per pot: if the difference is larger, Bill will lose all of his consumers as he is undercut by Ben. Thus, Bill will set his price no more than $5 above Ben's.

2. Bill must earn the same or more profits by charging a premium than by undercutting Ben slightly. If this were not the case, Bill would prefer to sell the 'generic' pot design.

So if Ben's price is $P_1$ and Bill's is $P_0$, these two conditions mean that:

$$P_0 = \$5 + P_1$$
$$(P_0 - \$2)40 = P_1 * 120$$

where (to make things simple) in the second equation we have assumed that by matching Ben's price Bill would capture the entire market. Taking the first equation and substituting it into the second gives a value for $P_1$ of $1.50. This means that $P_0$ would be $6.50. Notice at these prices, Bill would earn $180 and Ben would earn $120.

Thus, by differentiating his product Bill has sacrificed market share (dropping from a half to a third) but is able to earn greater margins. Moreover, this differentiation has caused both Bill and Ben to soften their price competition with one another. In the end, prices have risen for both.

What this demonstrates is that product differentiation can have an important strategic effect. Not only does it potentially make one's own product more valuable, in addition, by causing you to set higher prices, it leads rivals to follow suit.

### Horizontal differentiation

Sometimes both firms have 'loyal' consumers who prefer their product over their rival. To see how this might work, let's suppose that for Bill and Ben half of the market prefers one or the other's pots and is willing to pay a premium of $5 for that pot. Let's also suppose that for both Bill and Ben, producing pots costs $2 per unit.

Unlike the previous 'niche market' case, it is no longer the case that Bill and Ben's prices will differ when each is undercut-proof. However, it will still be the case that neither Bill nor Ben will want to undercut the other. But now, to undercut the other firm and increase sales each firm would have to charge a discount of at least $5 per unit. What this means is that, at their respective prices, both Bill and Ben must earn at least as much as if they undercut the other by $5 and captured the entire market. This means that each firm's price, $P$, must satisfy the following equation:

$$(P - \$2)60 = (P - \$5 - \$2)120$$

Solving this for $P$ gives $P = \$12$. At this price, both Bill and Ben earn $600 each. If one was to undercut the other at a price of $7 and capture the entire market, they would still earn $600 and so it would not improve their profits.

What this suggests is that if both firms can differentiate their products, this will soften price competition even further. As such, it may often be the case that product differentiation is a strategy that is worth imitating.

DIGGING

DEEPER

### A general model of price competition with differentiated products

Here we examine a more general model of product differentiation. This differentiation is captured by imagining that consumers are 'located' along a line between point 0 and point 1 and that each firm is located at the end (that is, Bill at 0 and Ben at 1). The distribution of consumers is depicted in Figure 9.5.

**Figure 9.5**

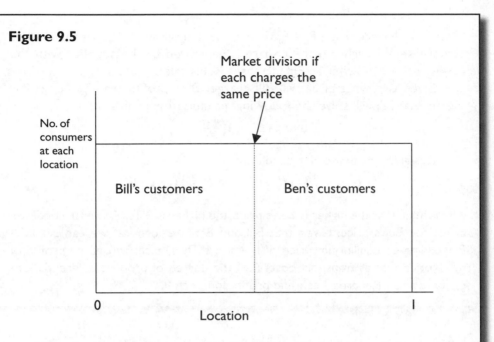

Market division if each charges the same price

No. of consumers at each location

Bill's customers

Ben's customers

0    Location    1

We will also assume that each seller has a marginal cost of $c$ in servicing each of their customers and that each consumer has to face a 'transportation' cost, $t$, per unit of distance they need to travel to purchase from a supplier. Thus, a consumer located at point ¼ would incur costs of $t/4$ to purchase from Bill and $3t/4$ to purchase from Ben. What this means is that for that consumer Bill's price could be almost $t/2$ higher than Ben's before that consumer would switch from Bill to Ben. In general, for a consumer located at $x$, the transportation costs associated with going to Bill would be $tx$ and to Ben, $t(1-x)$. In this respect, $t$ is a measure of the degree of product differentiation. While location and associated transportation costs may be a cause of such differentiation, 'location' could be associated with different consumer preferences and the transportation cost might be a measure of how close those preferences are aligned with the product offerings of Bill and Ben.

Given this, let's look at the demand for Bill's product. Let's hold Ben's price fixed at $P_1$ and think about how Bill's sales change as his price, $P_0$, changes. The easiest way to conceptualise this is to consider a consumer who would be indifferent between purchasing from Bill or Ben when prices are $P_0$ and $P_1$. For that consumer, located at $x$, this would mean that the 'full costs' (price + transportation cost) associated with each supplier are the same:

$$P_0 + tx = P_1 + t(1-x)$$

Solving this for $x$ gives: $\underline{x} = \frac{1}{2t}(P_1 - P_0) + \frac{1}{2}$. $\underline{x}$ is the number of consumers who Bill will get at if he charges a price of $P_0$ when Ben is charging $P_1$ (Ben gets $1 - \underline{x}$. Notice that if $P_1 = P_0$, then $\underline{x} = \frac{1}{2}$ and Bill and Ben split the market. Otherwise, the higher market share is generated by the supplier with the lowest price. Moreover, as Bill increases $P_0$, his sales, $\underline{x}$, fall.

Given this, what price will Bill charge? Bill's profits are $(P_0 - c)\,\underline{x}$. This means that Bill will solve the following maximisation problem:

$$\max_{P_0} (P_0 - c)\left(\tfrac{P_0 - P_1}{2t} + \tfrac{1}{2}\right)$$

This gives the first order condition:

$$\left(\tfrac{P_1 - P_0}{2t} + \tfrac{1}{2}\right) = (P_0 - c)\tfrac{1}{2t} \text{ or } P_0 = \tfrac{1}{2}(t + c + P_1)$$

Notice that the higher is Ben's price, the higher is Bill's. A similar condition arises for Ben's price. Given that Bill and Ben are identical we can set $P_1 = P_0$, yielding an equilibrium price of $P = t + c$. Thus, each firm earns profits of $t/2$. Notice that as transport costs (i.e., the degree of product differentiation) become small, $P$ approaches $c$ and profits approach 0.

## Strategic investments

The above discussion demonstrates how greater product differentiation may be mutually advantageous to competing firms. This represents a form of 'before the game' strategic commitment that can make both firms better off.

That situation does not necessarily apply to all strategic investments. In some cases, the investments can make both firms worse off. In others, it can make one firm better off at the expense of the other. What happens depends upon the nature of competition – price or quantity competition – as well as the nature of the investment itself.

To illustrate this, we focus here on incentives for firms to invest in ways of reducing their marginal production costs. We will consider price competition before describing what happens under quantity competition.

### Price competition

Let's consider the earlier situation where both Bill and Ben have a set of 'loyal' customers and their marginal production costs are $2 per unit. Recall that in that case, the market price for pots was $12 and each firm earned $600 in profits.

Bill is considering an investment that will reduce his marginal costs to $1 per unit. Everything else about the market will stay the same. Recall that the equilibrium prices in this instance arise when neither Bill nor Ben has an incentive to undercut the other. We will let Bill's price be $P_0$ and Ben's $P_1$. In this case, Bill will not have an incentive to undercut Ben if $(P_0 - 1)60 = (P_1 - 5 - 1)120$ and Ben will not have an incentive to undercut Bill if $(P_1 - 2)60 = (P_0 - 5 - 2)120$. Solving these two equations simultaneously gives $P_1 = \$11.34$ and $P_0 = \$11.67$. Thus, Bill's profits become \$640 and Ben's \$560. Thus, Bill is better off and Ben is worse off than before.

Notice, however, that Bill is not as well off as he might have anticipated. When he sells 60 units, a \$1 reduction in marginal cost might have netted him \$60 in additional profits. Instead he only earns \$40 more. The reason is that his lower marginal cost has created an incentive for both himself and, in response, Ben to lower price. The new equilibrium price is lower than before, and consequently both Bill's and Ben's profits are reduced.

What happens if Ben makes a similar investment? In this case, with both Bill and Ben having marginal costs of \$1, to prevent undercutting, each firm's price must satisfy $(P - 1)60 = (P - 5 - 1)120$ or $P = \$11$; so price competition is even tougher. Thus, each earns profits of \$600. Ben's profits are increased while Bill's fall. Notice that, given that Bill has made the strategic investment (for a seeming increase in profits of \$40) it is similarly worthwhile for Ben to follow suit (increasing his profits from that point by \$40). Hence, we can expect Ben to do so.

Suppose then that these investments cost each firm \$30. If one makes the investment while the other does not, that person earns \$610 while the other earns \$560. If both make the investment, each earns \$570 while if neither make it, each earns \$600. We can represent this situation as a simultaneous or sequential move game (see Figure 9.3). In either case, notice that it is a dominant strategy for either firm to invest; that is, regardless of what the other firm is doing, each can earn an additional \$10 by investing. The unique equilibrium involves both investing even though each would be better off if neither invested. In this respect, this game is akin to the 'Prisoners' Dilemma' game considered in Chapter 4.

**Table 9.3** Investment game

|       |        | Ben | |
|-------|--------|--------------|--------------|
|       |        | **Invest** | **Don't** |
| **Bill** | Invest | \$570, \$570 | \$610, \$560 |
|       | Don't | \$560, \$610 | \$600, \$600 |

This demonstrates what is known as a 'super trap'. While individually investment in cost reduction may make sense, when a rival's reaction is considered the increased profits from this activity can be diminished as the strategy is imitated. Moreover, the rival has an incentive to imitate that investment if you do so.

### Quantity competition

Interestingly, the story is somewhat different in the case of quantity competition. Under price competition, while there was a potential direct benefit from reducing costs, there was a negative strategic effect as the other firm reacted by reducing its price. Under quantity competition, the strategic effect is the opposite. In response to your reduced costs and hence, greater incentive to raise quantity, a rival firm will decrease its quantity. This gives you a strategic benefit of greater market share without the reduced margin.

The easiest way to see this effect is to consider the reaction curves for Bill and Ben as in Figure 9.7 (although this time imagining that there are some positive production costs). If Bill invests in cost reduction, this has the effect of shifting his reaction curve outwards. In equilibrium, his quantity is higher and Ben's is much lower.

**Figure 9.7** Effects of a cost reduction for Bill

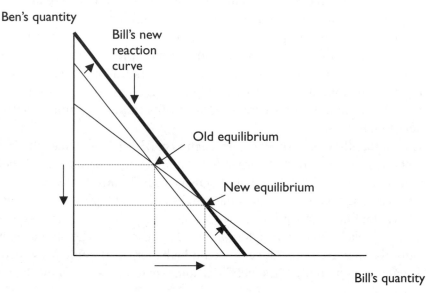

Ben's quantity

Bill's new reaction curve

Old equilibrium

New equilibrium

Bill's quantity

In the Advanced box below, it is demonstrated that this cost reduction improves Bill's profits by more than the reduction in Ben's profit. What this means is that should Ben want to follow on with his own cost reduction investment, the returns to doing so would be lower. If the investment costs are sufficiently high, it may be that Bill's investment pre-empts Ben from following suit. In this case, the strategic benefits to Bill from a first move in such investment may be very high.

ADVANCE

### Effect of cost reduction in quantity competition

Continuing on our earlier example of quantity competition, suppose that $n = 2$ and that firm 1 reduces its costs by . In this case, the reaction curves for firms 1 and 2 are:

$$q_1 = \frac{A - bq_2 - c + \Delta}{2b}$$

$$q_2 = \frac{A - bq_1 - c}{2b}$$

Solving these for the equilibrium quantities gives: $q_1 = \frac{1}{3b}(A-c+2\Delta)$ and $q_2 = \frac{1}{3b}(A-c-\Delta)$ so that $Q = \frac{2}{3b}(A-c+\Delta/2)$ and $P = \frac{1}{3}(A+2c-\Delta)$. Finally, firm 1's profit becomes $\frac{1}{9b}(A-c+2\Delta)^2$ and firm 2's profits are $\frac{1}{9b}(A-c-D)^2$. Notice that firm 1's profits are larger as $\Delta$ rises; in particular, the increment to firm 1's profit is $\frac{1}{9b}(A-c+2\Delta)2\Delta$.

In contrast, if firm 2 were to follow on with a similar cost reduction its profits would become $\frac{1}{9b}(A-c+\Delta)^2$ so that the increment was $\frac{1}{9b}2(A-c)\Delta$. This is less than the increment firm 1 obtained. Thus, the incentive to engage in cost reduction is lower for a follow-on investor.

What this means is that, unlike the price competition case, investment in cost reduction by one firm does not necessarily make it more likely the other firm will follow suit. They might but the returns to doing so are diminished. If the investment costs are sufficiently high, firm 1 might invest and pre-empt firm 2.

## Tacit collusion

The above analysis of strategic pricing treated the game played between rival firms as a one-shot game. In many industries, the interactions between firms are repeated over time and firms can observe one another's pricing on a quarterly, monthly and sometimes daily basis. If this is the case, the game between rivals is a repeated one and, as we saw in Chapter 4, this can have implications for the types of strategies players might employ.

We can illustrate this most easily with the case of price competition. For Bill and Ben, price competition led to a situation where each set their price equal to marginal cost and earned no profits. If, instead, each was able to explicitly collude and share the monopoly outcome (in that case, achieved at a price of $60), then each would earn profits of $1800 (or $60 x 30). What prevented this outcome from being sustainable without an explicit agreement was that either Bill or Ben had an incentive to undercut the other and charge $59, achieving total sales of 61 pots and denying the other any sales at all. In this case, the firm discounting would receive profits of $3599 (= $59 x 61).

When competitive interactions are repeated over time, it is no longer reasonable for Bill to expect that Ben, having observed the price drop to $59, would continue to keep their price at $60. One option would be for Ben to drop his price to $58. However, another would be to employ a trigger strategy. This strategy would be as follows: if in the last period Bill keeps his price at $60, continue to price at $60 but if Bill charges any lower price, drop price to $0 forever.

If Bill believed Ben was playing this trigger strategy, then when considering dropping his price to $59, Bill would anticipate that this would only be profitable for one period. Following that Ben would drop his price to $0 and Bill would earn no profits forevermore.

Suppose that pricing is set monthly and the interest rate is 2% per month. In this case, Bill will find it profitable to continue pricing at $60 if:

$$1800 + \frac{1800}{1.02} + \frac{1800}{1.02^2} + ... = \$91\,800 \geq \$3599$$

Notice that, for this (quite high) interest rate, Bill prefers to keep price high rather than grab market share for a month.

A similar calculation would apply for Ben if Bill was playing a trigger strategy. In this way, a collusive outcome can be sustained. Notice that the outcome is not because of an explicit agreement but because of an implicit or tacit one.

In general, the difference between half of the monopoly profits and competitive profits may not be as stark as this example. Suppose there are n firms in an industry. Let industry profits in a monopoly outcome be $\Pi^m$, individual competitive profits be $\pi^c$ while the short-term profits a firm could grab if they deviated from monopoly pricing be $\pi^d$. Then if each firm is playing a trigger strategy and the interest rate is $r$, no firm will deviate if:

$$\tfrac{1}{n}\Pi^m + \tfrac{1}{1+r}\tfrac{1}{n}\Pi^m + \tfrac{1}{(1+r)^2}\tfrac{1}{n}\Pi^m + ... \geq \pi^d + \tfrac{1}{1+r}\pi^c + \tfrac{1}{(1+r)^2}\pi^c + ...$$

$$\Rightarrow \tfrac{1+r}{r}\tfrac{1}{n}\Pi^m \geq \pi^d + \tfrac{1}{r}\pi^c$$

$$\Rightarrow \tfrac{1}{n}\Pi^m - \pi^c \geq r(\pi^d - \tfrac{1}{n}\Pi^m)$$

This says that a firm will not deviate if the per period profit gain from collusion is greater than the interest earnings for a single period deviation from the collusive outcome.

This analysis can give you an idea of when an industry you might be dealing with may be prone to non-competitive pricing. The idea is that collusion is sometimes easier to sustain in the sense that firms in an industry have more to gain from collusion than the 'punishment' that might arise if they deviate and compete. The following factors will all make tacit collusion more likely:

- The lower the interest rate (i.e., the more the future is weighted relative to the present): in this case, the short-term benefit to a potential deviator is not worth much
- The lower the speed at which prices can be adjusted so that the time a deviator could earn profits is short, and hence not valuable relative to future collusive profits
- The fewer firms there are in the industry
- The lower the competitive profits that will result if collusion breaks down
- The more transparent the firms' pricing to one another; allowing them to react more quickly to discounting by any one of them
- The more equally sized the firms are (see the 'Digging deeper' box below).

If you identify that many of these conditions are present, you might be vulnerable to collusive pricing even where a monopolist is not present.

DIGGING

DEEPER

### Different sized firms

Suppose that there are two competitors in an industry with market shares of $s \leq \frac{1}{2}$ and $1 - s \geq \frac{1}{2}$ (say arising from different capacities or costs). Suppose that their common interest rate is $r$ and that the collusive industry profits is $\Pi^m$. Firms play a 'tit for tat' punishment strategy. One possible strategy is to collude unless someone competes and then compete forevermore. Let's assume that competitive profits are 0 and that a deviating firm can gain all of $\Pi^m$ for a short period. In this case, a firm with market share of $s$ will be willing to collude if:

$$s\Pi^m(1+\tfrac{1}{1+r}+\tfrac{1}{(1+r)^2}+...) \geq \Pi^m + \tfrac{1}{1+r}.0 \Rightarrow (1-s)\Pi^m \leq \tfrac{1}{r}s\Pi^m$$

This reduces to $\frac{1}{1+r} \geq 1-s$. Firms are more likely to collude and weight future collusive profits over current competitive gains if their discount rate is low. This calculation shows that a firm with market share $s$ is more likely to collude when its market share is close to that of the other firm. Put simply, smaller firms are more likely to deviate from collusive outcomes.

## Summary

When engaging in strategic pricing, firms need to consider the reactions of rivals to price changes. As we have demonstrated here, the ultimate outcomes in an industry can be markedly different depending upon whether other firms are expected to maintain their price (price competition), maintain their quantity (quantity competition) or to react aggressively (tacit collusion). Ironically, the stronger the potential competitive response, the more likely it is for firms to 'toe the line' and maintain higher prices.

The chapter has also demonstrated that anticipating how strategic investments such as product differentiation and cost reduction may impact on the nature of price competition can influence the returns to those investments. In some cases, the strategic benefits from an investment may be higher even if rivals follow suit (e.g., product differentiation). In other cases, those benefits may be lower as competition is intensified and may cause others to respond in a similar way, eliminating all investment returns (e.g., for cost reduction under price competition).

The idea is that when considering strategic pricing or actions that may impact on price competition, a careful analysis of possible rival responses is required. To look only at the direct or immediate profits from an action and not the longer-term consequences can lead to a mis-evaluation of possible investment returns.

# Informative pricing

The previous chapters in this part have shown how firms set prices both non-strategically and strategically. In so doing, it has been assumed that the structure of the industry remains the same. Specifically, that means that different pricing choices do not lead to entry or exit of firms from the industry.

In reality, however, many firms and agents look to prevailing prices in order to tell them something about continued prospects in the industry. The canonical examples are of workers who look at prevailing wages in an industry to work out if it is worth acquiring the skills for that industry or farmers who look at commodity prices to determine what crops they should plant.

The role of prices as signals that drive individual behaviour is one of the central notions of economics. In the 1940s, an Austrian economist – Friedrich von Hayek – argued that the chief virtue of the market system was the ability of prices to aggregate important information from a wide variety of sources and send signals to agents as to the decisions they should make to maximise their own surplus.

Here we examine the informational role of prices in determining whether firms or agents should enter or exit an industry. When is it the case that one can look to prevailing prices to answer this question? After all, if, upon entry, the nature of price competition changes then the current price may not be a very accurate signal as to entry prospects at all. Moreover, if current high prices arise because of an incumbent's advantage with respect to many customers, then you may not be able to attain those prices upon entry. Hence, prevailing prices may not signal the prices you will receive for your products. A key consideration regarding the accuracy of the price signal is the absence or presence of high barriers to entry.

## No barriers to entry

Prevailing prices can provide a good signal of the profitability of entry when barriers to entry are low. To see this, here we consider two instances of low entry barriers allowing an accurate signal before turning to consider how entry barriers may prevent that signal.

### Perfect competition

Consider an industry with many firms, each of whom operates on a small scale. You are considering entering that industry and observe the prevailing price of $P$. You also know that your average unit costs (that is, your fixed costs plus variable costs divided by expected unit sales) should you enter on a small scale would be $c$. In this situation, your entry decision is easy: enter if $P \geq c$, otherwise do not enter.

The reason why the entry decision is easy is that with many firms each operating on a small scale, your entry is (i) unlikely to result in a significant change in price, and (ii) unlikely to provoke a response from current incumbents. This is because each is small and their own decisions have an insignificant impact on price. A situation where firms have no impact on the prevailing price regardless of whether they produce nothing or at their full capacity is a situation of *perfect competition*.

This is not to say that the decisions of a number of firms do not add up. If $P > c$ for many potential entrants, then as more and more enter the prevailing price will fall (as supply in the industry expands while the demand curve stays the same). In the long-run, $P = c$. In this situation, firms with average costs below $P$ will continue to earn profits but marginal firms (i.e., ones just indifferent between entering or exiting) will earn no surplus.

Similarly, should there be a decline in demand, it may be the case that for many firms in the industry $P < c$. In this case, those firms will exit the industry. This will reduce supply and cause $P$ to rise. In the end, the long-run equilibrium will be such that the marginal firms are earning zero profits.

As mentioned earlier, there are many industries where there are many firms operating at a small scale that fit the model of perfect competition. In these markets, prevailing prices act as a signal to firms as to their activities. If prices are such that they can make a profit from entry, then firms will enter. This situation operates in many commodity markets but also in financial markets. There, investors take prevailing prices of shares as signals as to whether they should become owners of those shares or not. Investors' trading decisions do not individually have an impact on price but in aggregate cause shares to increase or fall in value reflecting the aggregate information and beliefs investors have about their ultimate rate of return.

## Potential competition

The perfect competition case demonstrates how small-scale entry can lead to a situation where price equals average cost for many incumbent firms in the long run. But what would happen if there was just a single incumbent who enjoyed economies of scale over the entire market demand? Would that constitute an entry barrier for other firms allowing that incumbent to set its prices above average costs?

There is a situation in which no such barrier would exist. Suppose that a firm priced at $P^m$, as in Figure 10.1. Notice that that firm enjoys economies of scale in that average costs decline over the whole range of possible market demand. This might arise because that firm has a fixed cost component and a constant unit cost component in their production technology; i.e., their technology is a natural monopoly. That firm would be earning a positive economic profit.

**Figure 10.1** Perfect contestability

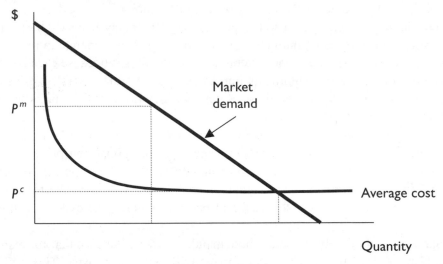

However, suppose also that there existed potential entrants with access to the same production technology. If there were no sunk costs associated with entry or exit, then an entrant could enter the market with a price below $P^m$ and capture the entire market. That entrant could realise sufficient scale economies at that price to undercut the incumbent.

What is important here, however, is that the same 'winner-take-all' entry strategy could be used by a potential entrant (or indeed an incumbent) until such time that it was not profitable. If each had access to identical technologies, that would result in a price such as $P^c$, which would just equal average costs.

This describes the operation of a *perfectly contestable market* where even a monopolist is subject to the discipline of potential competition should they raise their price by too much. Of course, the way in which the monopolist is driven to price at average cost (just as in a perfectly competitive market) is the fear of hit and run entry where the monopolist suddenly finds themselves with no consumers. In reality, however, the operation of this may not be that sudden as customer inertia slows the process down. Nonetheless, the fear that large-scale entry may cause a firm to lose too many customers to achieve sufficient scale themselves can be a discipline on their pricing.

Notice that what this means is that, like in perfectly competitive markets, prevailing prices in perfectly contestable markets are signals to entrants about whether entry will be worthwhile.

## Barriers to entry

As discussed in the last section, the absence of entry barriers means that prevailing prices reflect the average costs of incumbents. This gives entrants a signal as to what type of competition they might face upon entry and whether they will be able to build sufficient market share to make entry profitable. However, when entrants face tougher production requirements or more difficulty in securing customers than incumbents, prevailing prices may not be a good signal of the conditions entrants will face upon entry. Consequently, entrants face a much more difficult decision.

Here we explore two of the main sources of entry barriers: customer lock-in that prevents entrants from competing for significant numbers of customers and sunk costs that incumbents have already incurred and so may not be easily recoverable for entrants in post-entry competition.

### Customer lock-in

When consumers have learned to use a firm's product, those consumers may find it costly to switch to another firm's product and may need a significant price discount to do so. This type of switching cost may also arise when consumers' own complementary products, which are compatible with the incumbent's product but not the entrant's product, have formed habits that make switching costly or have entered into long-term contracts with incumbents. When switching costs are significant, customers may be effectively locked-in to the incumbent and not be contestable by entrants.

To see how this works, suppose that an incumbent has unit production costs of $C$ while an entrant has unit costs of $c < C$. Suppose also that the prevailing price charged by incumbents is $P > C$. Ordinarily, this would imply that entry would be profitable. However, suppose that, for consumers, if they were to switch to the entrant they would face a cost of $S$ per unit of consumption.

In this case, upon entry, the entrant will need to set their price, $p$, lower than $P - S$. Otherwise, customers will be better off staying with the incumbent. So, at a minimum, entry will only be profitable if $P - S > c$.

However, things are more difficult than this because the incumbent may respond to entry by dropping their price, $P$. In a worst-case scenario for the entrant, this price could fall to $C$. In this case, entry will only be profitable if $C - S > c$ or $C - c > S$. Thus, profitable entry requires a significant cost advantage on the part of the entrant. If this advantage is not present the incumbent can get away with charging a price well in excess of their costs. This prevailing price will not be itself a good signal to entrants as to the profitability of entry. They will have to look at non-price factors such as switching costs and their estimate of the incumbent's actual unit costs in order to make this decision.

### Sunk costs

One of the key conditions for perfect contestability is that there exist no sunk costs associated with entry or exit. This is a key condition because, in principle, even small sunk costs can allow an incumbent to operate free of the discipline of potential competition.

To see this, suppose that an entrant faced a sunk cost of $E > 0$. This might be costs associated with building a plant, advertising or research and development. Other than that the entrant's costs are the same as the incumbent. In this situation, one might think that the incumbent would price just low enough to make it not worthwhile for an entrant to enter and still be able to earn sufficient profits to cover $E$. This type of price is called a *limit price*; a price just low enough to deter entry. Obviously, the higher is $E$, the higher the limit price can be.

However, this type of limit price assumes that the incumbent is not able to adjust its price post-entry. Suppose, however, that such an adjustment is possible. If this is so then an incumbent may be able to keep its price at an unconstrained monopoly level, $P^m$, and entry from an equally efficient entrant may never occur.

To see this we need to work backwards and consider what post-entry pricing looks like. That price will be set by competition between the incumbent and entrant. If this competition is in prices, then price may fall below average costs. In this situation, those prices would be unsustainable and eventually one firm would exit the market. If both firms have equal costs, the entrant will only enter when the costs of the 'price war' are greater than the costs of a continued monopoly. The problem is that this means that even should the entrant prevail, its costs associated with entering and staying in the market would exceed any monopoly profits it may earn later on. Not surprisingly, under these circumstances an entrant would probably not choose to enter.

The more efficient an entrant is than the incumbent (in terms of lower costs), the more likely that an entrant will find it profitable to enter an industry even where modest sunk costs are present. But those sunk costs do represent a barrier to entry. Moreover, even the prospect of efficient entry is not a reason for an incumbent protected by sunk costs to price lower than the unconstrained monopoly level. After all, that price can fall post-entry and need not fall before then.

What this means is that the prevailing price may be a very poor signal as to the profitability of entry. Thus, in contrast to the perfectly competitive or contestable cases, the presence of sunk costs or customer inertia can mean that the current price reflects market power caused by barriers to entry rather than what an entrant might expect to earn in that market.

### Endogenous sunk costs

The presence of sunk entry costs, even when there are some economies of scale, will become less of an entry barrier as markets grow in size (say, due to population growth). In reality, in many industries, while a few firms compete in a market, the number of firms does not grow as quickly as the market does. What happens is that incumbent firms grow in size.

This occurs because sunk entry costs are not an exogenous or fixed amount. Instead, the amount an entrant will have to 'pay' to enter is in part a function of the actions of incumbents; that is, sunk costs are endogenous, arising out of incumbent choices. So, while an incumbent may not set its price low to forestall entry, it may make strategic investments that raise sunk entry costs.

R&D and advertising expenditures represent sunk costs that improve product quality. Moreover, the greater those expenditures, the higher is product quality in the eyes of consumers. What this means is that over time, incumbents will make continual improvements to product quality. For an entrant this means that the sunk costs associated with matching or beating that product quality are also growing over time. Not surprisingly, this escalation by incumbents has the effect of reducing the probability of entry as incumbents move first to improve offerings to their growing customer bases.

## Manipulating price signals

In some situations, entrants may still find it worthwhile to enter even when they face sunk entry costs. This occurs when they know that their cost advantage is very significant and that they can profitably undercut incumbents. This possibility, however, is a problem for some incumbents as the entrant may misjudge their cost advantage and enter. In this situation, the entrant may ultimately wish they had not entered but both the incumbent and entrant will end up competing with one another. This 'mistake' therefore costs the incumbent its monopoly profits.

Here we demonstrate how some incumbents can use prevailing prices to signal their competitive strength. This enables them to still earn healthy profits but also allows them to manipulate the entry decision in their favour. That is, an appropriately set price can deter entry but still result in ongoing profits. This situation arises because the incumbent knows its costs but the entrant needs to guess them; that is, there is asymmetric information.

To see how this works consider a market with $N$ identical consumers, each of whom value a unit of a good at $100. If there is currently a single seller in that market and they can set a posted price, that price will be $100.

There is also a potential entrant in the market whose unit costs are $20 per unit. It is common knowledge among potential entrants that the incumbent's unit costs may be $20 or $50 and that the probability of it being the low cost outcome is ½. Entrants also understand that consumers value the product at $100 per unit.

Suppose there are some small entry costs, $E$. Also, suppose that, should the incumbent's costs be $50, then an entrant could enter and charge $49 and still earn enough profits to cover those entry costs (i.e., ($49 – $20)$N > E$). In this case, sunk entry costs do not appear to be a barrier to entry for a low-cost firm.

The problem is that the entrant does not know whether the incumbent is high or low cost. If the incumbent is a high-cost firm, then upon entry, the incumbent will be unable to match the entrant's price. But if it can match the price, then the entrant will have discovered that the incumbent is a low-cost firm. In this case, the price to consumers will fall to $20 and the entrant will not make sufficient profits to cover sunk costs.

Absent other information, the decision to enter is a decision made under uncertainty. Figure 10.2 shows the decision tree facing the entrant. Working backwards, notice that if ½($29)$N > E$, then the entrant will enter and not otherwise.

**Figure 10.2** Entry decision under uncertainty

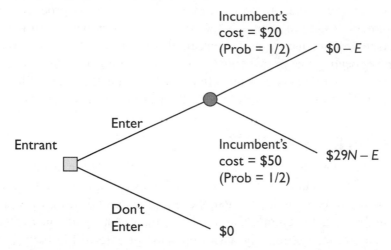

This, however, is a problem for the incumbent. If the incumbent indeed has low costs, the entrant might gamble and enter. But this causes the incumbent to lose its profits as well. The entrant may regret the entry decision, but will have no reason to exit given that entry costs have already been incurred.

What an incumbent could do, in this instance, is use their current price as a signal of the low costs. For instance, setting $P = \$50$ or lower would send this signal as a high-cost firm would never find this worthwhile. However, it need not go this far. All a low-cost incumbent needs to do is:

1. Set $P$ such that a high-cost firm would find it unprofitable even if this led to entry, and

2. set $P$ such that the incumbent still finds it optimal to deter entry and not instead charge $100.

If that price can be found, a low-cost incumbent will be able to send a credible signal to potential entrants and deter entry.

How do we find that price? The simplest way to see how this works is to imagine that there are two periods of time: a pre-entry and a post-entry period. We will also assume that incumbents do not discount the future. In this case, for the chosen price to be one that a high-cost firm would not choose to set (and instead keep its price at $100), the following inequality needs to be satisfied:

$$(\$100 - \$50)N > (P - \$50)N + (P - \$50)N$$

Or

$$P < \$75$$

This is condition (a) above. If the low-cost incumbent sets a price lower than $75, a high-cost incumbent would not want to mimic this price even if it deterred entry.

In addition, the price chosen by the low-cost incumbent must still make it profitable for it to want to deter entry and not instead charge $P = \$100$. This requires that $P$ satisfy:

$$(P - \$20)N + (P - \$20)N > (\$100 - \$20)N$$

$$\text{Or } P > \$60$$

Any price above $60 satisfies condition (b). Putting the two conditions together, if the incumbent sets a price between $60 and $75, then this will be a credible signal to entrants that it is, indeed, low cost *and* will deter entry.

What is interesting here is that the incumbent can set a price of $74, well below the unconstrained monopoly price of $100. In effect, this is a limit price. What makes it worthwhile is that the low-cost incumbent knows that the potential entrant is unsure of the incumbent's costs and may enter by 'mistake'. So the incumbent sacrifices profits in the short term to signal its 'competitive strength' to the entrant.

Ultimately, this means that the incumbent's pricing is constrained by potential competition and in fact does provide a signal of the profitability of entry for entrants. In addition, entry does, in fact, occur when it is needed the most – i.e., when the incumbent has high costs – as such incumbents have no incentive to sacrifice short-term profits to deter entry.

## Paying for entry

Above we demonstrated how sunk entry costs, even when modest, can be a significant entry barrier as entrants become concerned about recovering those costs in a tough post-entry environment. The fact that entry might be deterred is also a problem for consumers. In some markets, those consumers may be large and may find it worthwhile to subsidise entry costs so as to encourage competitive entry.

For example, suppose there is a large buyer for a product and many smaller buyers. Currently, there is only a single supplier in the industry and that supplier charges all consumers $P^m$ per unit. There are also sunk entry costs of $E$ and that post-entry price would fall to marginal cost, so entrants do not find it worthwhile to enter.

In this case, if an entrant's marginal cost is $c$, and the large buyer's demand is $x$, then if $(P - c)x > E$, it may be worthwhile for the large buyer to pay the entrant to enter. This could be achieved by offering the entrant a guaranteed margin on all sales to the large buyer or by an upfront payment. Thus, large buyers may themselves be a mechanism by which entry barriers can be overcome.

## Summary

Prevailing prices can sometimes provide good information to entrants as to the profitability of entry. When there is perfect competition or perfect contestability, prevailing prices reflect incumbent costs. Thus, an entrant can get an accurate assessment of any post-entry cost advantages. Even when this information may not be transparent, some incumbents may set prevailing prices to signal post-entry cost conditions.

However, when barriers to entry are significant, the prevailing prices may be no guide to post-entry competitive decisions. In this case, only entrants confident in their superior cost efficiency or product quality will enter. However, these judgments will rely on more than simply price information. Assessments will have to be made about customer lock-in and also incumbents' true cost conditions.

# Part IV

# Contracting

In the previous parts, we have considered how economic value can be created through cooperation, how valuable trading opportunities might be missed through pre-emptive strategic actions (e.g., hold-up problems) and the impact of private information limiting the types of contracts that might be written.

This part develops these ideas further to consider what instruments might be used to enhance value creation when contracts are incomplete or are imperfect because one party to a transaction has more information than another. We first consider this in relation to external contracting – that is, contracting between firms. In this situation, our economic framework shows that some of the popular rationales for outsourcing and integration – that is, changes of asset ownership among firms – do not stand up to closer scrutiny. However, when contracts are incomplete and hold-up is an issue, ownership can serve as an instrument to assure an 'at risk' party of sufficient value appropriation to reward them for value-creating actions. Hence, ownership is a means of mitigating lost value that results from contractual incompleteness.

We also examine the use of incentive contracts that link pay to performance as a means of enhancing value creation. We demonstrate that, in some circumstances, value created can be maximised with appropriately structured incentives but that in many circumstances this is not without cost. Some performance measures are imperfect and either confer unwanted risk on agents or alternatively are capable of value-reducing distortion. These issues tend to cause parties to mute incentives and not achieve the total value that might otherwise be possible if there were no informational issues.

Relational contracts can sometimes fill these gaps and overcome incentives problems caused by contractual incompleteness or informational issues. However, we show that building a trusting relationship so that private interests are aligned, in general, requires patience and transparency, either of which may be lacking in certain situations.

# 11 External contracting

The focus of previous chapters has been on the prices that are formed for transactions that take place in the *market*. These prices involved an explicit exchange of goods and services for a monetary payment. In contrast, many transactions in the economy take place within firms. To be sure, those firms deal in the marketplace, transacting between consumers and suppliers. However, agents, groups and divisions within the firm also exchange goods and services with one another. While there may be 'prices' – transfer prices – involved in such transactions, these prices are often implicit. Moreover, to the extent that one part of the firm is paying another, from the point of view of the firm's overall profit, the price does not necessarily matter.

In this chapter, we conceptualise whether a transaction can be viewed as taking place within a firm or in the market. Our particular concern is the circumstances under which this matters. Specifically, we ask the question first raised by Nobel laureate, Ronald Coase: *when is it more efficient for a transaction to take place within a firm or in the market?*[1] He was particularly concerned with the prevailing wisdom among economists in the early 20th century that markets were more efficient in organising economic activity than command or centrally planned structures. Yet the largest and most successful firms in capitalist economies were organised in the latter manner. Coase argued that transactions have different costs associated with them depending upon whether they are undertaken by the firm or in the market. So when the costs of transacting are lower in the firm than the market, that transaction will take place within the firm and vice versa. The usefulness of this insight, however, requires us to consider more precisely what these transactions costs are.

Before considering this, we will examine how to analyse transactions and classify a transaction on the basis of whether it is a within-firm transaction or market transaction. Based on the added value framework already developed in this book, we will then look at the relative efficiency of these transactions. In so doing, it will be demonstrated that when parties can freely negotiate over all relevant productive variables, within firm and market transactions are equally efficient – they lead to outcomes that create precisely the same value. The only difference is *distributional*: some agents may be better off (i.e., their added value is higher) when organising transactions within a firm.

Towards the end of this chapter we will point to two types of environments that alter this conclusion: market imperfections and contractual incompleteness. For the moment, however, we will concentrate on developing the irrelevance result that firm boundaries do not matter for efficiency – a result also attributable to Coase – so as to provide a benchmark and basis for which to discuss the role of transactions costs. This we develop by use of a simple example. Then we will show that this insight is particularly useful in reconsidering some commonly held rationales for outsourcing and integration.

## A definition of the firm

Determining whether a transaction takes place within a firm or not is a difficult matter. One might point to the existence of negotiations as an indicator of market behaviour. However, many firms have decision-makers with diverse interests, and different groups or divisions may negotiate with one another over strategies, budget allocations and the like.

Another viewpoint considers the firm as a 'nexus of contracts'. The firm makes contracts with suppliers, customers and complementors. It is the conduit through which all of these agents realise value. While this is certainly true, there is a sense in which every transaction involves some measure of contracting. Hence, this does not necessarily inform us where a firm starts and where it ends. If a firm has an ongoing relationship with a customer or supplier, is that person or organisation part of the firm or in the market? The boundaries based on this definition are unclear.

In this book, we take a simplistic approach to firm definition that has proved useful in analysing many issues to do with contracting between and within firms. We identify the firm with the collection of assets that is under the control of a decision-maker or set of decision-makers. In this view the firm is defined by the collection of assets that are owned or controlled by certain decision-makers. An individual decision-maker is part of the firm if their exit from negotiations involving the firm's assets also removes those assets from productive activities (or otherwise results in their sale). An agent is not part of the firm if their exit means that they are excluded from the use and returns that might be generated from an assets use.[2] This is a *property rights* approach to firm definition.

## The importance of property rights

We will illustrate how to conceive of firm boundaries in terms of asset ownership shortly. Before doing this, it is worth clarifying what we mean by ownership and property rights over assets.

In modern economies, when you own or have property rights over an asset this gives you two separate legal rights:

- *Residual rights of control*: when you own an asset you can control what uses it is put to (at least to an extent). There may be contractual, legal and even moral constraints on the way you use an asset that limit your control. So what ownership really gives you is the ability to use the asset in ways that are not precluded by these other restrictions. An excellent example of this is the control ownership of a car yields. A car's owner may drive the car wherever and whenever they want, subject to road rules. They may allow others to drive the car subject to licence and insurance restrictions. In effect, ownership confers a lot of freedom but this freedom is constrained in some well-specified dimensions.

- *Rights to residual returns*: owners of assets have the ability to exclude the assets from uses. This means that in order to generate returns from the use of an asset you do not own, you are forced to negotiate with the owner. You may negotiate over access to the asset or the transfer of its ownership. This gives the owner of the asset potential strength in negotiations and allows them to claim the residual returns an asset's use may generate.

The dual rights over control and returns give ownership value in negotiations. When you own an asset you bear the full financial impact of its performance. This gives you high incentives to maintain an asset and ensure that it is used in a way that maximises your returns. In any negotiations, if there is a breakdown, you can take the asset with you. This gives you bargaining power and the ability to claim a high fraction of the asset's contribution to value.

These features of ownership can be illustrated by considering your bargaining position when you evaluate your firm's outsourcing decision. Suppose that your photocopying needs require two inputs: a machine (the photocopier) and a person to operate the machine. If the firm outsources its photocopying, it employs a firm who owns the photocopier and employs the labour input. On the other hand, if the firm does its own photocopying, it owns the machine and employs someone to operate it. If the firm is unhappy with the quality and speed of copying, in the outsourcing case it has to negotiate with the photocopying firm and will have to sack both it and, with it, its employee if it is dissatisfied (even though the employee may not be at fault). On the other hand, with its own photocopying, the firm bears responsibility for the performance of the copier and cannot sack it. It can only sack the employee. As we will see below, this can influence the share of the value generated by photocopying services that the firm itself receives, although it may not affect the total value created from photocopying per se.

## A simple motivating example

Suppose there are two agents – a manufacturer and a marketer. By using a particular machine, the manufacturer can produce a good that the marketer can sell on the open market. The machine is essential to production; the good cannot be manufactured without access to it. On the other hand, we assume that the machine, if operated without the manufacturer and the marketer, could not earn positive profits elsewhere. Nonetheless, if either the manufacturer or the marketer uses the machine in production, they can earn a positive profit.

### Effort and value created

What the various levels of effort on the part of the marketer and manufacturer mean for profits are summarised in Table 11.1.

**Table 11.1** Effects of different levels of marketing and manufacturing efforts

| | | Marketer | |
|---|---|---|---|
| | | Low | High |
| **Manufacturer** | Low | $0 | $100 |
| | High | $50 | $200 |

The manufacturer has the ability to lower production costs while the marketer can expend effort in increasing revenue. In particular, if both the manufacturer and marketer contribute a high level of effort, this generates profits of $200. This is in contrast to the outcome where neither agent exerts a high level of effort. In this case, no economic profit is generated. This is equivalent to the value the machine could earn if neither agent utilised it or its output.

If only one agent utilises the machine or its output, production and marketing are still possible. However, in each case, the profits earned are as if the other agent provided a low effort level. One reason for this could be that while there are many agents who can easily substitute a low effort level of service, only the manufacturer and marketer have the ability to, if they wish to, provide a higher effort level in their respective activities. This means that, without the marketer, the manufacturer can, by utilising the machine, earn $50 in profits while the marketer on its own can earn $100 in profits. Notice that, if both agents provide a high level of effort, profits are greater than the sum of their independent earnings. Hence, the agents are complementors.

There are costs involved in expending effort, however. We assume here that the monetary equivalent of the manufacturer's costs in providing a high effort rather than low effort for cost reduction is $20, while the marketer's cost of providing higher rather than low effort is $80. This means that it is always value creating for each agent to provide a high effort level. Even if they utilise the machine without the cooperation of the other agent, the value created from high effort exceeds the cost of that effort (i.e., $100 > $80 and $50 > $20, respectively).

## The effect of ownership

As mentioned earlier, in this book we take the view that the ownership of non-human assets or capital defines a firm. In this simple example, there is only one such asset – the machine. Given this, there are four ownership possibilities:

- *Ownership by the manufacturer*: the manufacturer owns the machine and employs the marketer to sell its output (or alternatively, sells the product to the marketer who retails it).
- *Ownership by the marketer*: the marketer owns the machine and employs the manufacturer to use it to produce output that the marketer retails.

- *Joint ownership by the manufacturer and marketer*: the manufacturer and the marketer both own the machine, its output and any resulting revenues. They negotiate the division of those revenues among themselves.
- *Ownership by a third party*: a third party owns the machine and employs the manufacturer and the marketer to produce and sell output from it (or alternatively, sells the product to the marketer who retails it).

In each case, as depicted in Figure 11.1, the boundary of the firm is different. This is because the asset is linked to the decisions of the marketer, manufacturer, both or neither. Each structure, therefore, represents a different type of integration and employment configuration.

What ownership of the asset means is that during any negotiations over who receives what proportion of total value created, the agent with the asset can threaten to exclude other agents from use or access to it. As the machine is essential to the creation of value, ownership of the machine makes the owner essential in any negotiations. Note that under joint ownership, the use of the asset requires the agreement of both agents. This makes both agents essential. Recall that when this occurs an agent's added value becomes equal to total value created.

**Figure 11.1** Ownership and firm boundaries

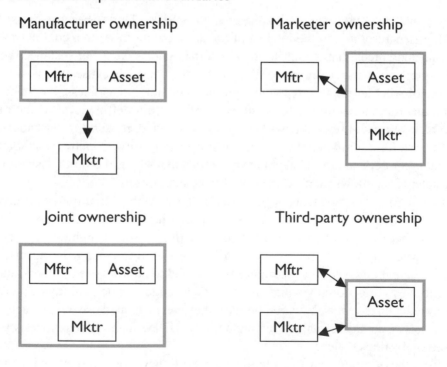

### Added value and ownership structure

The added values of each agent and their expected earnings under an assumption of equal negotiating ability are listed in Table 11.2 for each ownership structure. Note that total value created is the value realised when both the manufacturer and marketer choose high effort levels, that is, $200 – $80 – $20 = $100.

**Table 11.2** Added values and expected earnings (equal negotiating ability is assumed)

| Ownership structure | Manufacturer's added value (expected surplus) | Marketer's added value (expected surplus | Third party's added value (expected surplus) |
|---|---|---|---|
| Manufacturer ownership | $100 ($65) | $70 ($35) | $0 ($0) |
| Marketer ownership | $80 ($40) | $100 ($60) | $0 ($0) |
| Joint ownership | $100 ($50) | $100 ($50) | $0 ($0) |
| Third party ownership | $80 ($30) | $70 ($20) | $100 ($50) |

Notice that, in each case, total value created is $100. This is because, regardless of ownership structure, it is in the interest of the asset owner to write a contract with each agent that guarantees that a high level of effort is undertaken. For instance, when the manufacturer owns the asset, it exerts a high effort level because this is worthwhile regardless of whether it has agreement with the marketer. Nonetheless, the marketer can raise the manufacturer's profits by $100 by exerting a high effort level. If the marketer were to receive a fixed reward regardless of effort exerted, it would never choose a high level of effort. In order to benefit from the positive externality given by the marketer, it is in the manufacturer's interest to negotiate a contract that shares the surplus generated with the marketer. This allows total value created to be maximised.

Similar sharing arrangements occur under each ownership structure and it is possible for the asset owner to contract with agents to supply a high effort level. Agents, therefore, receive a higher reward (or any reward at all) only if they exert a high effort level.

What ownership does affect is the *distribution* of value among the agents. This is because the agent that owns the asset can always withdraw it from use by others, and hence that agent is essential for any value creation. Their added value is always equal to total value created. Other agents, however, because they can be denied use of the machine, may find themselves outside of value-creating activity. Hence, their added value is typically less than total value created.

So, from the point of view of an individual agent, they would rather own the machine than not. This allows them a greater share of any value created. However, in each case, ownership does not matter for the efficiency with which the firm is run. In all cases, both the marketer and manufacturer will be encouraged and negotiate to provide a high effort level.

## The Coase Theorem

This general outcome is a variant of the *Coase Theorem*. We can state that theorem as follows:

> *If all relevant variables (i.e., effort) are contractible, then ownership of an asset only affects the distribution of value and not the value realised under each structure.*

What this means is that the firm, defined by the asset's ownership, will be equally productive regardless of where its precise boundaries are. This suggests that as a benchmark, the dividing line between firm and market does not matter. Assets will be productive regardless of whether their outputs are traded among agents or directly to final consumers.

DIGGING DEEPER

### The Coase Theorem and externalities

In our simple example, the manufacturer and marketer's respective effort choices affected value created, and hence the returns an asset owner could expect to earn. When an agent's private actions affect social returns, we say that the action potentially imposes an externality on others. Through effective contracting the affected party can either compensate or provide inducements for the other party to undertake a socially desirable action. The result is that socially desirable actions are undertaken, although the distribution of the gains depends on each agent's relative bargaining position.

When Coase originally made this observation,[3] he was concerned with some very pervasive externalities associated with environmental harm. He considered the costs imposed on a farmer if cattle from a neighbouring farm stray on its land. Such straying could be overcome if a fence was built. Suppose the total damage caused by the cattle to the neighbour is valued at $100 but the fence cost is $50. Then it is socially desirable for the fence to be built. But will the fence actually get built? Coase argued that it would regardless of whether the farmer was held liable for the damage caused to the neighbour.

To see this: suppose the farmer was legally liable for the $100 damage. In effect, this gives the neighbour the right to enforce property rights. Then the farmer would build the fence rather than pay a penalty to the neighbour.

On the other hand, suppose the farmer was not legally liable and had a right to let cattle go wherever they happened to. Then the neighbour would find it desirable to pay the farmer $50 to build the fence or, indeed, build the fence himself. The end result is that, regardless of the assignment of property rights (i.e., liability rule), the socially desirable outcome is realised.

The same thing would hold if the cost of the fence were $200 rather than $50. In this case, it is not socially desirable for the fence to be built. If the farmer is liable for the damage caused, he will simply opt to pay the $100 penalty rather than build the fence. If the farmer were not liable, the neighbour would not decide to pay for, or build the fence, as the benefit he receives ($100) would not outweigh the costs of so doing.

This powerful result is known as the *Coase Theorem*. It demonstrates why the assignment of property rights does not matter for efficiency concerns but is important from a distributive point of view. When the farmer is liable, he is worse off relative to when he is not liable.

## Misconceptions about firm boundaries

There are many important decisions made by businesses that affect the boundaries of the firm. These include decisions to spin-off and focus on core competencies, to merge with another firm to realise synergies and whether or not to outsource a given function or service. When such decisions are made, they are made with a view to enhancing efficiency or value created. Distributional concerns do not necessarily come into play as, in each case, asset ownership or property rights are being traded. If purchasers of an asset were to find themselves in a superior bargaining position after the transfer, they would have to compensate the seller prior to an exchange taking place. Such exchanges of asset ownership or property rights would, therefore, only occur if this enhanced overall value created.

The logic of the Coase Theorem questions the value-creating or efficiency rationales behind decisions about firm boundaries. To be sure, the Coase Theorem only holds under certain conditions and below we consider these. Nonetheless, some of the basic rationales for spin-offs, mergers and outsourcing rest on other criteria. In particular, decisions to spin-off functions are often based on arguments regarding the need to realise economies of scale; decisions to merge, on the other hand, are motivated by a concern to generate economies of scope; while decisions to keep a function in-house often are based on arguments regarding supply assurance and imperfect competition. Here we review the logic of each of these arguments in the light of the Coase Theorem to highlight misconceptions that some people have regarding firm boundaries.

### Realise economies of scale

One reason that it is argued why firms should spin-off divisions or outsource functions is to allow those parts of the business to realise economies of scale. Recall that a technology can realise economies of scale if the long-run average cost of producing a greater level of output is falling as output rises. Therefore, one rationale behind outsourcing is the desire to allow that function or division to sell to other firms, thereby expanding output and lowering average costs. Broadly speaking if a function or division serves many customers that means that the associated fixed costs need not be duplicated.

To evaluate this argument let us return to the photocopying outsourcing decision discussed earlier. Imagine that business A has bought a photocopier but that they do not use it all of the time. Business B is considering buying a photocopier but do not believe they will utilise its full capacity either. If A's photocopier could be used to supply B's needs as well, then both firms would be better off. A and B are complementors in their ability to utilise a single photocopier.

One way for A and B to realise these gains is for A to outsource its photocopier and sell it to a firm that would be dedicated to photocopying only. That firm could then sell copying services to both A and B. Moreover, since this firm would face lower average costs than A did for photocopying, both A and B would better off, in terms of the price they pay for copying.

However, outsourcing is not necessarily the only way for A to realise scale economies. It could simply contract with B directly for B to utilise A's photocopying function. So A could go into the copying business. In principle, value created by this structure would be the same as outsourcing and hence, would make no difference to A or B. Each firm's photocopying expenses would be the same regardless.

To be sure, there may be other reasons why outsourcing photocopying services is a good idea. The point here is that economies of scale alone cannot justify such a decision. This is because these economies could be realised regardless of whether A outsources or undertakes photocopying services in-house.

### Realise economies of scope

An often-cited reason why two firms that are not direct competitors merge is to realise synergies or gains from economies of scope. Indeed, a similar rationale is used to justify the social value of mergers between competitors to anti-trust authorities. Economies of scope arise when it is cheaper to use the same plant or assets to produce two or more goods than it would be if each good were produced completely separately. One common situation of scope economies arises when two goods utilise the same resource that itself is subject to scale economies. As such, a merger is justified as the way of ensuring that those shared resources are not duplicated among firms.

Seen in the light of the Coase Theorem, however, we quickly realise that a merger is not the only way to realise scope economies. Two firms that identify the resource or asset that gives rise to such economies, or indeed the complementarities between their goods in the marketplace, need not merge to realise those gains. A contractual arrangement among them can do the job in exactly the same way that the economies of scale could be realised in the earlier photocopier example.[4]

Once again, there may be reasons why value created might be lower when two firms are separate than when they merge. However, scope economies alone cannot explain why a merger is the only way to realise such efficiencies. Scope economies, like scale economies, can potentially be realised between contractual arrangements among firms and do not necessarily require all production to take place inside a single firm.

## Supply assurance

While scale or scope economy arguments are sometimes used to justify outsourcing, the need to assure supply is sometimes held up as a reason for having a particular function in-house. Once again, consider our photocopier example. Suppose that firm A was concerned with outsourcing because during times when it required a lot of photocopying it could not be assured that the independent copying firm would divert resources to it rather than to B or otherwise charge it a higher price. On the other hand, if it merely contracted with B for services, A could easily opt not to supply those services to B during high demand times. It would not be subject to any shortages or higher prices.

To see this, imagine that the marginal cost of providing a unit of photocopying services (say, 1000 copies) was $100. On a normal day, A would demand 750 copies while B would demand 100 copies. On a peak day, however, A would demand 1000 copies while B continued to demand 100 copies. On these days, if its copying was in-house, A could assure those 1000 copies were made by simply not providing those services to B on those days. But the key question is: would it want to?

Consider the behaviour of an independent copying service. Suppose that users of copying services had all of the bargaining power and could make take-it-or-leave-it price demands. In this case, in normal demand periods, both A and B could demand a price of 10 cents per copy. In high demand periods, however, total demand would exceed the capacity of the photocopier. Suppose A's willingness-to-pay for copies was $150 for 750 copies and $120 for the next 250 while B's was $140 for all of its 100 copies. In this case, total value created would be maximised by supplying A 900 copies and B 100 copies. So A's demand would not be satisfied. Moreover, at this level of demand, the copying firm would be able to raise B's price to 12 cents rather than 10 cents per copy.

If A had the copying service in-house, it could refuse to supply B during these time periods, justifying this on the basis that its own willingness-to-pay for the extra copies of 12 cents per copy exceeded its production costs of 10 cents per copy. Unfortunately, this would not be profit maximising behaviour for A. This is because its opportunity cost of supplying itself those 100 copies is its production cost ($10) plus profits it could earn by charging B 12 cents per copy ($2). So while A would earn an accounting profit by supplying itself, its economic profit from doing so would be negative.

Once again, where the boundaries of the firm lie does not alter value created (i.e., willingness-to-pay less opportunity cost). A could choose not to maximise value created but this would result in a reduction in its profits. It is simply too costly for A to assure its own supply when B values copying services above A's own marginal value.

# Market imperfections and integration

As we demonstrated in Chapter 9, when markets are very competitive, prices are close or equal to marginal costs of production. This means that when you consider your contracting options with suppliers or retailers along the vertical chain, you do not have to face the consequences of market imperfections; that is, dead-weight losses that might be associated with the exercise of monopoly power. If the firms you contract with have monopoly power, however, there may be losses in value associated with the exercise of that power. As such, it is sometimes argued that one reason for integrating (vertically) with suppliers, customers or complementors is to avoid the adverse consequences of the exercise of monopoly power.

Here we evaluate that argument. We demonstrate that it has some legitimacy when you operate in mass markets when contracting with other firms. Those firms are forced to use simple posted prices of the type described in Chapter 8. However, when pricing and consequent contracting possibilities are enriched, market imperfections are not a reason to integrate.

## A vertical pricing problem

Suppose there are two firms in a vertical production chain. An upstream firm produces an input that is turned on a one-for-one basis by the downstream firm into units of a final good. We assume that each firm is a monopolist; that is, the upstream firm is the only supplier of the input and the downstream firm is a monopolist in the final goods market. These assumptions are made to simplify matters, and similar considerations to those discussed here apply to any market where upstream and downstream firms have some monopoly power. It is also assumed that the final goods market is a mass one, so the downstream sets a single price for all customers there. Finally, it is assumed that each firm has a constant marginal cost. The downstream firm's marginal cost is $c$ per unit while the upstream firm's marginal cost is zero.

## Vertical integration

Consider first what would happen if the upstream and downstream firms were vertically integrated. The marginal cost of the integrated firm is the sum of the marginal costs of the upstream and downstream firms; in this case, $c$. The demand curve facing the integrated firm is the market demand curve for the final good produced by the downstream unit. Recall from Chapter 8 that, when choosing its price, the integrated firm equates its marginal cost to marginal revenue based on the market demand curve; as any mass market monopolist would. Figure 11.2 depicts this price and quantity as $P_I$ and $Q_I$ respectively. Notice that the integrated firm's profit is the area, $(P_I - c)Q_I$.

Figure 11.2: The double marginalisation problem

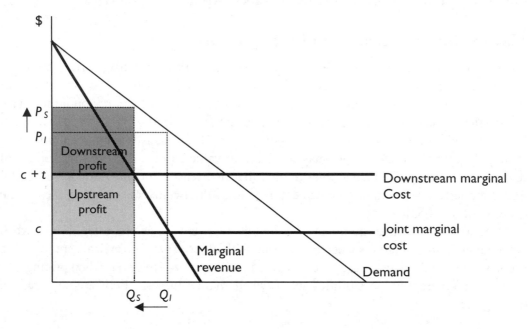

### Vertical Separation

Now suppose that the upstream and downstream firms are vertically separated. The downstream firm sets its price, $P_S$, to maximise its profits only and disregards any effect this might have on the profits of the upstream firm. The upstream firm charges a supply price of $t$ per unit to the downstream firm; once again, in so doing it disregards any adverse effect a higher price may have on the downstream firm's profits. As a result, the upstream firm surely charges a price, $t$, above its marginal cost of 0. If it did not do this it would not earn any profit. This, however, means that when the downstream firm chooses the final good price, it charges a mark-up over $c + t$, its marginal cost, rather than the 'true' marginal cost of $c$. This means that the final good price is higher and output lower than it would be if the firms were integrated.

As a result, however, the sum of upstream and downstream profit is necessarily less than the profit that would be realised by a vertically integrated monopolist. This is because monopoly profits are at a maximum only when the price charged to final consumers is $P_I$. Under vertical separation, the final good price is too high. As a result, industry profits are lower.

### Double marginalisation

This suggests that vertical integration might be preferable to both firms and their customers. The problem under vertical separation is that when each firm thinks about raising their price, they neglect the negative impact this has on the profits of the other. So, as was the case with complementors setting prices independently in Chapter 4, the prices set by each firm are too high from the point of view of maximising joint profits. This is the *double marginalisation* problem.

There is, however, an alternative to integration as a way of overcoming the problem of double marginalisation. The upstream firm can propose a two-part tariff (with a fixed charge as well as a usage rate) rather than a simple per unit price for the sale of the input to the downstream firm. The reason profits are lower under vertical separation is that the downstream firm does not use the 'true' marginal cost when choosing its output level. If the usage rate equals the upstream firm's marginal cost (in this case it would be zero), the downstream firm would choose an output of $Q_I$. In the absence of a fixed fee, its profit would equal the industry profit maximising level. The fixed fee is then used to allow the upstream firm to share in those profits. Given that those profits are always greater than the sum of profits under vertical separation, there is a fixed fee that would leave both firms better off. From the point of view of the industry, when a two-part tariff can be negotiated, the outcome is the same as under integration.

Seen in this light, the problem with market imperfections is only a problem when contracting or pricing possibilities are restricted to simple linear prices. When a non-linear price such as a two-part tariff can be negotiated, there is no difference from the firms' and consumers' perspective between a situation where there is vertical integration or vertical separation.

## Incomplete contracts and integration

While market imperfections may in some situations provide a motivation for integration, there is another important context where ownership structure can have an impact on total value created. This arises when contracts are incomplete.

In Chapter 7, we discussed how hold-up problems can arise when key decisions of agents cannot be contracted upon. In that situation, anticipating subsequent negotiations that do not consider the costs associated with those actions, agents may make decisions that do not maximise total value created.

One possible solution to such hold-up problems occurs when an agent taking a non-contractible action also owns key assets in the value chain. It is perhaps easiest to see this by returning to our simple motivating example. In our earlier discussion, we assumed that the effort levels of the marketer and manufacturer were contractible. This meant that in any negotiations, the costs associated with those actions would be part of the negotiations and may be shared among the agents concerned. However, it is also possible that those effort choices may be non-contractible. In this situation, the costs associated with them would not be part of any negotiation over value created and would be borne privately by the agents concerned.

This situation involves a two-stage game whereby the manufacturer and the marketer first choose their effort levels and incur any costs associated with a high effort level. They then negotiate with the asset owner over their participation in subsequent production based on the effort levels chosen. If both agents choose the high effort level, then the resulting negotiation will be over $200 in total value created. This is because, even though the manufacturer has incurred costs of $20 and the marketer costs of $80, those costs are sunk and cannot be withdrawn during negotiations. However, if either agent were to leave at that point, the benefits of that effort would also be lost. This gives the added values in those *ex post* negotiations as:

| Ownership structure | Manufacturer's added value (expected surplus) | Marketer's added value (expected surplus) | Third party's added value (expected surplus) |
|---|---|---|---|
| Manufacturer ownership | $200 ($125) | $150 ($75) | $0 ($0) |
| Marketer ownership | $100 ($50) | $200 ($150) | $0 ($0) |
| Joint ownership | $200 ($100) | $200 ($100) | $0 ($0) |
| Third party ownership | $100 ($16.67) | $150 ($66.67) | $200 ($116.67) |

There are several things that should be noted here. First, the manufacturer and marketer appropriate the most private surplus when they own the asset. Second, they appropriate the least private surplus when the third party owns the asset.

These facts are significant as it is their expected level of surplus that determines whether they undertake high effort or not. So the manufacturer is most likely to undertake that high effort if they own the asset but as a non-owner the marketer's effort incentive is lower. The reverse is true when the marketer owns the asset. Thus, while ownership can solve the hold-up problem for one agent it creates an additional hold-up problem for others. In the end, the owner should be an agent who (a) needs to appropriate a large share of value in order to justify a high effort level, and (b) an agent whose effort level is important for creating high total value. While we do not work through it here – you might attempt that on your own – it turns out that, in fact, giving the marketer ownership results in both productive agents engaging in high effort. In contrast, under any other ownership structure, the marketer puts in a low level of effort.

What this also indicates is the detrimental effect on incentives that third party ownership gives. The third party has no action to take and so the level of surplus they appropriate does not directly impact on total value created. However, any surplus they receive is surplus a productive agent does not receive. This reduces their expected private surplus, and hence reduces total incentives to undertake non-contractible actions that might create more value. In this sense, third party ownership is almost always undesirable, leading to an inefficient outcome.

## Markets for ownership

The Coase Theorem tells us about the efficiency of different ownership structures: that is, they are equally efficient. This means that if the productive and outside agents were to collectively decide on ownership, they would be indifferent as to which one to choose.

However, in many situations, there is no such collective decision on ownership. Instead, asset markets dictate the ownership structures that emerge. The easiest way to consider this is to suppose that initially an outside or third party owned the asset. There are many such third parties. Suppose that the initial owner decided to sell the asset in an auction. In this case, what would each agent bid?

A third party would be willing to pay an amount equal to their expected earnings from ownership. In this case of our simple example above, this would be $50. In contrast, the willingness-to-pay of a productive agent would be the amount they expected to earn as an owner less what they would earn as a non-owner. Suppose that these productive agents expected a third party to own the asset if they did not. Then, in our example, the willingness-to-pay for the marketer would be $40 (= $60 – $20) and for the manufacturer $35 (= $65 – $30). Each of these is below a third party's willingness-to-pay, and hence in an open auction we would expect the third party to win the auction and own the asset.

Notice, however, that if the productive agents could get together prior to the auction and agree to joint ownership should they win, then they would be willing to pay (jointly) $50 (=2 x $50 – $20 – $30); the same as a third party. In this case, either ownership outcome is possible.

In reality, it is much harder for productive agents to coordinate joint bids in asset markets the more of them are required for efficient production. This gives third parties an advantage in markets for ownership. Perhaps this explains why so many of the largest corporations are owned by passive investors whereas smaller firms tend to be owned and managed by individuals or partnerships.

## Summary

In the absence of hold-up problems caused by incomplete contracts, outsourcing or external contracting does not appear to hold any benefits over internal sourcing or integration. Arguments for outsourcing or integration based on scale and scope economies and supply assurance should, therefore, be treated warily. It should always be asked whether any issue could be resolved by a contractual arrangement as opposed to a change in ownership.

Ownership does give owners greater bargaining power. This means that when actions are not contractible, owners will appropriate a greater proportion of the surplus in subsequent bargaining, and hence will have a greater incentive to undertake value-maximising actions.

This suggests that outsourcing or integration may be desirable in different circumstances. Ultimately, the issue is whether individual incentives to undertake non-contractible actions can best be motivated by conferring ownership on those individuals. Hence, the analysis of the desirability of changes in ownership should begin with a careful consideration of what actions are contractible and how these are influenced by ownership.

## Endnotes

[1]    Coase Ronald (1937), 'The Nature of the Firm', *Economica*, Vol 4, pp 386–405.

[2]    This means that most employees are not considered to be part of the firm under this definition. They have a relationship – contracting or otherwise – with the firm in much the same way any supplier would.

[3]    See Coase, Ronald (October 1960), 'The Problem of Social Cost', *Journal of Law and Economics*, Vol 3 , pp 1–44.

[4]    For a discussion of this point in relation to diversification in the petroleum products industry see Teece, David J. (1980) 'Economies of Scope and the Scope of the Enterprise', *Journal of Economic Behavior and Organization*, 1 (3), pp 223–47.

# 12 Incentive contracting

Thus far, this book has painted a very simple picture of contracting. In a perfect contracting world, cooperation can be achieved between two or more parties by identifying the actions each must take to maximise total value created and then ensure that each party is adequately compensated for their participation in their cooperative venture. In this respect, each agent receives some additional surplus for their cooperation; this is their incentive to participate.

It is often the case, however, that agents also need to be compensated to take value-creating actions. In Chapter 6, we saw what would happen when this type of compensation is not possible. When actions are non-contractible, the risk of hold-up means that total value is not maximised. In Chapter 11, we saw how ownership might be used to mitigate this type of problem.

In many situations, actions are not simply contractible or non-contractible but somewhere in between. For instance, while it might be difficult for you to specify all of the actions a photocopier repairer should take, it may be possible for you to specify the outcomes you want (e.g., that the photocopier works immediately after repair and also in the weeks following some repair activity). In this situation, while the outcome may not be a perfect representation of the actions or effort you desire (e.g., the photocopier may break down for a new reason), it may be sufficiently correlated with it to make some form of contracting feasible. For a photocopier repairer, payment may only occur if the photocopier works well for a specified period of time.

In this chapter, we examine such situations. Their common feature is that there is one player (the agent) who has *private information* regarding the quality of the goods or services provided to another player (the principal). In this sense, contracting is incomplete. However, whereas with hold-up problems, it was considered impossible to contract *in advance* on the different outcomes from an agent's actions, here such contracting is possible. That is, while it may not be possible for a principal or, for that matter, a court of law, to observe what precise actions an agent has taken, it is possible for them to observe some consequence of those actions. So you may never know precisely what (if anything) your photocopier repairer did on a job but you (and others) will know whether the photocopier ran well following that job. It is this measurable outcome that can be contracted upon.

These types of situations are given various names that all mean the same thing. In general, the principal is someone who procures work or services from an agent. The agent can typically improve the quality of the product for the principal – and hence their value – by expending more costs. Not surprisingly, absent compensation for higher costs, the agent would prefer to save these and reduce the quality of the product provided. This gives rise to what insurance companies have called a *moral hazard* problem. In insurance, this is the idea that having been insured, agents do not undertake sufficient effort in care (e.g., car owners may choose to drive more recklessly or park in unsafe neighbourhoods). More generally, these problems arise because of a fundamental conflict of interest between the goals of the principal and the goals of the agent. This matters when the agent has information that the principal does not have (e.g., your car repairer may take advantage of your lack of knowledge by replacing parts that are working well). This more general problem is called a *principal-agent* problem or simply, an *agency* problem.

As we will see in this chapter, agency problems require special types of contracts – *incentive contracts* – to ensure total value created is maximised. We see incentive contracts throughout the economy. Salespeople and real estate agents paid on commission are a pervasive example, as are executives awarded stock options. Many companies offer performance bonuses while others offer career paths with higher pay and responsibility in return for good performance. Finally, many utility companies are regulated in a way that offers them incentives to reduce costs.

Incentive contracts take a measure of performance (based on outcomes) and relate that measure to the pay received by the agent. There are two main issues in this regard. First, how strong should the relationship of performance to pay be and, second, what performance measures should you look to include in incentive contracts? As we will see throughout this chapter, agency problems cannot simply be solved by putting in strong performance incentives. These incentives have additional costs in terms of value created that must be weighed against any benefits they bring.

## Putting outcome-based incentives into contracts

To begin, it is useful to consider the way in which an outcome-based performance measure impacts upon the compensation paid to agents. We will represent an outcome-based performance measure by a variable $x$. $x$ will denote things like the number of units sold by a salesperson, the growth in stock value by a funds manager, or the unit cost of a manufacturing plant. Conceptually, $x$ may comprise many different measures, the selection of which depends upon the situation. We will look at the selection of performance measures later in the chapter. For the moment, we concentrate on the relationship between $x$ and the pay received by an agent.

Perhaps the most familiar form of outcome-based incentives arise when an agent receives a bonus for superior performance. That is, pay is some base level or wage, $b$, plus an additional bonus $B$ if $x$ exceeds some level $\underline{x}$. The relationship between pay and performance can be graphed. This type of scheme is depicted in Figure 12.1 (a). Even if performance is low, the agent receives $b$ but if performance exceeds the threshold, they receive $b + B$. Thus, the relationship is a step function.

**Figure 12.1**

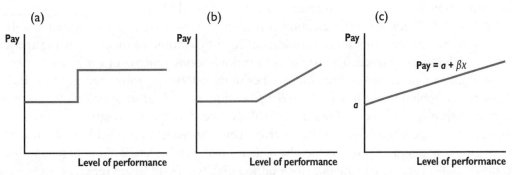

(a)    (b)    (c)

How does this impact on an agent's incentives? Imagine that in order to achieve a level of measured performance, $x$, the agent must incur private costs of $C(x)$. $C(.)$ is an increasing function so that performing better costs the agent more in terms of effort expended. In this situation, if $B = 0$, so that the agent only received a base pay unrelated to performance, the agent would choose their effort so that $x = 0$; as there would be no reason for the agent to perform better.

Having $B > 0$ causes the agent to consider a higher level of effort. One way to consider this is to compare an agent's choice between $x = 0$ and $x = \underline{x}$. This is a simple decision where the agent will choose $x = \underline{x}$, only if $b + B - C(\underline{x}) > b - C(0)$ or

$$B > C(\underline{x}) - C(0).$$

That is, the bonus exceeds the additional private costs the agent must incur to achieve the threshold level of performance. Not surprisingly, you can see from this inequality that the agent is more likely to perform better the higher is $B$ and the lower is $\underline{x}$.

Notice that this performance decision does not depend upon the base pay, $b$. Regardless of whether the agent performs well or not they receive this base pay so it does not impact on their performance decision. What it does impact on is their decision to engage in the activity altogether. That is, if their alternative outside employment would give them $\underline{b}$ in pay, then they would only participate in this contract if:

$$b + \max\{B - C(\underline{x}), -C(0)\} \geq \underline{b}.$$

Thus, raising base pay, $b$, can be used in inducing the agent to participate in the activity. However, the expected bonus can also assist in this as the agent looks forward to how the incentives impact upon their overall pay.

Of course, in conducting this analysis, we have considered the agent as having a choice between 0 or $\underline{x}$. In actuality, the agent can target any performance outcome. However, with a base plus threshold-bonus scheme, other performance outcomes will never be chosen by the agent. If the agent were to consider performing above 0 but less than $\underline{x}$, they would not expect to receive any bonus, and hence the additional costs of achieving modest performance would not be worth expending. Similarly, performance strictly greater than $\underline{x}$ would not give the agent more pay than $b + B$ but would involve additional cost. Thus, with a step function pay to performance relationship, the agent is effectively choosing between a very low level of performance and the threshold level.

This is a problem for value creation if it is in fact the case that the principal values superior performance more than the additional costs that would be incurred by the agent in achieving that performance. The pay plus threshold-bonus scheme incentivises the agent but only up to a point. If the principal wishes to encourage performance above $\underline{x}$, then a performance schedule that has a bonus, $B = \beta(x - \underline{x})$ if $x > \underline{x}$, is more appropriate. This type of relationship is depicted in Figure 12.1 (b). Notice that the agent still receives a base pay and only receives a bonus if their performance exceeds a threshold level. However, the greater the agent's performance above that level, the higher is their bonus. A good example of this type of scheme is a stock option plan where the agent receives greater pay as the stock price exceeds some threshold but does not receive a bonus otherwise.

The advantage of this type of scheme is that the agent is incentivised beyond a threshold level. The rate of that incentive is given by $\beta$, the slope of the pay for performance function above the threshold. In general, the slope of the pay for performance function describes the intensity of incentives given to the agent. Notice that below the threshold, the slope is 0. This means that incentive intensity is very low as additional performance does not yield greater pay. In contrast, above $x$, the slope is given by $\beta$. The greater is $\beta$, the greater is the agent's incentive intensity. As a point of comparison, in the step performance scheme in Figure 12.1 (a), the agent's incentive intensity is low except for a point just below $\underline{x}$, where it becomes infinite. An agent at that point will be highly motivated to perform slightly better.

The problem with these schemes is that while they motivate agents to perform beyond a threshold, they may demotivate them in performing to that threshold if that target is set too high. To counter that risk, the principal and agent may agree to a pay to performance relationship that gives the agent pay of $b + \beta x$. This scheme is depicted in Figure 12.1 (c). Notice that no threshold is set. All that is agreed upon is base pay plus a performance-related pay with incentive intensity of $\beta$. Many sales commissions or piece rate systems look like this scheme.

What this demonstrates is that there are many different possible pay to performance schemes. Schemes that set a threshold are easy for agents to understand but may not motivate agents for superior performance. Schemes that have no threshold can be motivating but require very careful consideration of the incentive intensity built in so that the principal is not paying for performance they do not actually value.

What this also demonstrates is that similar pay to performance schemes may be expressed in different ways. For instance, a step performance scheme in Figure 12.1 (a) may be expressed as a base plus bonus scheme or as a base minus penalty. The latter would offer the agent a base pay of $b + B$ but a penalty of $B$ if performance is below a threshold, $\underline{x}$. This threshold penalty scheme would give the same pay to performance relationship as the threshold bonus scheme. Thus, in economic terms, they would be regarded as equivalent.

For the rest of this chapter, we will focus on pay to performance schemes of the type depicted in Figure 12.1 (c). In so doing, we will discuss the trade-offs in setting the incentive intensity, $\beta$, as well as the selection of performance measure(s), $x$. How each of these are chosen depends critically on the nature of performance measures available. Some performance measures are 'noisy' in the sense that they reflect a principal's objectives but only imperfectly. Other measures are 'distorted' in that they do not perfectly reflect a principal's objectives and could be manipulated by the agent. We deal with each situation in turn.

## Noisy performance measures

Agency problems arise because the principal and agent cannot contract directly on the agent's activities and must instead use an outcome-based measure of those activities. Having decided upon that measure, the agent is 'free' to choose their activities as they see fit. Of course, their choice will be guided by the impact of those activities on the performance measure and the relationship between that measure and their pay.

If the performance measure perfectly reflected the agent's activities, there would be no real agency problem. In this case, the principal and agent would simply contract on the outcome and achieve the same value that they would if they could have contracted on the agent's actions directly.

The agency problem arises because the available performance measures are different from the agent's activities. One critical way in which a measure may be different is that it is not perfectly correlated with those activities: that is, the measure is noisy. Our earlier example of a photocopier repairer provides an illustration of this. The measure in that instance is the reliability of the photocopier following the agent's activities. If the agent expends effort in thoughtfully and diligently repairing the copier, the chances that it breaks down in the near future are reduced. If the agent does not expend this effort, the probability of a breakdown is much higher. However, it could easily be the case that a higher level of effort is expended but the photocopier breaks down despite this. Similarly, a repairer could expend a low level of effort and luck out with no breakdowns. Thus, the relationship between effort and reliability is not perfect. There is noise caused by the fact that there are many reasons photocopiers may break down that are unrelated to repair activities. The problem is the principal can't identify responsibility for any fault. A measure based on reliability is an imperfect or noisy signal of the agent's real performance.

### Incentive intensity

We begin by considering the impact of noisy performance measures on incentive intensity. Suppose that the number of days that no breakdown occurred following a repair job on a photocopier was $x = e + \varepsilon$ where $0 < e + \varepsilon < 1$, e was the repairer's effort level and $\varepsilon$ was a random variable with mean of 0 and variance of $\sigma$. What this says is that there is a correspondence between higher repairer effort and reliability (in terms of breakdown-free days) with greater effort leading to greater reliability. However, there is also a random element that on average has no effect on reliability. The cost of the repairer's effort is private and represented by a function, $C(e) = \gamma \frac{1}{2} e^2$. Finally, suppose that the willingness-to-pay for each breakdown-free day was $f$.

It is instructive, for a point of comparison, to consider what outcome maximises total value created if the principal and agent can contract upon $e$. In this case, they would choose $e$ to maximise the principal's willingness to pay less the agent's cost or $f E[x] - C(e)$ or $fe - \gamma \frac{1}{2} e^2$.[1] Using some simple calculus,[2] the value of $e$ that maximises total value created is $e^* = f/\gamma$. Thus, total value created would be $\frac{1}{2\gamma} f^2$.

In contrast, if effort was not contractible while $x$ was, the agent may receive pay of $b + \beta x$. Having accepted this contract, the agent would choose $e$ to maximise their own payoff of $b + \beta E[x] - C(e) = b + \beta e - \gamma \frac{1}{2} e^2$. Using calculus, the level of effort that maximises this is: $\hat{e} = \beta / \gamma$. This means that the higher is the agent's incentive intensity ($\beta$), the greater will be their chosen effort. Notice again that base pay, $b$, does not influence this effort choice as it does not vary with the performance measure, $x$. As such, $b$ has no impact on total value created.

In negotiating a contract, the principal and agent will want to choose $\beta$ to maximise total value created taking into account how this will impact upon the agent's effort. That is, they will want to maximise: $f\hat{e} - \gamma \frac{1}{2} \hat{e}^2 = \frac{1}{\gamma} f\beta - \frac{1}{2\gamma} \beta^2$. This gives $\hat{\beta} = f$; that is, that value created will be maximised if the agent receives an incentive intensity equal to the principal's willingness to pay. This will lead to effort of $f/\gamma$ and total value created of $\frac{1}{2\gamma} f^2$. This is the same outcome as the case where effort is contractible.

This illustrates something very important about incentive intensity: the goal in setting incentives is to create a situation where the agent's private incentives are aligned with the outcome that will maximise total value created. In this case, an additional unit of effort from the agent, on average, creates an additional $f$ units of value for the principal. The agent's payment for those additional units ($\beta$) should equal the additional value created ($f$).

As we have set up this simple example there are no impediments to using an incentive contract to achieve the same outcome as a contract based on the agent's actions. As $x$ is on average a good reflection of the agent's effort, it becomes a good measure upon which to base an agent's incentives. However, in reality, this means that the agent's pay will be variable as $x$ is sometimes higher than would be the outcome from their effort alone and sometimes lower. In contrast, if a contract could be based directly on effort there need be no variability in the agent's pay.

Variability of this kind becomes a problem if agents are risk averse. A risk averse agent places greater value on a certain payment than on an uncertain payment with the same average. That is, this agent faces private costs associated with uncertainty over pay. One way of considering this is to suppose that uncertainty creates a cost, $\frac{1}{2} \lambda \operatorname{Var}[\beta x] = \frac{1}{2} \lambda \beta^2 \sigma$, to the agent. Here $\lambda$ is a measure of the agent's degree of risk aversion. Notice that this cost does not change the agent's choice of effort (as $e$ changes the mean of $x$ but not its variance) so that given $\beta$, it is still the case that $\hat{e} = \beta / \gamma$. What it does change is total value created, which becomes $\frac{1}{\gamma} f\beta - \frac{1}{2\gamma}\beta^2 - \frac{1}{2}\lambda\beta^2\sigma$. Maximising this with respect to $\beta$ gives $\hat{\beta} = \frac{1}{1+\lambda\gamma\sigma} f$. Notice that incentive intensity is decreasing in $\lambda$ (the agent's risk aversion), $\sigma$ (the variance of the performance measure, $x$) and $\gamma$ (the agent's marginal effort cost).

Thus, in comparison to the case where the agent was not risk averse, here giving the agent a higher incentive intensity puts more of the agent's pay under uncertainty and reduces total value created. The cost of uncertainty is greater the more averse to risk the agent is and the more noisy is the performance measure. In the end, the agent is induced to provide a lower level of effort than before.

This illustrates a very important principle in outcome-based incentive contracting. When one party is more risk averse than another, it enhances value to insure that party against risk and uncertainty. However, when that same party needs to be subject to outcome-based incentives and performance measures are noisy, providing insurance and providing incentives for effort are conflicting goals. The resolution of this trade-off involves reducing the power of incentives on the risk averse agent to balance against the costs associated with uncertainty that such incentives bring.

### Performance measures

This insight regarding the potential costs of providing incentives to risk averse agents also provides a guide as to appropriate performance measures to include in incentive contracts.

First, if you have two possible performance measures that equally reflect the principal's objectives, it is better to base incentives on the less noisy measure. In this situation, the costs associated with uncertainty are lower and more high-powered incentives can be provided.

Second, if it is possible to add other variables to the contract those measures should only be added if they reduce the variance of the overall performance measure in the contract. For example, a sales contract based on revenue earned may benefit from measures that include the overall state of sales in the industry. The idea of this is that uncertainty will be reduced the tighter the link between an agent's sales effort and revenue earned. If that revenue is affected by industry conditions (e.g., there happens to be a high demand for the product this season) then including those measures will reduce uncertainty. Thus, if revenue earned by the agent is low but industry demand is also low, the agent may receive a higher commission than if industry demand was high. Similarly, if revenue earned is high but industry demand is also high the agent will receive a lower commission than if industry demand happened to be low in that instance. The inclusion of such a variable can be effectively used to provide the agent with insurance without distorting their incentives.

Third, it may be desirable to base an agent's incentives on their relative performance as compared with other similar agents performing similar tasks. Relative performance measures are useful in so far as they provide a tighter relationship between an agent's effort and the performance measure itself. For instance, if the uncertainty associated with a performance measure includes elements that are common across a set of agents then using relative performance measures can filter some of that uncertainty. For instance, the market conditions facing sales agents may be influenced by common factors such as the effectiveness of national marketing campaigns and customer delivery operations. In this case, it is their ability to achieve higher sales as compared with other sales agents that is a better measure of their performance than sales alone.

That said, if there is no such common element, including the performance of others in an agent's incentive, contracts may create additional variability in pay. This will, in turn, raise the costs of having high incentive intensity. Thus, care must be taken in considering measures to include. Including additional measures can easily be costly if they do not assist in improving how the overall performance measure relates to effort expended.

## Distorted performance measures

While the cost associated with the variability in pay is a necessary feature of incentive contracting and one reason incentives may be muted, another arises because of the perverse effects on behaviour strong incentives may encourage. Consider these examples:

CASE

Business history is littered with firms that got what they paid for. At the H.J. Heinz Company, for example, division managers received bonuses only if earnings increased from the prior year. The managers delivered consistent earnings growth by manipulating the timing of shipments to customers and by prepaying for services not yet received. At Dun & Bradstreet, salespeople earned no commission unless the customer bought a larger subscription to the firm's credit-report services than in the previous year. In 1989, the company faced millions of dollars in lawsuits following charges that its salespeople deceived customers into buying larger subscriptions by fraudulently overstating their historical usage. In 1992, Sears abolished the commission plan in its auto-repair shops, which paid mechanics based on the profits from repairs authorised by customers. Mechanics misled customers into authorising unnecessary repairs, leading California officials to prepare to close Sears' auto-repair business statewide.

In each of these cases, employees took actions to increase their compensation, but these actions were seemingly at the expense of long-run firm value. At Heinz, for example, prepaying for future services greatly reduced the firm's future flexibility, but the compensation system failed to address this issue. Similarly, at Dun & Bradstreet and Sears, although short-run profits increased with the increases in subscription sizes and auto repairs, the long-run harm done to the firms' reputations was significant (and plausibly much larger than the short-run benefit), but the compensation system again ignored the issue. Thus, in each of these cases, the cause of any dysfunctional behavior was not pay-for-performance *per se*, but rather pay-for-performance based on an inappropriate performance measure.[3]

The root cause of this undesired behaviour is the type of performance measure incentives were based on. All such measures are imperfect but in these cases the measures could be manipulated by the actions of the agent other than the desired action. Thus, those measures were not simply noisy but they were capable of being distorted by the agent. Not surprisingly, it can often reduce total value created to provide agents with incentives based on such distorted performance measures.

## Incentive intensity

Let's consider what distorted performance measures means for incentive intensity. Returning to our earlier copier repair model, suppose that the driver of a performance measure, $x$, is now $e + a$. In this case, we have removed the intrinsic uncertainty ($\varepsilon$) associated with the measure but in its place put another action, $a$, that the agent can take to influence that measure. For instance, $a$ may be a quick fix for the photocopier that will improve reliability but only over the short-term or only in a way that increases the rate of depreciation of the copier. In this case, $a$ would have additional costs for the principal, $\delta$ x $a$, that would not be observed until it was too late. If $\delta > f$, then total value created is reduced if $a > 0$; i.e., the costs associated with depreciation are higher than the principal's willingness to pay for additional reliability. We will assume here that $a$ carries the same effort cost for the agent as $e$.

In this case, for a given incentive intensity, $\beta$, the agent would choose both of its actions to maximise: $\beta x - C(e) - C(a) = \beta(e+a) - \frac{1}{2}\gamma e^2 - \frac{1}{2}\gamma a^2$. This gives $\hat{e} = \beta/\gamma$ and $\hat{a} = \beta/\gamma$. Thus, raising $\beta$ increases the agent's effort on both action types. In terms of total value created, this becomes $fx - \delta a - C(e) - C(a) = f\beta/\gamma - (\delta - f)\beta/\gamma - \beta^2/\gamma$. The $\beta$ that maximises this is: $\hat{\beta} = f - \delta/2$. Thus, the expected costs associated with the agent taking the 'bad' action mutes incentives overall for both the good and bad actions.

This situation is a reflection of a general principle: 'you get what you pay for'. In this case, if you pay for reliability you get reliability even at the cost of additional depreciation. In effect, the principal's willingness to pay for agent effort is now $f - \delta/2$ and so incentives are set on this basis. Not surprisingly, if what you pay for is worth less to you, you pay less and encourage less of it.

A similar set of issues arises when agents can explicitly engage in multiple tasks. For example, teachers can divide their time in terms of what they teach students. So if you pay them incentives based on standardised tests or student evaluations, this will change how they allocate their time. If this means that they shift time away from constructive learning activities then it may be better not to have an incentive contract in place at all. Similarly, a builder given a bonus for meeting a time deadline may cut corners to do so. The costs associated with that may be so high that if may be better not to have a time-based bonus and to sacrifice that objective.

### Performance measures

What do distorted measures mean for the types of measures included in incentive contracts? Recall that with noisy measures, the principle behind what measures should be included versus what should be excluded was whether having a wider or smaller set of measures reduced noise. For distorted measures, the same would be said with regard to the potential for a distortion to arise. However, much care needs to be taken in making these judgements.

For instance, it may be seem like a good idea to take into account factors seemingly out of control of the agent (such as overall market demand or the price of key inputs) when devising a performance measure. That reduces the noisiness of those measures and hence any costs arising from an agent's risk aversion. It may also seem fair to not punish or reward agents for factors out of their control.

However, even if a factor may be out of an agent's control, their response to it may be important and within their control. A truck fleet manager cannot control petrol prices but if those prices were to rise, their attention should be moved to consider fuel economy measures. As such, insuring them from such rises by making their pay independent of the price of petrol may mean that they are insufficiently motivated to deal with consequences of petrol price fluctuations. Responding to change is often part of an agent's job and that can mean leaving their rewards open to factors seemingly out of their control.

What this means is that principals and agents must trade-off the potential value creating aspects of insuring risk averse agents against unnecessary pay fluctuations with the potential distortions such blanket insurance policies may create in terms of an agent's initiative and response to unforeseen circumstances. In either case, when both issues are extreme, as noted earlier, the potential for high-powered incentives to be value-creating is reduced.

# Screening

Thus far, we have considered how incentive contracts can be used to increase total value created between a principal and agent. In the absence of an incentive contract, cooperation and trade may simply not be possible as the agent may have no incentive to undertake value creating actions. An incentive contract, by linking pay to performance, creates that incentive. However, incentives are themselves not without cost. Hence, while they improve total value created, they cannot achieve what might be done if a hypothetical complete contract could be written.

But incentive contracts can also perform another valuable function for principals: they can act as a screening device. The easiest way to see this is to imagine that there are two types of agents that might be employed by a principal: some with low and some with high intrinsic skills. Not surprisingly, a principal would like to hire those with high intrinsic skills but perhaps cannot easily tell one type of agent from another before hiring them. This lack of information can cause principals to shy away from such transactions altogether or insist on low compensation that reduces the pool of available agents to be hired.

But a high intrinsic skill agent will be able to achieve high performance more easily than an agent with low skills. In this situation, high skill agents may find an incentive contract that links pay to performance attractive whereas a low skill agent will not. Consequently, by offering an incentive contract with a high incentive intensity, the principal can sort among agents. Only agents who believe they will achieve high performance will accept such contracts. As such, the incentive contract itself helps screen potential agents for the attributes principals might desire. And these include not just skill level but motivation, risk-taking and diligence. Agents with these qualities will find incentive contracts a more attractive proposition than those who do not possess them.

Principals engaged in external contracting may use a fixed price contract rather than a cost plus contract as a similar screening device. Fixed price contracts involve the agent committing to a price for a service regardless of how circumstances might change throughout the contract term. The agent is responsible for all costs and will work to contain them. Cost plus contracts insure the agent against cost increases but they also provide low incentives to contain costs. If principals offer only a fixed price contract, they will screen out those subcontractors who do not believe they can contain costs.

## Incentives for teams

Thus far, we have considered incentive contracts from the perspective of motivating a single agent. In many situations, the principal is engaging a team of agents to supply a service. In addition, while it may easy to find measures of the team's performance, it may be very difficult to isolate the performance of any one agent. This gives rise to a *free riding problem*.

Free riding can occur when agents' individual effort benefits others and those others realise that. In this situation, agents anticipate the effort contribution of others and reduce their own effort accordingly. In the end, incentives for higher performance are muted.

To see this suppose that there are two agents, *A* and *B*. By expending \$1 in effort costs, each agent can lift the team's output, $Q(n)$, where $n$ is the number of agents expending higher effort and $Q(0) = 0$. Suppose that $Q(2) - Q(1) > 1$ and $Q(2) > 2$. In this case, it is value-maximising for both agents to expend high effort. How can the principal motivate them to do so?

Suppose that the principal bases pay to each agent on performance, $x = Q$. If the team achieves output of $Q(2)$ each agent receives $B(2)$. If the team achieves output of $Q(1)$ each agent receives $B(1)$. To be motivated to provide higher effort when it expects the other agent to contribute higher effort, $B(2)$ must satisfy, $B(2) - 1 \geq B(1)$. In addition, should the other agent not contribute higher effort, to be motivated to do so, $B(1) \geq 1$. Comparing these two conditions, for them both to be satisfied, it must be the case that $B(2) \geq 2$. However, if $Q(2) < 4$, there is no way to compensate for team performance in this way without 'breaking the bank'. Unless the agents wish to have negative base pay, providing sufficient group incentives involves doubling up on individual incentives; a costly proposition indeed.

The problem in team compensation is that individual performance cannot be separated from the group. As such, to motivate the team, not only does the team bonus have to be sufficient, it has to be sufficient to motivate each agent individually. In the end, the total sum of bonuses may well exceed the total value produced by the team.

In reality, this means that it is very difficult to motivate a team by the use of incentive contracts. This can be done, but achieving high-powered incentives may simply be too costly for the principal. Sometimes the alternative is to redesign the team task to consist of separate individual tasks. However, in this instance, providing incentives to individuals may reduce their incentives to help other team members.

## Summary

Incentive contracts are a means of overcoming agency problems. However, they do so imperfectly. First, as performance measures are noisy, risk averse agents face pay variability; something costly to them. Second, if performance measures can be distorted by agent actions, rewarding high performance on those measures may not give principals the value they desire.

In reality, writing incentive contracts can provide value-creating opportunities but their design requires careful thought and attention to detail. In addition, to work as incentives, linking pay to performance must be done in a credible fashion. The difficulties of achieving such credibility are the subject of our next chapter.

### Endnotes

[1]    $E[x]$ is the expected value or mean of $x$. As $\varepsilon$ has a mean of zero, this expected value is simply $e$.

[2]    To find the maximum, you take the derivative of total value created with respect to $e$. This gives a condition: $f = \gamma e$ as the condition defining the maximum.

[3]    Baker, G., Gibbons, R. & Murphy, K.J. (1994), 'Subjective Performance Measures in Optimal Incentive Contracts, *Quarterly Journal of Economics*, 109, pp.1125-56.

# 13 Relational contracting

The previous two chapters have considered contracting as a 'once-off' transaction. In many situations, parties to a transaction deal with one another over and over. If they write a long-term contract initially, then their ongoing relationship can be governed by those contract terms. However, ongoing transactions are sometimes a series of short-term contracts. This is especially the case in employment relationships. There is an ongoing contract but pay and performance terms are usually set at regular intervals.

This chapter examines what happens when agents are parties to repeated transactions with one another. On the one hand, this raises commitment issues that can thwart the ability to put appropriate incentives in place. On the other, the ongoing nature of the relationship offers a new set of instruments that can be used to enhance value created. Just as repeated games can allow parties to cooperate in situations where cooperation would otherwise be impossible (as in Chapter 4), repeated transactions allow parties to commit where otherwise commitment was not possible. Put simply, reneging on implicit agreements can cause the relationship and any value it was creating to end. This gives parties an incentive to continue to perform well.

## Committing to incentives

To begin, we consider why it may be difficult to commit to incentives in a once-off transaction. Suppose that a principal promises a bonus, $B$, that will be paid if the agent's 'performance' exceeds some threshold. In many employment relationships, performance measures that are related to pay bonuses are not objective; that is, they are not an independently verifiable quantitative measure. Instead, performance is measured against qualitative criterion by the agent's superior. In this respect the criteria for an agent's performance is subjective.

The advantage of subjective performance measures is that they can be a means of providing incentives where quantitative or objective measures are not available or are problematic for other reasons (e.g., they are subject to the type of distortions we discussed in Chapter 12). The problem is that subjective performance, while observable to other parties, may not be capable of independent verification. In this respect, the contract may be incomplete (as discussed in Chapter 11). In this case, there is a risk the agent will be held-up.

Hold-up here would occur if the agent did, in fact, perform well on the basis of the subjective performance criteria but the principal refused to pay the bonus, $B$, as that promise was not really enforceable. That is, the principal may claim that the performance criteria were not met and being subjective the agent may not be able to verify their good performance in a court.

To see this, suppose that by expending effort at a cost of $c$, the agent can raise the value of work for a principal from $v_L$ to $v_H$; where $v_H - v_L > c$. The principal can observe this value and so can pay a bonus, $B$, based on it. However, this performance cannot be verified independently by a court. The principal also pays the agent a fixed wage of $a$.

Given this, the game between the principal and agent is as in Figure 13.1. Solving it by backwards induction, if the agent expends effort, the principal has a choice between paying the bonus or reneging. Notice that reneging will always be chosen as the principal receives $v_H - a$ regardless and can simply avoid paying the bonus, $B$, to the agent. Knowing this the agent will never choose to expend effort as this only results in a reduction in their payoff by the amount of $c$. Ultimately both the principal and agent are worse off than they would be if the principal could commit to paying the bonus. It is because the principal cannot commit to this that a hold-up problem arises and there is a loss in total value created.

**Figure 13.1** Once-off subjective performance bonus

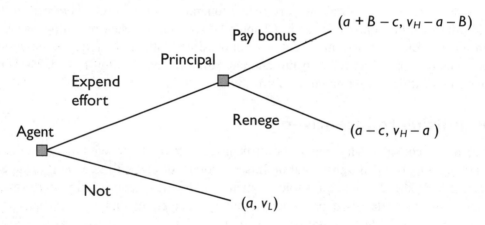

Notice that this problem cannot be resolved by paying the agent upfront for their higher effort. Figure 13.2 depicts the game where the principal moves first and chooses to pay a high wage $(a + B)$ or not $(a)$ and then the agent chooses their effort level. In this situation, having received a higher wage, the agent has no incentive to expend higher effort as this costs them $c$ while all of the increased value goes to the principal. Anticipating this, the principal does not offer the higher wage and total value created remains low.

Reneging can sometimes take a more subtler form than a simple refusal to pay a bonus or a claim that performance was insufficient to warrant one. Instead, the principal might use the fact that performance objectives were met this year to change the threshold criterion for performance next year. This type of reneging can also happen with objective measures such as quotas. As performance is met one year, the principal might increase the required quota for next year. This situation where good performance is met with a raising of performance standards is called the *ratchet effect*; the idea being that criteria are being ratcheted up over time.

**Figure 13.2** Once-off incentive pay

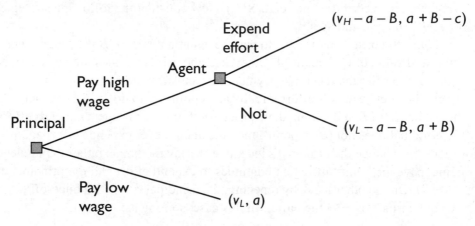

The problem is that if agents recognise the possibility of the ratchet effect – that is, that good performance today will be punished with more stringent performance requirements tomorrow – they will be demotivated today. Even if they are paid a bonus, agents will anticipate the higher requirements that result from good performance and shade their effort accordingly. In the extreme, agents may choose to keep their performance low and forego any short-term bonus. When the principal cannot commit not to ratchet up performance criteria, the effect is potentially the same as if they were to renege on bonuses altogether.

At the heart of all of these problems is a lack of commitment. The principal cannot commit to continue the incentives put in place and, anticipating this, agents do not respond to those incentives. However, if the principal and agent have an ongoing relationship it is possible that each could use the value of that as a means of resolving this commitment problem.

## Continuing the relationship

The incentive problems highlighted so far come from the fact that formal contracts cannot provide the necessary commitments to payments and actions. When the principal and agent are in an ongoing relationship, it is possible that an implicit or relational contract can provide incentives where informal contracts cannot. The idea is that the principal and agent pay and perform according to their agreed-upon obligations for fear of damaging or terminating the relationship. Here we examine when such relational contracting is feasible and value-creating.

### Subjective performance bonuses

Suppose that the game in Figure 13.1 is repeated. Suppose also that both the principal and agent discount the future on the basis of an interest rate of $r$ (that is, the present value of $1 to be received in every future period is $1/r$). Now consider the following strategies on the part of the principal and agent:

- *Principal*: the principal 'agrees' to pay the agent a bonus of $B$ if the agent expends effort and value of $v_H$ is realised. Otherwise, the principal does not pay a bonus but continues to offer the incentive payment in each subsequent period.
- *Agent*: the agent expends effort initially and continues to do so if the principal pays them a bonus of $B$ in the immediate past period. If ever the agent expends effort but the principal does not pay a bonus, then the agent never expends effort again.

How does this change the principal's incentives to pay the bonus rather than renege? If the principal pays the bonus, the agent continues to expend effort and the principal earns $\frac{1+r}{r}(v_H - a - B)$. On the other hand, by reneging, the principal receives a once-off payment of $(v_H - a)$ but earns $\frac{1}{r}(v_L - a)$ thereafter. In this case, so long as:

$$\frac{v_H - v_L}{1+r} \geq B$$

the principal will continue to honour the performance bonus scheme and the agent will continue to expend effort and perform well.

The above condition suggests that relational contracting may not always be feasible. In particular, the highest level of the bonus is $B^* = \frac{1}{1+r}(v_H - v_L)$. If this is less than $c$, then the agent will not be motivated to expend effort. Thus, if the interest rate, $r$, is too high (that is, principal and agent weight the future too little), then a relational contract will not resolve the once-off commitment problem.

### Many agents

Suppose that a principal employed many agents; each on a subjective bonus scheme. Suppose also that agents could observe whether their co-workers performed well and deserved a bonus or not. In this case, it becomes easier to sustain a relational contract.

To see this suppose that if all agents expend effort, total value to the principal is $nv_H$; where $n$ is the number of agents. If none expend effort, total value is $nv_L$. Suppose that the strategies are now as follows:

- *Principal*: the principal 'agrees' to pay the agent a bonus of $B$ if the agent expends effort and value of $v_H$ is realised. Otherwise, the principal does not pay a bonus but continues to offer the incentive payment in each subsequent period.
- *Any agent*: the agent expends effort initially and continues to do so if the principal pays themselves and any other agent who expends effort a bonus of $B$ in the immediate past period. If instead, *any* agent expends effort but the principal does not pay them a bonus, then the agent never expends effort again.

In this case, an agent considers not only the principal's behaviour with regard to themselves but also with regard to their co-workers. Should the principal renege with any one agent then all agents will no longer expend effort.

Given this, in considering whether to renege on the bonus payment to any one agent, the principal realises that while they might receive a once-off benefit of saving $B$ the cost is a loss in total surplus from all agents. Such reneging will not be worthwhile to the principal if

$$n \frac{v_H - v_L}{n + r} \geq B$$

If we imagine that it may be more difficult for the principal to renege on an individual agent's bonus than on its entire workforce (i.e., together workers could verify reneging to an independent court), then this condition will sustain a relational contract. Comparing this with the earlier condition, it is easy to see that the feasible bonus is higher when *multilateral* enforcement of the relational contract is possible.

Many firms often use relational contracts and work practices with all of their employees. The cost of this is that it becomes difficult to lay off workers during economic downturns and instead some firms opt for 'fairer' adjustment in poor economic times (e.g., shorter work weeks across the board). This is also a reason why firms may opt for two tiers of workers including permanent employees – who are part of the relational contract – and temporary workers who are not. As the temporary nature of that work is explicit, permanent workers do not react should those workers be laid off in a downturn.

### Using objective and subjective measures

In some relational contracts, objective measures appear alongside subjective ones. This can happen when 'key performance indicators' are identified. These are then objectively measured but how they translate into overall performance is essentially subjective.

At one level, the existence of good objective performance measures can undermine the use of subjective ones. Recall that a principal will consider the loss in future value created were it to renege on a promise. That loss will be mitigated if the principal could substitute the incentive payment based on a subjective evaluation for a good objective measure of performance. Hence, good objective measures may undermine the ability to create a self-enforcing relational contract.

On the other hand, we noted in Chapter 12, that some objective measures are subject to distortion or 'gaming' that may reduce the value of incentives. Subjective evaluation can mitigate this. In this situation, it may be that the gain in total value created from a joint use of objective and subjective measures is so great that it reinforces the relational contract. Put simply, the combination of measures makes the relationship so valuable that the principal does not want to risk damaging it by reneging.

### Efficiency wages

Relational contracts can also work by having the principal choose to pay the agent a higher wage but to threaten to dismiss the agent should performance not be sufficiently high. To see this, consider a repeated version of the game in Figure 13.2. The strategies of the parties become:

- *Principal*: continue to employ the worker at a wage of $w$ if high performance is observed in the previous period. (Here we are setting $w = B$ and $a = 0$.) Otherwise dismiss the worker.
- *Agent*: expend effort to achieve high performance so long as have received a wage of $w$ that period.

In this situation, the agent is promising the principal that they will work hard if they receive a sufficiently high wage. Their payoff from working hard is $(w-c)(1+r)/r$. If they 'shirk' for a single period, they receive $w$. Hence, the agent will work rather than shirk if $w \geq c(1+r)$.

Thus, the lowest wage the principal can pay and still receive high effort is $w^* = c(1+r)$. $w^*$ is termed an efficiency wage by economists. Notice that it exceeds (by $rc$) the level of wages that would just compensate the agent for their effort cost. The idea is that a wage premium needs to be paid to induce the agent to work hard each period. Not surprisingly, that premium needs to be higher the more agents discount the future (that is, the higher is $r$). However, in a more realistic model, it would also be higher the longer it takes for the principal to detect poor performance and the better are the agent's outside employment prospects.

When wealth constraints are not an issue, the efficiency wage premium can be mitigated by bonding arrangements. In this situation, prior to employment, the agent would put up a bond that would be forfeited should the agent leave the firm. The bond itself becomes a means of assuring the relationship. This is sometimes used when there are large employee-specific training costs and the principal is concerned that an agent may leave employment too soon.

## Summary

Relationships provide a scope for trust to be built. This chapter has shown how trust – if it can be sustained – can be a means of substituting for formal contracts in encouraging agents to take actions that maximise value created. The key economic issue is whether trust can in fact be sustained: that is, is a relational contract feasible?

Feasibility depends upon farsightedness and transparency. When principals and agents weigh the future more heavily relative to the present, they will be concerned about maintaining the value of the relationship more than any short-term gain they might privately receive from reneging or shirking. In addition, the quicker principals and agents can detect poor behaviour on the part of the other, the quicker they can terminate the relationship. As such, transparency between them can increase the self-enforcing nature of relational contracts. With these characteristics, relational contracts can be a potent force in enhancing total value created from a transaction or series of transactions.

# Index